D1593312

The
CHARLIE PARKER
Companion

Six

Decades of

Commentary

Edited by
CARL WOIDECK

SCHIRMER BOOKS
An Imprint of
Simon & Schuster Macmillan
New York

Prentice Hall International
London Mexico City New Delhi Singapore Sydney
Toronto

Schirmer Books
An Imprint of Simon & Schuster Macmillan
1633 Broadway
New York, New York 10019

Library of Congress Catalog Card Number: 97-41859

Printed in the United States of America

Printing Number
10 9 8 7 6 5 4 3 2 1

Library of Congress Cataloging-in-Publication Data
The Charlie Parker companion : six decades of commentary / edited by Carl Woideck.
   p.   cm.
  Discography: p.
  Includes bibliographical references (p.   ) and index.
ISBN 0-02-864714-9 (alk. paper)
1. Parker, Charlie, 1920–1955. 2. Jazz—History and criticism.
I. Woideck, Carl.
ML419.P4C45   1998
788.7'3165'092—dc21   97-41859
                                                              CIP
                                                              MN

Contents

Contents
viii

Acknowledgments

Profound thanks go to my editor at Schirmer Books, Richard Carlin. His faith, good will, and patience as I encountered frustrating conditions helped make this book possible.

An anthology like this is not conceived of and written in a vacuum. For it to succeed, it requires creative input and help from many individuals. Thanks go to Lewis Porter of Rutgers University for helping me find this opportunity to edit and publish. Dan Morgenstern, director of the Institute of Jazz Studies, helped me to move this project forward with the right gestures. The staff at the institute—Don Luck, Ed Berger, and Vince Pelote—gave valuable in-person and long-distance help. Thanks also go to the contributors to this collection and to the copyright holders who gave permission to print their material for this anthology: John Fitch, Phil Schaap, Max Harrison, Scott Asen, Bob Rusch, and Frank Alkyer.

My deepest appreciation goes to my wife, Marian Smith, whose support during this project's various stages made the process less difficult, and whose wide appreciation for music made creating this book far more enjoyable.

Introduction

Saxophonist Charlie Parker was one of the most innovative and influential of all jazz musicians. More than fifty years after his death, listeners are still strongly drawn to his music and find it deeply moving. Musicians young and old continue to find inspiration in Parker's art and study it for inspiration. Charlie Parker's contributions to music were far-reaching melodically, rhythmically, and harmonically. Like Louis Armstrong, Parker influenced players on all instruments, not just on his own. Fewer than ten years elapsed between Charlie Parker's first recording date as a leader in 1945 and his last one in 1954, but during that time he created an enduring body of recordings. Many musicians excel at one or two facets of jazz. Parker was a master of every aspect of the music. He could improvise on up-tempo numbers with breathtaking speed and exhilaration ("Ko Ko," "Kim"); he could play the blues with great poetic depth ("Parker's Mood," "Now's the Time"); and he could explore the heartfelt romance of ballads ("Embraceable You," "Out of Nowhere").

This book is a collection of articles, surveys, interviews, and reviews about Charlie Parker and his music. I came across many of the individual pieces found here while writing my book *Charlie Parker: His Music and Life* (University of Michigan Press, 1996). In addition to a biographical sketch of Parker, that book includes considerable analysis of Parker's music. However, for this anthology, I have chosen only nontechnical material that will be interesting and accessible to all readers.

As editor, I have tried to find the best works on Parker available. It is important to me to include the actual thoughts and words of Charlie Parker, and I am very pleased to include key articles that feature extensive quotations by Parker. Period reviews of an artist tell us a lot about how the artist was perceived at the time, and I am happy to offer a fine group of concert and record reviews. Of course, not all the writings that I wanted were obtainable. Most publishers and authors were extremely cooperative in making their works available, but not surprisingly I occasionally had to make compromises in my choices while always considering the overall strength and balance of this anthology. Of course, I don't agree with every opinion expressed within these covers. A few somewhat negative record reviews, for example, were included to give perspective to the critical reception of Parker's music. I hope all the pieces in this anthology stimulate thought and discussion about Parker's music. Above all, I hope that the contents of this book will inspire the reader to listen to, experience, and absorb the music of Charlie Parker.

Carl Woideck

PART ONE

Chasin' the Bird

Parker's Career
and Influence

BIRD LIVES! (1987)

Gary Giddins has written on a wide variety of jazz topics in many articles and books. He was a contributing editor at Down Beat *magazine and has written many excellent pieces for* The Village Voice. *Giddins's* Celebrating Bird: The Triumph of Charlie Parker *(where this chapter originally appeared) is, as of this writing, the single most accessible nontechnical account of Charlie Parker's life and music; Giddins's writing is clear and inspired, and he shows a special insight into Parker. This succinct introduction to Parker and his music is an excellent way to begin* The Charlie Parker Companion.—CW

The witness to his death heard a clap of thunder at the moment of Charlie Parker's passing. The companion of his last years remains in spiritual contact with him after more than thirty years. His childhood sweetheart and first wife continues to hear his music as nothing more or less than the "story of our lives together." Such indications of veneration and awe, shot through by an unmistakable religious symbology, suggest the extent to which Parker's posthumous life is clouded with romance. Deification did not begin with his death. Parker, who enjoyed remarkably little public recognition in life, was nonetheless attended by disciples and hagiographers. Many musicians, a few critics, and a coterie of enthusiasts—most of them drawn from the tight-knit, defensive world of jazz—were inspired by his music to the often voluble rapture that finds comfort in the elaborations of myth.

Parker's status as a prophet was largely inadvertent, a byproduct of his self-acknowledged destiny to become "a great musician." As an apprentice in Kansas City jazz circles, he got off to a slow start. He impressed fellow apprentices with little more than his confidence and determination; others thought him lazy, obdurate, and spoiled. But the young man was favored with supernatural abilities, and the tempo of his life quickened soon enough. Resolve gave way to obsession and a desire to succeed equaled only by a vertiginous desire to fail. He hurled himself at the gates, falsifying his age to gain entry into the most competitive nightclubs, daring Kansas City to reject him, and maximizing every rejection as a stimulus for new feats. He forged ahead with astonishing assurance. At sixteen, he was laughed off a bandstand; at seventeen, he made converts—including Jay McShann, a stranger in town, who eventually offered him the chance to reject Kansas City. The fledgling, who many years later would answer a query about his religious affiliation by declaring himself "a devout musician," was too conscious of his genius, too possessed of pride, too much the product of racial repression and maternal sanction not to suspect that a larger world awaited him—a world he could recast in his own image.

It's no surprise to learn that Parker was embarrassed by the insipid onomatopoeia *bebop,* which got tarred to modern jazz and which survives his scorn. He never proselytized for modernism in any guise. Impatient with those who attempted to stampede him into aesthetic cubbyholes, he jousted with critics—celebrating the traditions of jazz in one interview (*Down Beat,* 1948) and dismissing those traditions in another (*Down Beat,* 1949). Asked to distinguish between his music and that of his predecessors, however, he invariably demurred: "It's just music. It's trying to play clean and looking for the pretty notes" (1949). His willingness to let people draw their own conclusions is suggested in his one surviving television appearance, when he disdainfully tells the dotty emcee, "They say music speaks louder than words, so we'd rather voice our opinion that way." Everyone agrees that he knew his own worth and had neither the need nor the desire to politick on behalf of a new movement. On the contrary, he kept himself humble with an attentive enthusiasm for those modernists—Stravinsky, Hindemith, Schönberg, Bartók—who were skilled in the compositional techniques he coveted. Yet at twenty-five, he was the acknowledged leader of a new music; at thirty, his brilliance was recognized by musicians around the world; at thirty-four, when he died, he was regarded as an elder statesman who had yet to be superseded by his descendants. No sooner was he buried—in Easter season—than the graffiti appeared: *Bird lives!*

Parker's followers dogged his footsteps, often armed with tape recorders to preserve his improvised performances (but not those of his accompanists, most of whom also have claims on posterity). Some put words to his music. One such lyricist, a singer who called himself King Pleasure, made a profession of the practice and paid Parker the dubious but canonical tribute of predicting his death in his words to "Parker's Mood." Parker sought allied musicians (and could be stern with those who failed to make the grade), but he did not seek followers and tended to be contemptuous of idolizers. He had little use for cult foppery—beret, beard, jive talk—or cult arrogance. If he seems to have attracted converts rather than mere fans or imitators, the reason is obvious. Parker was the only jazz musician since Louis Armstrong whose innovations demanded a comprehensive reassessment of all the elements of jazz.

It's natural for a saxophonist to influence saxophonists, or a drummer drummers. But Parker, like Armstrong before him, engineered a total shift in the jazz aesthetic. The autodidactic country boy from Kansas City brought modernism to jazz, and forced players on every instrument to face their worst fears or realize their most prized aspirations in his music. Established players satisfied with approved jazz styles encountered not only new levels of harmony, melody, and rhythm in Parker's work—all of which evolved from precedents easily found in classic jazz—but an iconoclastic sensibility that threatened to undermine generally accepted standards of excellence. Younger players were more open to the shock of recognition that, to paraphrase Melville, binds not only the community of geniuses but that of apprentice artists impatient to express their own powers in a world paralyzed with orthodoxy. Small wonder, then, that so many musicians of Parker's generation (and not a few elders) tell of how he changed their lives with a way of playing music they scarcely imagined. The witnesses are many, but the language is similar:

JAY MCSHANN: When I first came to Kansas City, I went to all the clubs to meet all the musicians. So one night I stopped in a club and Bird was blowing. That was in 1937, and he was *playing*, and you know the first time you hear Bird, you *hear* it—you've got to hear it. I asked him, "Say, man, where are you from? You don't play like anybody else in Kansas City." He said, "Well, I've been down in the Ozarks with George Lee's band. It's hard to get musicians to go down there, because it's quiet and musicians like to be where the action is, but I wanted to do some woodshedding so I went down there with George. That's probably the reason you think I sound different."

DIZZY GILLESPIE: I had a friend, Buddy Anderson, who played good trumpet with Jay McShann, and we'd jam together in Kansas City. He wanted me to hear this saxophone player, but I wasn't too interested because I'd been hearing Don Byas, Lester Young, Chu Berry, Coleman Hawkins, and Ben Webster, and I said, "Not another saxophone player!" Until I heard him. Jesus! Knocked me off my feet. We played all day that day. . . .

RED RODNEY: Dizzy kept telling me about this saxophone player I had to hear. . . . He took me up to New York with him and I met Charlie Parker. When I heard him play I near fell out the window. Oh, my God! Everything came together at one time. I knew then. I knew where it was and who it was and what I had to do.

BUDDY DE FRANCO: He was just three years older than me but he seemed so much more mature and older. . . . When I got to know him I got to realize that he was more than just an innovator and a musician. He was a deep, extremely knowledgeable person, though self-taught. I don't think he had professional training and teaching, but his fingers were perfect. His technique was just *perfect*—as though he had years of schooling. To me it's incredible that he's the one person in jazz who influenced the entire jazz world. Every bit of it.

JOE NEWMAN: Jay McShann had his band at the Savoy Ballroom and Rudy Williams, a well-known alto player at the time, said, "Come on with me, man, I want you to meet this alto player." He introduced me to Bird and the first time I heard him play I couldn't believe it, because he was doing something different from what everybody else was doing, and it was obvious his style was going to force things in another direction.

THAD JONES: I was in the army on an island called Guam, traveling with a GI show. There were about six of us, all in our tent, preparing for the evening and listening to the radio, and all of a sudden Dizzy comes on playing "Shaw 'Nuff" with Charlie Parker. And, you know, I can't describe what went on in that tent. We went out of our minds! . . . It was the newness and the impact of that sound, and the technique. It was something we were probably trying to articulate ourselves and just didn't know how. And Dizzy and Bird came along and did it. They spoke our minds.

Of course, Parker's travail as prophetic genius, accepted only by a coterie in his own country, was hardly as unambiguous as that of the traditional romance. Nor, tragically, were his converts satisfied with imitating just his music. The usual tale of the exceptionally gifted and sensitive young artist who is emboldened by despair and suffering, and ultimately overcomes self-doubt and public indifference, is too conventional, too perfunctory (perhaps too European) to suit Charlie Parker. Parker achieved his hipster sainthood in part by transcending, in word if not in deed, a full measure of Augustinian vices. If Parker's career was a frantic quest for musical fulfillment, it was continuously detoured by self-destructive impulses so gargantuan that they also became the stuff of legend. The bop king had another, by no means secret, identity as the junkie king, and many votaries unable to get close to him musically were eager to share the communion of drugs. "Do as I say, not as I do," Parker warned friends when they asked about that part of his life. He kept it private, refusing to partake with those he respected, at least until they were as far gone as he was. Despite his warnings, many persisted in the sometimes fatal belief that Parker drew part of his seemingly inexhaustible greatness from teaspoons of white powder.

Disconcerted commentators can be forgiven the inclination to link Parker's gluttonies to racism and an absent father. Still, something basic in Parker's individuality resists the familiar simplifications of fast-Freud analyses. The hugeness, majesty, and authority of this man are diminished when the culpability for his downfall is removed from his shoulders and placed on those of an uncomprehending commonalty. Racist and Philistine societies are all alike; every artist is unique. The shift in blame from Parker to the mass tethers him to the very prosaicness his art so unequivocally counters. Always one step ahead of the mob, he cut himself down before they could. Still, it must be emphasized that as a black man in mid-twentieth-century America, Parker suffered more than personal injustices. He also endured a constant debilitating slander against his art. Minority citizens healthily buffered by their own communities do not look to the oppressive majority for a sense of identity. The artist, however, seeks recognition in the community of artists, which defies, or ought to defy, the conventionalism, mediocrity, and pettiness that are inseparable from race and nationalism. In that community, a far worse fate than neglect is acknowledgment followed by expulsion for lack of an acceptable pedigree. By all accounts, Parker could not be cowed by the insanity of white supremacism. But the frustration he experienced on behalf of his music was lifelong and stifling.

Parker was bred in one of the richest musical communities in American history: Kansas City in the 1930s. In addition to constant access to dozens of the most individual and accomplished musicians in the country, he could hear the rest of the world's best jazz musicians on records and radio. As a provisionally popular music, jazz wasn't merely available; it was virtually inescapable. But partly because of its popularity, it was also reputed to be lacking in seriousness: a folk music at best, a fad for adolescents at worst. The combination of Jim Crow racism and the public's inability to distinguish genuine achievement from meretricious imitation invariably favored the exposure of white bands. Since the most successful of those bands diluted their music with trite novelties and feeble showmanship, jazz itself was widely construed to be a low art. In Europe, Japan, and elsewhere, jazz was celebrated as a vital music. In the United States, jazz was confined to gin mills and dance halls. It was practically banned from concert halls until 1938, when—significantly enough—the Benny Goodman band played Carnegie Hall, and from conservatories for much longer. It was ignored by most classical music critics, and still is.

When he died, in 1955, Charlie Parker was arguably the most influential musician in the country. Jazz musicians copied him so shamelessly that the pianist Lennie Tristano made an oft-quoted remark to the effect that Parker could have invoked plagiarism laws. On more than one occasion, Charles Mingus made a show of firing his musicians on the bandstand for relying on Parker clichés. Studio musicians were no less mesmerized by Parker's ideas, as witness the wholesale use of bebop harmonies and melodic figures (once considered terrifyingly complex) as fodder for movie and television scores, as well as arrangements for pop and rock-and-roll records. It's doubtful that the host of the *Ed Sullivan Show* knew his entrances were cued by Parkeresque phrases, or that moviegoers who watched *The Helen Morgan Story* realized the 1920s torch singer was crooning to 1950s bop licks, or that kids dancing to "The Hucklebuck" recognized the melody as Parker's "Now's the Time." Forty years after Parker and Gillespie popularized Latin rhythms, salsa bands continue to feature solos played in their styles. As Parker's influence extended into the repertory of "legitimate" ensembles—for examples, David Amram symphonies with passages for Parker-styled improvisations and John Lewis fugues and ballets—Gunther Schuller coined the term Third Stream to suggest a new pluralism inspired in large measure by Parker's music. Indeed, his impact transcended music. In the 1950s, numerous novelists, poets, and painters cited him with metaphorical urgency, often as the embodiment of a psychic breakthrough.

Yet the various rewards with which a society pays tribute to its artists were denied Parker. The academic musical world, notwithstanding individual admirers such as Varèse, never knew him. Countless jazz and popular performers who worshipped him achieved a renown that persistently eluded Parker. In fact, the cultural racism that sneers at jazz had sniped at his heels from the moment he obtained a saxophone: he never had the option of studying at the two conservatories in Kansas City because neither accepted black students. When, at the peak of his influence, *Life* ran an article on bop, Parker wasn't discussed. When *Time* cast about for a cover story on the new jazz, it turned to a white musician with a "classical" education, Dave Brubeck—a slight that especially riled Parker. If the mainstream press ignored him, the jazz press wasn't much more perspicacious. He won few jazz polls, even when all the winners reflected his guidance. The best-known jazz club of the era (Birdland) was named for him, yet in concert appearances with Gillespie he was usually billed second and in smaller type. When he died in New York City, where he'd lived most of his adult life and achieved his greatest successes, a minority of local newspapers published obituaries. Of those that acknowledged his passing, only the *New York Post* got his age right (the others gave fifty-three) or attempted to suggest his impact on the music of his time. Two papers failed to learn his first name and buried him as Yardbird Parker.

Posterity made up for that neglect in a hurry, not with an accurate rendering of facts, but with a rush of memories, many of them self-serving, a mad pastiche of discipleship and true love. "I knew him better than anyone," is the most frequent pledge a Parker biographer hears. But the fairest warning he can expect is that of the far from dispassionate observer who said, "You will talk to a million people and you will hear of a million Charlie Parkers." One wonders if it is even possible to peel away the Charlie Parker created in death by family and disciples, hagiographers, and voyeurs, and if so to what purpose? Would a Charlie Parker reduced to life size be more easily apprehended, understood, and admired, or even closer to the truth, than the one of legend? The one irreducible fact of his existence is his genius, which will not cater to the routine explanations of psychologists, sociologists, anthropologists, or musicologists. But a basic ordering of facts, as best they can be adduced with limited resources in the face of conflicting claims (most of them plenary), may complement the music of Charlie Parker and engage the imagination of listeners who know the ravishing pleasures of his art.

CHARLIE PARKER: THE BURDEN OF INNOVATION (1970)

Martin Williams had a tremendous impact on the appreciation of jazz in the United States and beyond. In addition to writing many articles and reviews for Down Beat, Evergreen Review, *the* New York Times, *and* Saturday Review, *in 1958 he and Nat Hentoff founded and edited* The Jazz Review, *often considered to be the finest of all jazz magazines. In 1970, Williams began working for the Smithsonian Institution; his legacy there includes the* Smithsonian Collection of Classic Jazz *and its revised edition.—CW*

It is now possible to discuss Bix Beiderbecke as a musician, but Beiderbecke has been dead since 1931. When Charlie Parker had been dead less than a year they still spoke of him often, but it became more and more unusual for anyone to discuss his music. They were beginning to speak of him as a god, perhaps because it saved them the trouble of reflecting either on his playing or on his life. Some prayed to him as a saint, but surely a saint must have a clear self-knowledge and acceptance of his destiny. Some said, in *non sequiturs* that passed for insight, that he was destroyed by big business and advertising. An uptown barkeep muttered, "I got no use for a man who abuses his talent." They proclaimed, "He never practiced." (But he *did* practice, of course, and in his youth he practiced day and night.) They said of the more careless performances and the reed squeaks, "He was a man in a hurry." Perhaps he once said it better: "I was always in a panic." His friends said, "You had to pay your dues just to know him." In a sense you have to pay them even to listen to him. Perhaps that is as it should be.

A Negro celebrity has said that Charlie Parker represented freedom. It is hard to be sure exactly what he meant, for surely there was little true individuality in the life of the man, so constantly was he, it seems, the victim of his own passions.

For Parker's music, perhaps *freedom* would not be the best word, but there should be no question that his music represented high individuality and an independent, inner determination. Charlie Parker the saxophonist was a conquering Tamerlane interpreting and revising the whole world on his own terms. He was, if you will, the bird that seemed to soar with grace and ease along its own flightlines. But a bird, it might be appropriate to add, does not always have its feet on the ground.

Parker the musician had made the first decision of maturity, knowing what he wanted and knowing how he could best obtain it. Those who knew him, those who tell you that you had to pay your dues to know him, will usually tell you also that he did exactly what he wanted to do, when he wanted to, regardless. And the negative side of knowing only what one wants and how to get it is a kind of heedlessness, a self-indulgent unawareness of the consequences or effects of one's actions.

This is not the place for an evaluation of Parker's personality and personal life, but perhaps in that life he did live the negative side of his self-determined musical persona.

What saves one from the ultimate, implicit *self*-destruction of heedlessness is of course the second step of maturity, knowing the consequences and effects of one's actions, and taking the responsibility for them. In any case, heedlessness was not a part of Charlie Parker's music. His music said that, although the choices are greater and more exciting, more promising, than one had thought, so are they more challenging and demanding, and they do have musical consequences.

Parker was indeed a complex being, yet his personal life seems to have been a chaos in which moments of perceptive kindness vied with moments of anger and panic, moments of gentleness contrasted with moments of suspicion. The opposites in him were indeed far apart, tragically far apart. But his music, for all its freshness, its expanded emotion and its liberated feeling, its originality, its seemingly unending invention, at its best presented an image of unexpectedly subtle and complex order and wholeness.

In his one-chorus improvisation on "Embraceable You," Parker barely glances at Gershwin's melody. He begins with an interesting six-note phrase which he then uses five times in a row, pronouncing it variously and moving it around to fit the harmonic contours of Gershwin's piece. On its fifth appearance the six-note motive forms the beginning of a delicate thrust of melody which dances along, pauses momentarily, resumes, and finally comes to rest balanced at the end with a variant of that same six-note phrase. From this point on, Parker's solo interweaves that opening musical motive in remarkable permutations and in unexpected places. Sometimes he subtracts notes from it, changes notes within it, adds notes to it. But it is the core of his improvisation, and, speaking personally, I have seldom listened to this chorus without realizing how ingeniously that phrase is echoed in Parker's remarkable melody.

I think we sense such subtle musical order even though we may not hear it directly. Of course that order has nothing to do with repetitiousness. It represents a kind of organization and development quite beyond popular song writing. It fulfills the sort of compositional premise which a composer might take hours to work out on his own. But Parker simply stood up and improvised the chorus. And a few moments later, at the same recording session, he stood up and played another chorus in the same piece, quite differently organized and, if not quite a masterpiece like the first, an exceptional improvisation nevertheless.

Improvisation has a meaning of its own; if we know that a piece of music is being at least partly made up for us on the spot, that we are attending the act of creation, we hear that music with special receptivity. But in the final analysis, an improvised music needs to be improvised well, and the final defense of improvisation in jazz is that the best jazzmen can improvise superbly; they can compete with less spontaneous melodists and even surpass them.

Of course, I am not contending that creating melodic order by a recurring motive, by "sequencing," is new in jazz. And I am not contending that it is new with jazz, but I do believe jazzmen rediscovered it for themselves. Some of King Oliver's best solos (let us say "Dippermouth Blues") use recurring motives and develop sequential phrases exceptionally well. Nor am I contending that the approach always works. There is a first take of "Hallelujah," with Charlie Parker as a sideman in a Red Norvo group, on which he seems repetitiously and monotonously hung up on a single idea. But hear the second take of "Hallelujah."

The six-note phrase is not the only principle of organization on Parker's first "Embraceable You." The chorus begins simply and lyrically, gradually becomes more intricate, with longer chains of melody involving shorter notes, to balance itself at the end with a return to simple lyricism— a kind of curve upward and then downward. The second take of "Embraceable" has quite different contours, as Parker alternates the simple lyric phrases with more complex, virtuoso lines, and variations in light and shade, tension and release.

A great deal of misinformation has been put into print about music in which Parker was a major figure. It was at first called, onomatopoetically, bebop, then modern jazz. It has been said that the boppers often made their compositions by adopting the chord sequences of standard popular songs and writing new melody lines to them. So they did, and so had at least two generations of jazzmen before them. It has been said that they undertook the similar practice of improvising with only a chord sequence as their guide, with no reference to a theme melody itself—in classicist terms "harmonic variations," in the terms of jazz critic André Hodeir "chorus phrase." But the practice had become a norm and commonplace by the late 'thirties to men like Teddy Wilson, Henry "Red" Allen, Roy Eldridge, Johnny Hodges, Ben Webster, Lester Young, Coleman Hawkins, Charlie Christian, and hundreds of others; indeed one might say that in their work it had reached a kind of deadlock of perfection. For that matter, one can find choruses of nonthematic improvising in the recordings of players who were leaders in the 'twenties and earlier—Louis Armstrong, Earl Hines, Bix Beiderbecke, Jack Teagarden, Sidney Bechet, even Bunk Johnson.

The practices are, basically, as old as the blues. Certainly King Oliver's three classic 1923 choruses on "Dippermouth Blues" have no thematic reference to the melody of that piece. One might say that jazz musicians spent the late 'twenties and the 'thirties discovering that they could "play the blues" on chords of "Sweet Sue, I Ain't Got Nobody," "Sweet Georgia Brown," "You're Driving Me Crazy," "I Got Rhythm," "Tea for Two," and the rest.

What Parker and bebop provided was a renewed musical language (or at least a renewed dialect) with which the old practices could be replenished and continued. The renewed language came, in part, as have all innovations in jazz, from an assimilation of devices from European music. But a deliberate effort to import "classical" harmony or melodic devices might have led jazzmen to all sorts of affectation and spuriousness.

Like Louis Armstrong before him, Charlie Parker was called on to change the language of jazz, to reinterpret its fundamentals and give it a way to continue. He did that with a musical brilliance that was irrevocable. But he did it simply by following his own artistic impulses, and Parker's innovations represent a truly organic growth for jazz and have little to do with the spurious impositions of a self-consciously "progressive" jazzman.

The music of Charlie Parker and Dizzy Gillespie represented a way for jazz to continue, but that way was not just a matter of new devices; it also had to do with a change in even the function of the music. Parker's work implied that jazz could no longer be thought of only as an energetic background for the barroom, as a kind of vaudeville, as a vehicle for dancers. From now on it was somehow a music to be listened to, as many of its partisans had said it should have been all along. We will make it that, Parker seemed to say, or it will perish. The knowledge that he was sending it along that road must have been at times a difficult burden to carry.

Today we are apt to see Parker as the most important of the pioneer modernists, chiefly because his influence has proved more general, widespread, and lasting; and because, for most of his brief and falling-star career, his talent grew and his invention seemed constant. Rightly or wrongly, we are apt to think of Dizzy Gillespie's influence as chiefly on brassmen, Parker's on everyone. And we know that Thelonious Monk's ideas were rather different from either Parker's or Gillespie's, and that their real importance would emerge only later.

It is perhaps hard for some of us to realize now, so long after the fact, what a bitter controversy modern jazz brought about, but it is instructive to look briefly at that controversy. Among other things, its opponents declared that the modernists had introduced harmonic values that were alien to jazz. Well, once jazz has embraced European harmony in any aspect, as it did far longer ago than 1900, it has by implication embraced it all, as long as the right players came along to show just how it could be unpretentiously included and assimilated into the jazz idiom. But the curiousness of this argument is clearly dramatized in the fact that bop's opponents are apt to approve of pianist Art Tatum and tenor saxophonist Don Byas, both of whom were harmonically as sophisticated and knowledgeable as Parker and Gillespie. But Byas does not really *sound* like a modernist, because rhythmically he is not a modernist. And rhythm is the crux of the matter.

The crucial thing about the bebop style is that its basis came from the resources of jazz itself, and it came about in much the same way that innovation had come about in the past. That basis is rhythmic, and it involves rhythmic subdivision. Any other way would surely have been disastrous. We should not talk about harmonic exactness or substitute chords and the rest before we have talked about rhythm.

Like Louis Armstrong, Charlie Parker expanded jazz rhythmically and, although his rhythmic changes are intricately and subtly bound up with his ideas of harmony and melody, the rhythmic change is fundamental. "Bebop," however unfortunate a name for the music, does represent it rhythmically and hence rather accurately, much as "swing" accurately represents the rhythmic momentum that Armstrong introduced.

We may say that Armstrong's rhythms are based on a quarter-note. Parker's idea of rhythm is based on an eighth-note. Of course I am speaking of melodic rhythm, the rhythm that the players' accents make as they offer their melodies, not of the basic time or the basic percussion.

For that matter, to speak of rhythm, melodic line, and harmony as if they were entities is a critic's necessary delusion. But such separations can clarify much. To many ears attuned to the music of Coleman Hawkins or Roy Eldridge and the rhythmic conceptions they use, Parker's music seemed at first pointlessly fussy and decorative—a flurry of technique. Players at first found Parker's sophisticated blue lines like "Relaxin' at Camarillo" and "Billie's Bounce" almost impossible to play, not because of their notes but because their strong melodic lines demanded such a fresh way of accenting and phrasing. But once one is in touch with Parker rhythmically, every note, every phrase, becomes direct, functional musical expression. And of course I am giving only a rough rule of thumb; each style is more complex than such a description makes it seem. Parker, who showed that his notes and accents might land on heavy beats, weak beats, and the various places in between beats, was the most imaginative player rhythmically in jazz history, as his one dazzlingly intricate chorus on "Ornithology" might easily attest.

I do not think that one can hear the impeccable swing of a player like Lionel Hampton without sensing that some sort of future crisis was at hand in the music, that—to exaggerate only slightly—a kind of jazz as melodically dull as a set of tone drums might well be in the offing. In guitarist Charlie Christian, it seems to me, one hears both the problem and the basis for its solution, a basis which Lester Young had helped provide him with. Christian's swing was perfect. He was an outstanding melodist. And at times his rhythmic imagination carried him to the verge of some new discoveries.

To say that fresh rhythmic invention is basic to Parker's music is not to ignore the fact that he also possessed one of the most fertile harmonic imaginations that jazz has ever known. In this respect one can mention only Art Tatum in the same paragraph with him. Tatum must have been an enormous influence, one feels sure, harmonically and even in note values. But Tatum's imagination was harmonic and ornamental, and Parker—although he had a melodic vocabulary in which (as with most musicians) certain phrases recur—was perhaps the greatest *inventor* of melodies jazz has seen.

Still, one is brought up short by the realization that a "typical" Parker phrase turns out to be much the same phrase one had heard years before from, say, Ben Webster. The secret is of course that Parker inflects, accents, and pronounces that phrase so differently that one simply may not recognize it.

What was Parker's heritage? Such questions are always vexing for so original a talent. Someone has suggested that he combined on alto the two tenor saxophone traditions: the sophisticated and precise harmonic sense of Coleman Hawkins and his follower, Don Byas; and the rhythmic originality, variety, and looseness of phrase and penchant for horizontal, linear melody of Lester Young and his follower, guitarist Charlie Christian. But the closest thing on previous jazz records to Parker's mature phrasing that I know of are a handful of Louis Armstrong's most brilliant trumpet solos—"West End Blues" from 1928, "Sweethearts on Parade" from 1930, "Between the Devil and the Deep Blue Sea" from 1931, "Basin Street Blues" from 1933. In them we clearly hear Parker's melodic rhythm in embryo. No one jazzman, not even Roy Eldridge, undertook to develop that aspect of Armstrong until Charlie Parker.

However, it is fitting that Parker's first recorded solo, on "Swingmatism" with Jay McShann, does owe so much to Lester Young. Whatever his debt to others (and to himself) for the genesis of his style, Parker had obviously absorbed Young's language soundly and thoroughly. Charlie Parker's second recorded solo is also indicative—brilliant but perhaps exasperating. On McShann's "Hootie Blues" he played what might have been a beautifully developed and rhythmically striking chorus, one which introduces almost everything Parker was to spend the rest of his life refining. But the solo is not finally satisfactory; he interrupts it in the seventh bar to interpolate a trite riff figure. Granted that he showed the sound intuition of knowing that a contrastingly simple idea was precisely right at that moment in his melody, a simply commonplace one was not.

The best introduction to Parker's music is probably his remarkable pair of choruses on "Lady Be Good." Stylistically he begins rather conservatively, in a late swing period manner rather like Lester Young's, and he gradually transforms this into the style that Parker himself offered jazz.

These choruses are melodically fascinating in another aspect. Just as "Embraceable You" is organized around the interweaving and permutation of one melodic fragment, "Lady Be Good" uses several which emerge as the choruses unfold. Parker's first few notes are Gershwin's, but he uses these notes as the opening to quite a different melodic phrase. His second phrase is a simple riff. His third phrase echoes his opening Gershwinesque line, but in a kind of reverse-echo reassortment of its notes, and it also has something of the character of his second riff phrase—in a sense it combines and continues both. And so on.

At the same time this brilliance was delivered in the most adverse circumstances, at a "Jazz at the Philharmonic" concert in the spring of 1946 in Los Angeles. The solo thereby refutes what is patently true, that Parker's playing really belonged only in the small improvising quintets he established as the norm. The circumstances were made even more trying by the fact that, as Parker begins to move further away from the conventions of an earlier style, moving in his own direction, he is rewarded with a wholly unnecessary background riff from the other musicians on the stage at the time. It is apt to distract a listener, but it apparently did not distract Parker. Still, the solo is delivered with a kind of personal and technical strain and pressure in his alto sound that was foreign to Parker at his best.

Almost opposite to the "classic" development of a "Lady Be Good" is another public recording made with a far more appropriate group, the Carnegie Hall concert of 1947 with Dizzy Gillespie. Here is Parker the daring romantic, using passing and altered harmonies, complex movements and countermovements of rhythm, unexpected turns of melody. Much of it is delivered with an emotional directness that makes the complexity functional and necessary. The celebrated stop-time break on "A Night in Tunisia" played on the same occasion shows Parker's intuitive sense of balance at its best: an alternation of tensions and releases so rapid, terse, and complete that it may seem to condense all of his best work into one melodic leap of four bars. One knows that on this occasion Parker was out to "get" his friend and rival Gillespie, and Gillespie was playing as if he were not to be gotten. This personal element influences the aesthetics of the music, sometimes for the worse. There was at times a sharper than usual edge, an apparent strain, to Parker's sound.

No one who has listened with receptive ears to Charlie Parker play the blues could doubt that aspect of his authenticity as a jazzman. Nor should one fail to understand after hearing his music that the emotional basis of his work is the urban, Southwestern blues idiom that we also hear running through every performance by the Basie orchestra of the late 'thirties. "Parker's Mood" (especially take 2) is as indigenously the blues as a Bessie Smith record, more so than several James P. Johnson records. But one also senses immediately the increase in the emotional range of the idiom that Parker's technical innovations make possible.

Charlie Parker was a bluesman, a great *natural* bluesman without calculated funkiness or rustic posturing. It has been said that all the great jazzmen can play the blues, but that is obviously not so. Earl Hines has played wonderful solos in the blues form, but with little blues feeling. Neither did James P. Johnson, Fats Waller, nor any of the classic "stride" men. Johnny Hodges can play the blues; Benny Carter not. But without counting, one would guess that perhaps 40 percent of Parker's recordings were blues. The best of them are reassessments and lyric expansions of traditional blues phrases and ideas, ideas reevaluated by Parker's particular sensibility. The classic example is probably "Parker's Mood," but there are dozens of others. And his "written" (more properly, memorized) blues melodies are also a valid introduction to his work. On the first record date under his own name he produced two blues. "Now's the Time" is an obviously traditional piece (so traditional that its riff became a rhythm-and-blues hit as "The Hucklebuck") which is given an original twist or two by Parker, particularly in its last couple of bars. But "Billie's Bounce" is a strikingly original, continuous twelve-bar melody, in which phrases and fragments of phrases repeat and echo and organize the line, and in which traditional riffs and ideas leap in and out rephrased, reaccented, and formed into something striking, fresh, and unequalled.

Writing was an aspect of playing to Parker. He contributed durable pieces and durable melody lines to the jazz repertory. But likely as not, he contributed them simply by standing up and playing them out of his head when it came time to contribute them. A traditional or borrowed chord structure would take care of the basic outline; his own sense of order as an improviser would take care of melodic order; his own melodic and rhythmic imagination would take care of originality. "Scrapple from the Apple," one of his best and most influential melodies, began with the chords of "Honeysuckle Rose" but borrowed the bridge of "I Got Rhythm." His basic repertory included the relatively complex challenges of sophisticated structures like "How High the Moon" and "What Is This Thing Called Love?" But it also included the simpler challenges of the blues and "I Got Rhythm." He met both kinds of challenges successfully, both as a player and composer, and therein showed the range of an artist.

Parker's best piece of writing is "Confirmation," an ingenious and delightful melody. For one thing, it is a continuous linear invention. Pieces which use AABA song form have two parts, of course, a main strain and a bridge or release or middle. The main strain is repeated twice before the bridge and once after it, exactly or almost exactly. "Confirmation" skips along beautifully with no repeats, but with one highly effective echo phrase, until the last eight bars and these are a kind of repeat-in-summary to finish the line. And Parker uses the bridge of the piece not as an interruption or interlude that breaks up or contrasts with its flow but as part of its continuously developing melody. Finally, "Confirmation" was in no way predetermined by a chord sequence; its melody dictates one of its own. But note that the song form dictates a cyclical harmonic understructure, whereas Parker's melody is relatively continuous.

One frustration with Parker's recorded work is that, although a lot of it is kept in print, the brilliant records he made for the Dial label in 1946 and 1947 had been sporadically available and in a rather scattered manner. In the '70s, they reappeared, edited well, and we heard "Bird of Paradise" evolving from three takes of "All the Things You Are," and we heard the different variations on alternate takes of "Embraceable You," "Scrapple from the Apple," "Klact-oveeseds-tene," "Dexterity," "Moose the Mooche," and the rest.

Also from the Dial catalogue there was a far better take of "Quasimodo" than the one that was long generally available on reissues. But the leaping solo on "Crazeology" tells as much as any single performance about the ease with which Parker handled harmony, rhythm, and line. "Klact-oveeseds-tene" would be a wonder if only for Max Roach's drumming. It also has a breath-stopping Parker solo that at first seems built in brief spurts, placed ambiguously and vaguely around a bass line until he slides into the bridge. From that point he builds form simply by increasing complexity, and what previously seemed careless, disparate fragments of melody now take their place in a firm, logically developed line.

The collected Dial issues present the final takes of four pieces from a highly productive recording date. There is "Moose the Mooche" memorable not only for its writing but for Parker's bridge in the first chorus which seems to dangle us bitonally between two keys at once. There is the more tender Parker of "Yardbird Suite," lyric in both the theme and the improvisation, understandably the favorite Parker of Lee Konitz. There is the famous fourth take of "Ornithology," not only superb in its rhythmic ingenuity but in its alternation of long/short/long/short phrases, with some rests in between. There is "A Night in Tunisia," with its famous unaccompanied break, and, again, the spontaneity with which Parker juggles tension and release, complexity and simplicity. There is a very different Parker on each of these pieces. He develops each in a manner he considered appropriate to the piece at hand, and those who will not allow that Parker had that kind of artistic discipline should listen carefully.

The personnel of the quintet that made Parker's 1947 records offered a fine collection of foils and counterfoils to Parker. The talent of a then still-developing and sometimes faltering Miles Davis was, in its detached lyricism, sonority, and lack of obvious virtuosity, an excellent contrast. What is perhaps more important is that, in a growing capacity for asymmetry and displacement, Davis was able to carry and refine a part of Parker's rhythmic message in a unique manner, quite opposite from Dizzy Gillespie's virtuoso approach to the idiom of "modern" jazz. Pianist Duke Jordan was a balanced melodic player. Bud Powell or John Lewis replace him on some of the Savoy records from the same period, and with the former at least, the whole group quality changes; Powell's ideas, his touch, and his strong emotion are perhaps too much like Parker's. Max Roach was at the apex of his early career in the mid 'forties. The simplest way to put it is to say that he could *play* the rhythms that Parker used and implied, and he knew exactly when and how to break up his basic pulse to complement what the soloists were doing with it. To call what he does interfering or decorative is perhaps to misunderstand not only the whole basis of this music but the function of all jazz drumming from Baby Dodds forward. Hear Roach on "Crazeology" behind the "guest" soloist on that date, trombonist J. J. Johnson, then behind Miles Davis and throughout the piece. "Klact-oveeseds-tene" represents Roach's work at a peak development.

Surely one of the most interesting documents in jazz is the Savoy LP which preserves all the recorded material from the record date that produced "Ko Ko" and two blues we have already mentioned, "Now's the Time" and "Billie's Bounce." It might be enough just to hear the various final performances gradually shape and reshape themselves as the various takes are programmed in order, but the session was also one of Parker's best, and its climax was "Ko Ko." "Ko Ko" may seem only a fast-tempo showpiece at first, but it is not. It is a precise linear improvisation of exceptional melodic content. It is also an almost perfect example of virtuosity *and* economy. Following a pause, notes fall over and between this beat and that beat: breaking them asunder, robbing them of any vestige of monotony; rests fall where heavy beats once came, now "heavy" beats come between beats and on weak beats. "Ko Ko" has been a source book of ideas and no wonder; now that its basic innovations are familiar, it seems even more a great performance in itself. I know of no other Parker solo which shows how basic and brilliant were Parker's rhythmic innovations, not only how much complexity they had, but how much economy they could involve. "Ko Ko," at the same time, shows how intrinsically Parker's rhythms were bound to his sense of melody.

Parker's career on records after 1948 is a wondrous, a frustrating, and finally a pathetic thing. It was perhaps in some search for form beyond soloist's form, and for refuge from the awful dependency on the inspiration and intuition of the moment (as well as a half-willing search for popular success) that he took on the mere *format* of strings, the *doo-wah* vocal groups, the Latin percussive gimmicks. A major artist can find inspiration in odd places, but Parker with strings still includes the strings and banal writing for them. It seems a perversion of success to place a major jazzman in such a setting, whatever he thought about it or would admit to feel about it. (Yet hasn't Louis Armstrong had worse, and more often?)

There is an arrangement of "What Is This Thing Called Love?" whose triteness is gross indeed, yet Charlie Parker plays brilliantly in it (as he usually did in that piece and in its jazz variant, "Hot House")—in effect he was a great, creative musician battling pseudo-musical pleasantries. Then there is "Just Friends"—Parker's part of it beautifully developed—which is the only one of his records he would admit to like, and "In the Still of the Night" where he shimmers and slithers around tritely conceived choral singing like a great dancer in front of a chorus doing time-steps. The Latin gimmickry is not as bad, and on "Mango Manque" Parker adjusts his own phrasing admirably. But to what end? One cannot hear Dizzy Gillespie improvise without realizing that his phrasing was influenced by his experience in rhumba bands, but Parker's is always a development of jazz and jazz rhythms. It was perfectly natural for Gillespie to use Chano Pozo, the brilliant Cuban bongo player, as a second drummer; for Parker such things remain extrinsic effects, however well he adapts himself.

What remains otherwise from those years is often an expansive soloist. One cannot hear the fluent sureness of "Chi Chi," the easy conservatism of "Swedish Schnapps," the developed virtuosity of "She Rote" without knowing that a major talent is enlarging and perfecting his language. And there is the celebrated excitement of "Bloomdido" and "Mohawk" on the "reunion" recordings with Gillespie. But on several of these personal successes Parker is involved with Buddy Rich, a virtuoso drummer who simply did not feel the pulse in Parker's way.

By this time, Parker created a finely developed and natural means of expression out of a high virtuosity of short notes and intricate rhythms. It is from this Parker that Cannonball Adderley learned, much as it was from the earlier Parker that Sonny Stitt learned.

Even in the midst of the orderliness of Parker's best solos we sometimes return to the proposition that a lot of Parker's work is oddly incomplete. Sometimes a solo will leave us with a feeling of suspense rather than one of order restored or even of passion spent. Parker fulfilled a mission, surely, to salvage a music and set it on its course. Perhaps he was also the victim of that mission. In any case, one wonders if he really fulfilled his talent, even as one hears recordings on which he is so brilliant.

Perhaps to Charlie Parker invention sometimes came too easily, or perhaps he was tortured by its constancy. Perhaps, on the other hand, he did rely too completely on the intuitive impulse of the moment; it was his strong point, and he may therefore have come to believe it was his only point. Perhaps it was. When he could blow everyone else away just by standing up and playing, he admitted hearing no call to any other kind of challenge, and thereby he may have been persuaded to take on the spurious challenge of flirting with popularity by standing in front of those strings. In his utter dependency, night after night, on the inspiration he drew from the act of playing itself, in his frequent refusals to coast and determination always to invent, he may have given himself the kind of challenge that no man of sensitivity could respond to without inviting disaster. Or perhaps Parker the man might have learned from the liberation *with* order and proportion that we can hear in Parker the musician.

I have said that Parker and his associates not only evolved a replenishment of the jazz language, but that they proposed a change in the function of the music. Players undertook the former simply because they could, because they heard the music that way and therefore had to play it that way. There can be no question that they succeeded in permanently replenishing the jazzman's vocabulary and usage. But they undertook to bring about the change in the function of jazz a little more deliberately and a lot more self-consciously, and there remains a question of whether or not they succeeded. There was and is relatively little ballroom or social dancing done to modern jazz, but for a large segment of its audience it is not quite an art music or a concert music. It remains by and large still something of a barroom atmosphere music. And perhaps a failure to establish a new function and milieu for jazz was, more than anything else, the personal tragedy of the members of the bebop generation.

New Orleans jazz began as a communal activity, played by men who were not professionals. The transition from such a communal music to a musical vaudeville was not too difficult. The early modernists wanted to take still another step, but as performers they had little or no tradition on which to draw in making that step: they had few traditions of presentation, of personal conduct before an audience, of stage manner, even of programming, to guide them. They did not favor the hoopla presentations of the vaudeville stage, and, I suspect, they did not want to borrow outright the stuffiness of the contemporary concert hall. On the one hand, they repudiated what they thought of as the grinning and eye-rolling of earlier generations of jazzmen; on the other, they sometimes refused to make even a polite bow to acknowledge the applause of their listeners. At the same time, some of them, Parker included, apparently courted a public success and a wide following that were defined in much the same terms as the popular success of some of their predecessors.

But if they had little tradition on which to draw in presentation, they had a rich one on which to draw musically. I think they treated that musical tradition honorably, and obviously they left it richer still.

IRA GITLER

CHARLIE PARKER AND THE ALTO SAXOPHONISTS (1997)

Ira Gitler is probably the best writer we have on the modern jazz style called bebop. Although he was not on the scene for the genesis of modern jazz in the early 1940s, he began frequenting New York's 52nd Street in 1945 and in 1946 wrote a review for his high school newspaper of Dizzy Gillespie's Spotlite club quintet. In addition to visiting nightclubs and attending jam sessions, Gitler got experience in the business of music when he worked for Prestige Records from 1950 to 1955. Gitler's many subsequent articles and liner notes on modern jazz are laced with firsthand accounts of the music and the musicians. His book Jazz Masters of the Forties *is a valuable and highly readable guide to modern jazz, and his* Swing to Bop *is a fascinating history of developments in jazz told through oral history. This essay originally included information on modern jazz baritone saxophonists, but for reasons of maintaining focus, it was decided to emphasize Parker's artistic evolution and his influence upon those who played his particular sax, the alto.*

(Note: The Dean Benedetti recordings mentioned here are now available as a seven-CD set, The Complete Dean Benedetti Recordings of Charlie Parker, *Mosaic MD7-129. The recordings discussed in connection with Frank Driggs are often called the Wichita Transcriptions, and were most recently available in the United States on the CD* Early Bird *[see the Discography entry on page 270]. Also note that although Gitler writes that Parker's last night-club engagement lasted only one night, the group's bassist, Charles Mingus, stated that the job lasted two nights.)*
—CW

Although a man and his music are inseparable, often in writing about Charlie "Yardbird" Parker, more attention is given to the wild, lurid aspects of his life than to his music. The emphasis should be placed on his playing and composing, for he rose above the sordid to produce great and beautiful art. His friend and musical partner Dizzy Gillespie summed it up in an interview some six years after Parker's death. "You hear so much about him that I don't like to hear," Dizzy said, "about his addiction and all sorts of irrelevant nonsense. What kind of man was Beethoven? Perhaps he wasn't a very admirable individual, but what has that got to do with listening to his music?

"Not that I didn't think Bird was admirable. He was. But people talk too much about the man—people who don't know—when the important thing is his music.

"The Negro people should put up a statue to him, to remind their grandchildren. This man contributed joy to the world, and it will last a thousand years."

Others have expressed the feeling that there should be a statue of Parker. On his first visit here in the early fifties, French jazz pianist Henri Renaud was surprised when he found none standing on Fifth Avenue. But America's only native art form isn't taken seriously in its birthplace, and this was just one of the hardships Parker endured as a creative artist in a hostile environment.

Bird was a warm person, sensitive to public reaction. I remember talking to him one night at the Three Deuces in the summer of 1947, just after he returned from a seven-month confinement at Camarillo State Hospital in California, where he had recuperated from a nervous collapse. He stressed the fact that "the young people are getting with the music." It seemed very important to him to communicate the spirit of jazz to the next generation. For his music came from the very roots of jazz and always possessed its basic elements, no matter how oblique his flights may have seemed. His awareness of the entire jazz literature can be heard in his quote from Louis Armstrong's "West End Blues" in his own "Visa" solo from *Bird at St. Nick's*.

Parker was a giant figure who influenced countless lives, musically and otherwise. He affected jazz as totally as had Armstrong a generation before him, and he brought the alto saxophone to prominence the way Coleman Hawkins and Lester Young had with the tenor saxophone. Because of him, young musicians turned to the alto and tried to play like him. Later, many escaped to the tenor to avoid direct comparison.

His fans were legion; they would devour his every recording, and some were not content to stop there. One, Dean Benedetti, an alto player from California, followed Parker around the country, most often by Greyhound bus, just to capture his every note on a wire recorder. (Benedetti died of pneumonia several years ago, and the recordings were never brought to light.)

In the late forties I met a group of young Chicagoans who would listen to no other music but his. Some of the most extreme would rerecord his solos from the Dial and Savoy records on tape or wire and immerse themselves for hours in uninterrupted Parker. Among them were the hippies who would boast, through half-closed, watery eyes, "I got high with Bird."

Parker disapproved of both attitudes. He listened to all kinds of music and could find something of value in the worst surroundings. Saxophonist Gigi Gryce tells of a time when he and Bird were passing a rock 'n' roll joint. "He would stop to listen, and maybe it would be something the piano player was doing which he liked. He'd say, 'Man, do you hear that? It would be a gas to play with that guy.' "

That people emulated his narcotics addiction distressed him. During a 1947 interview with Leonard Feather, Parker said that a musician professing to play better when he was high on anything was a liar. It was true that many people copied everything he did, from his music to the drugs and kicks, but the entry of heroin into the jazz world had begun before Parker reached idolatry. There was an obscure sideman who, according to musicians, was active in "turning on" others, but I never heard of Charlie Parker recommending the drug to neophytes.

He started using heroin as a youngster, before he had a chance to know better. Parker was 34 when he died, but he looked a lot older. He had crammed at least twice that number of years of living into the thirty-four. He once was quoted as saying, "I began dissipating as early as 1932, when I was only twelve years old; three years later a *friend* of the family introduced me to heroin. I woke up one morning very soon after that, feeling terribly sick and not knowing why. The panic was on."

Before the panic, Parker had become interested in music. Born in Kansas City, Kansas, on August 29, 1920, he moved across the river to Kansas City, Missouri, when he was 7. His father, Charles Parker, Sr., was a vaudevillian who played piano and sang. He left home when Charlie was 9, and was fatally stabbed by a woman in a quarrel eight years later. Charlie's mother, Addie Parker, a nurse, raised him and encouraged him to play. Although Bird is reported to have played baritone horn in the Lincoln High band, according to his mother it was the larger tuba. "I didn't go for that," she said, "—was so funny coiled around him with just his head sticking out, so I got him another instrument."

That was an alto saxophone, the instrument through which Parker was to tell his story to the world. No doubt he had more than average talent for music, but it was not evident at first. After a year of study he began to play with the band of Lawrence Keyes, who because he played piano was saddled with the nickname 88. The band was made up of other high-school kids and was called the Deans of Swing. (Some of the members, like tenor saxophonist Freddie Culliver and singer Walter Brown, later graduated to Jay McShann's band along with Parker.) Bird was really a fledgling in 1934. Bassist Gene Ramey, who also worked with him in the McShann band, first heard him then and describes him as "the saddest thing in the [Keyes] band."

Since Parker himself told Leonard Feather that he "spent three years in high school and wound up a freshman" and since Keyes has said of him, "If he had been as conscientious about his schoolwork as he was about his music, he would have become a professor, but he was a terrible truant," we are led to wonder why he didn't develop at a faster pace on his saxophone. Ramey, however, remembers him as seeming to be "just like a happy-go-lucky kid."

Humiliation at the jam sessions so prevalent in the Kansas City of the thirties soon made him serious about his music. Parker told of the first time he ventured into a jamming situation. "I knew a little of 'Lazy River' and 'Honeysuckle Rose' and played what I could," he said. "I was doing all right until I tried doing double tempo on 'Body and Soul.' Everybody fell out laughing. I went home and cried and didn't play again for three months."

This was the reaction of a youth whom Ramey describes as "an only child, sheltered and coddled, and . . . not used to getting along with people."

Another time, Parker was jamming with members of Count Basie's band. Drummer Jo Jones waited until Bird started to play and then rendered his opinion of Parker's blowing by sailing his cymbal all the way across the dance floor. Jones's self-styled Major Bowes gesture caused Bird to pack up his horn and leave, his spirit dragging. This time, however, he didn't stop playing. In the summer of 1937, he joined the band of George E. Lee, the brother of singer Julia Lee, and went off to nearby Ozark Mountain resorts. With him Parker took all Count Basie's records, from which he learned Lester Young's solos inside out. (Years later, in the fifties, Lee Konitz walked into Bird's dressing room during the course of a tour and heard him play Young's solo from "Shoe Shine Boy" at twice the tempo of the original.)

When Parker returned to Kansas City a few months later, he was a changed musician. The band's guitarist, Efferge Ware, had taught him about chord progressions, and he had begun to practice assiduously. Soon he was commanding attention and respect from his cohorts. In those days, musicians used to go out into the middle of the city's Paseo Park and play all night without police interference. Some say Bird instituted this practice. Whether or not he did, he was a regular member of the fresh-air jamming group. Kansas City musicians were still doing it in the late forties, with the aid of a portable organ.

In 1937, Parker was in the band of Buster Smith, the alto saxophonist who was an early influence on his playing. Smith had known him for about five years before he joined the band. "Charlie would come in where we were playing," Smith has said, "and hang around the stand, with his alto under his arm. He had his horn in a paper sack—always carried it in that paper sack. He used to carry his horn home and put it under his pillow and sleep on it."

Professor, as Buster is called, was Bird's mentor during the latter's stay with the band. They divided the amount of solos equally. "He always wanted me to take the first solo," said Buster. "I guess he thought he'd learn something that way. He did play like me quite a bit, I guess. But after awhile, anything I could make on my horn, he could make too—and make something better out of it."

Smith, who still leads a blues band in Dallas, Texas, has told how he left for New York to find work, intending to send for the rest of the band when he had. Meanwhile, Parker started to play with McShann. This was 1938. After three months, Bird hit the rails and hoboed his way to Chicago. He showed up, right off a freight train, at the Club 65's breakfast dance. Both Budd Johnson and Billy Eckstine were present, and they have both related the story of how this raggedy man asked King Kolax's alto man, Goon Gardner, whether he could blow Goon's horn and then proceeded to "upset everybody in the joint." Gardner then got Bird some clothes, a few gigs, and a clarinet with which to play them. Soon thereafter, Gardner looked for Parker, but he had left town, clarinet and all.

Parker's next step is somewhat in doubt. Buster Smith remembers Bird showing up at his New York apartment in a bedraggled state. His legs were swollen because he had been wearing his shoes for so long. According to Smith and McShann, this was still 1938. Jay's recollection is that Parker "washed dishes in Jimmy's Chicken Shack in Harlem for a few months, while out front, Art Tatum was gassing everybody. Several months later he got a job with a group at Monroe's Uptown House [Clark Monroe's club on 138th Street]."

In Leonard Feather's *New Encyclopedia of Jazz* (1960), Parker is said to have first come to New York in 1939 and "for almost a year worked intermittently" at Monroe's.

Smith says that Bird went to Baltimore for three weeks, and then McShann sent for him. McShann states that Parker came back to Kansas City to play with Harlan Leonard's Rockets in the latter part of 1938 and that Tadd Dameron was writing for Leonard at the time.

Which is the accurate account is not clear, but before he died, Dameron said that he did not join Leonard until 1940. Considering that Parker rejoined McShann in late 1939 or early 1940 and stayed until 1942, Dameron's version of his first meeting with Bird raises some questions. "Bird was cleaning up the club," said Tadd. "I never knew he played horn until one jam session he pulls out this raggedy alto with this pipe tone he had then. I couldn't hear anyone but him because I could hear his message. So we got together and we were playing "Lady Be Good" and there's some changes I played in the middle where he just stopped playing and ran over and kissed me on the cheek. He said, 'That's what I've been hearing all my life, but nobody plays those changes.' So we got to be very good friends—he used to come over to my house every day and blow. This was in 1941. This was when war was declared—I remember it definitely. And my wife would cook. And the people used to knock on the door, and I'd say, 'Oh, I'm sorry we're making so much noise.' 'No,' they'd say, 'we want you to leave the door open,' because he was playing *so* pretty."

Dameron's reference to Bird's appreciation of the way he played those particular chord changes has a parallel story. In New York, Parker had jammed with a guitarist named Biddy Fleet in a variety of places, including the back of a chili house in Harlem. "Biddy would run new chords," said Parker. "For instance, we'd find you could play a relative major, using the right inversions, against a seventh chord, and we played around with flatted fifths."

In a 1949 *Down Beat* interview, Parker spoke of a particularly stimulating session with Fleet. Bird had been getting tired of the stereotyped changes in general use. "I kept thinking there's bound to be something else," he said. "I could hear it sometimes, but I couldn't play it." While playing "Cherokee" with Fleet, he found that by utilizing the higher intervals of a chord as a melody line and using suitably connected changes with it, he could make the thing he had been hearing an actuality. As Bird put it, "I came alive."

Whenever the exact moment was that Parker "came alive," the period of wandering just prior to 1940 and the time he spent with McShann gave his talent the nourishment necessary for him to develop as a fully mature artist in the mid-forties.

There were other McShann men who were also working with new ideas, like trumpeter Buddy Anderson, alto saxophonist John Jackson, and tenor saxophonist Jimmy Forrest. Dizzy Gillespie, in talking about his first meeting with Parker in a Kansas City hotel room—an occasion on which they spent the whole day playing the piano and discussing their ideas—also mentions Anderson. "Good trumpet player," he says. "Got tuberculosis—had to stop playing. Started playing bass—haven't seen him in years."

McShann has talked of Anderson and claims that he had an influence on Gillespie. "He played in the same style as Bird—only, on the trumpet," said Jay, who reported that Anderson was playing piano in Oklahoma City in the early sixties.

In 1941, McShann's Decca record of "Confessin' the Blues" sold eighty-one thousand copies. Mike Morales (calling himself the Vine Street Vulture) wrote in Down Beat: ". . . some of Jay's boys, Walt Brown, Gene Ramey, Gussie Johnson, Charles Parker and others, deserve a mention. They've helped Jay in his climb."

Parker's allegiance to the blues tradition, in evidence throughout his career, was no doubt strongly influenced by his experience with this band, although the blues had become part of his musical makeup long before. But the band's basically blues-oriented framework was obviously conducive to the early experiments of certain members.

Parker was in charge of the reeds, under McShann's system of separate rehearsal leaders for each section. Bird had "straightened up" in McShann's words. He had begun writing by this time, and "Yardbird Suite" was in the book, although it had another title and was never recorded by McShann. But later Bird showed the members of the band how to get high on nutmeg by taking great quantities of it in milk or Coke.

The earliest recorded documents of Parker are not available to the public, although record producer-writer Frank Driggs hopes to make them so someday. There are six titles, recorded at a Wichita radio station in 1940. Parker solos on five. They are not lengthy, and far from his fully formed style, but the seeds of the past (the Lester Young influence) and the ready-to-ripen fruit are there to hear. His "Moten Swing" solo is part Pres, part Bird, with a sound that is not yet solidified; his entrance on "Honeysuckle Rose" is very Youngish, but the solo contains occasional significant departures; on "I Found a New Baby," he exhibits his quickness—the pickups he employs at the beginning of phrases are a device he made extensive use of later; "Body and Soul" contains some typical runs—and a phrase he played ten years later on the same song at a restaurant in Sweden (issued on a Swedish label, Sonet); "Lady Be Good," his longest solo—a complete chorus—is notable for its flowing lines.

When McShann did his first recording for Decca in 1941, Parker was featured on "Swingmatism" and "Hootie Blues." The sides cut by the band a year later (July, 1942) in New York included "Sepian Bounce" and "The Jumpin' Blues," both of which contain solos by Parker. The first four bars of his "Jumpin' Blues" solo emerged as part of Benny Harris' "Ornithology" a few years later.

In 1942, Bob Locke, reviewing the McShann band in *Down Beat*, wrote: "Charlie Parker offers inspired alto solos, using a minimum of notes in a fluid style with a somewhat thin tone but a wealth of pleasing ideas."

During the McShann years, Parker is supposed to have acquired his nickname of Yardbird because of his fondness for chicken. Parker himself was said to have traced it back to his school days and a series of transformations from Charlie to Yarlie to Yarl to Yard to Yardbird to Bird. Another story has Parker, underage, avidly keeping up with the music in the Kansas City clubs by sneaking into the backyards behind the buildings and listening—sometimes even playing along. However he got his nickname, it stuck. Some called him Yard; most called him Bird. Those who were aware knew that he had brought a new language to jazz.

While McShann was playing at the Savoy Ballroom in New York in 1941, Gene Ramey relates, people like Gillespie, Chubby Jackson, and Big Sid Catlett would come to sit in. At the same time, Parker was doubling at Monroe's, playing after-hours sessions. He spoke to Leonard Feather of these years later. "At Monroe's I heard sessions with a pianist named Allen Tinney; I'd listen to trumpet men like Lips Page, Roy, Dizzy, and Charlie Shavers outblowing each other all night long. And Don Byas was there, playing everything there was to be played. I heard a trumpet man named Vic Coulsen playing things I'd never heard. Vic had the regular band at Monroe's, with George Treadwell also on trumpet, and a tenor man named Prichett. That was the kind of music that caused me to quit McShann and stay in New York."

Monroe's became Parker's main base of operations. In this period he also worked with Noble Sissle's band, doubling on clarinet. Some have reported that he was with Sissle for nine months, but the leader has placed the time as "maybe three or four weeks." Bird had but one solo in the book, and the relationship was not the most pleasant.

His next affiliation was much happier. At the urging of Billy Eckstine, Benny Harris, and lead altoist Scoops Carry, Earl Hines hired Parker for his band. (If you are familiar with Carry's solo on Hines's "Jelly Jelly," you can hear that Bird listened to him with more than half an ear.) Since both alto chairs were filled, Hines bought him a tenor. For ten months in 1943, Parker played with the band; but due to the ban set by the musicians' union, no recorded evidence exists.

While Hines was rehearsing at Nola Studios in New York, the modern clique continued to jam at the uptown clubs. One night tenor great Ben Webster heard Parker at Minton's and took the instrument from his hands. "That horn," he said, "ain't supposed to sound that fast." But that night, Webster walked all over town telling everyone, "Man, I heard a guy—I swear he's gonna make everybody crazy on tenor."

Bird is reputed to have said of the tenor, "Man, this thing is too big." After the Hines days he returned to it for only two record dates, both with Miles Davis, in August, 1947, and in January, 1953. Perhaps he did not feel comfortable on tenor, but he played it convincingly, especially on the earlier Davis session, which produced "Sippin' at Bell's," "Little Willie Leaps," "Milestones," and "Half Nelson," and part of Bird's influence on Sonny Rollins can be ascribed to these sides.

Parker was brilliant on all the reeds. Anyone who had heard him play Charlie Ventura's baritone saxophone one night at the Royal Roost in December of 1948 would have to agree that he handled the large horn with the same ease as he did the alto, without sacrificing any tonal character.

Dizzy Gillespie tells of Parker on tenor with Hines. "He played superbly with that band," Diz is quoted as saying. "I remember Sarah Vaughan would sing 'This Is My First Love' [probably 'You Are My First Love'], and Bird would play 16 bars on it. The whole band would be turned to look at him. Nobody was playing like that."

Parker was not neglecting his alto either. He would bring it to theater engagements and practice between shows. This diligent attitude was not standard procedure, however. Often he would miss shows completely or fall asleep onstage. He wore dark glasses, and as Billy Eckstine has recounted, "Earl used to swear he was awake. He was the only man I knew who could sleep with his jaws poked out to look like he was playing."

Because of his bad feet, he often would take his shoes off during a performance. Once when Scoops Carry awakened him to take his solo, Bird ran out to the microphone in his stocking feet.

Many times the men in the band would gang up on him for a mass "lecture" regarding his dilatory actions, but heroin had a good hold on Bird by then and presented them too formidable a foe.

When Eckstine left Hines in 1943 he tried to make it as a single, but by 1944 he decided that he wanted a big-band setting again. He understood and supported the new jazz movement because he had been so involved with it in Hines's band. He also felt that the time was right for the public to receive the full impact of the innovations. He had picked up trumpet with Hines, but now he was playing valve trombone in an exuberant, if not particularly inventive, manner. In June of 1944 he formed his own band with the help of Budd Johnson, the man Parker had replaced in the Hines band. An effort was made to get as many of the Hines alumni as possible. Gillespie was one. Parker, who had played with Cootie Williams and Andy Kirk in the interim and was now working with Carroll Dickerson at the Rhumboogie in Chicago, was another. Both joined as the nucleus of a band that was to feature some of the best of the up-and-coming youngsters during the three years of its existence. Sarah Vaughan was one of them, and as with Hines, she sang "You Are My First Love." Parker again played his solo, this time on alto. Art Blakey, Eckstine's drummer, referring to a Saturday night in Chicago, has said, "That man came out and took sixteen bars and stopped the show. The house was packed. People applauded so loud we couldn't go on. We had to do it all over again."

An October 1, 1944, review by Johnny Sippel in *Down Beat*, written while the band was at the Regal Theatre in Chicago, notes. "Driving force behind the reeds is Charlie Parker, destined to take his place behind Hodges as a stylist on alto sax. After hearing this band doing six shows during the week at the Regal, your reviewer didn't hear repeats on many of the choruses which Parker did. His tone is adequate, but the individualizing factor is his tremendous store of new ideas."

Parker never recorded with Eckstine, for he did not stay with the band very long. His roots were in Fifty-second Street, where the new music now had its unofficial headquarters. Parker soon was leading his own trio, with

Joe Albany on piano and Stan Levey on drums. Albany says that they played Monday nights at the Famous Door and that Baby Lawrence used to come in and dance with them. Levey places the club as the Spotlite and says, "This was Bird's first gig as leader, and it was also the first chance I really had a chance to hear him play. Oh, I'd heard his record of "Swingmatism" with Jay McShann, but that was all. My first impression of Charlie's playing was that he was a sort of Pied Piper. I'd never heard anything like it. I didn't really know what he was doing, but it made me feel good to listen to him."

On September 15, 1944, Parker recorded with guitarist Tiny Grimes for Savoy. "Bird used to come in and jam with me all the time," said Grimes, who worked extensively on Fifty-second Street between 1944 and 1947. "When I got this date, I called him to make it." With Parker and Grimes were Clyde Hart, an important transitional pianist in the early forties; Harold "Doc" West, a drummer who had been with Bird in the McShann band; and bassist Jimmy Butts. Grimes sings on two numbers, "Romance Without Finance" and "I'll Always Love You Just the Same," and Parker solos convincingly on all four sides. These titles are far from the kind of original material that he was to record with Gillespie five months later. "Tiny's Tempo," by Hart, is a riff blues, typical of the previous era, and Parker's "Red Cross," based on "I Got Rhythm," combines a "Mop Mop" figure (Leonard Feather has attributed the piece "Mop Mop," copyrighted by Coleman Hawkins, to Parker) with a tricky run. Although his tone is not fully developed—it has not yet lost all its baby fat, so to speak—Bird's ideas suggest what he was going to do in the very near future. Undoubtedly, some of the freedom of his rhythmic phrasing is hampered by the more conservative time feeling of his mates.

In the company of Gillespie, Hart, guitarist Remo Palmieri, bassist Slam Stewart, and drummer Cozy Cole, some five months later, Parker played in the manner to which he later made us accustomed. The material recorded is more in keeping with the improvisatory inclinations of Parker and Gillespie, and naturally the playing that springs from songs like "Groovin' High" (based on the chords of "Whispering") and "Dizzy Atmosphere" is more consistently representative. Even the standard ballad "All the Things You Are" is fitted out with a new introduction and coda. An insight into how the two sessions differ can be found by comparing the approaches of Grimes and Palmieri.

In May, 1945, a significant event took place. Parker and Gillespie appeared with their own quintet on Fifty-second Street at the Three Deuces. With them were Al Haig, piano; Curly Russell, bass; and Stan

Levey, drums. When the group recorded for Guild Records the versatile veteran Sid Catlett replaced Levey on the session that produced the swift, intricate "Shaw 'Nuff," "Salt Peanuts," and Tadd Dameron's beautifully integrated composition called "Hot House." In addition, Sarah Vaughan sang a "Lover Man" that perhaps did not have the polish of her later singing but did have a pure beauty that her work has not always shown since.

"Shaw 'Nuff" and "Hot House" were definitive statements of the new music, recorded documents of the quintet's stay at the Deuces, and a culmination of the ideas that had been developing in the first half of the decade. Parker and Gillespie execute the unison work with fiery perfection and complement each other's solos marvelously. In an interview with Maitland Edey, Jr., Gillespie said, "I guess I probably played my best with Charlie Parker. He would inspire you; he'd *make* you play. And he always used to play before I did, so I had to follow him." Gillespie also traced his and Bird's ideas, and related how they became interdependent, from their first meeting in Kansas City. "At first we stressed different things," he said. "I was more for chord variations and he was more for melody, I think. But when we got together each influenced the other."

When he was asked the important differences between bebop and the jazz that preceded it, Gillespie put everything into perspective. "Well, chords," he stated. "And we stressed different accents in the rhythms. But I'm reluctant to say that anything is *the* difference between our music of the early forties and the music before that, of the thirties. You can get records from the early days and hear guys doing the same things. It just kept changing a little bit more; one guy would play a phrase one way, and another guy would come along and do something else with it. . . . Charlie Parker was very, very melodic; guys could copy his things quite a bit. Monk was one of the founders of the movement too, but his playing, my playing, and Charlie Parker's playing were altogether different."

Two other significant recording sessions took place in 1945. In June, an all-star date, combining older-style players like Teddy Wilson, Red Norvo, Slam Stewart, and Flip Phillips with Parker and Gillespie, was done for Comet and issued on two 12-inch 78-rpm records under Norvo's name. The titles are "Congo Blues," "Hallelujah," "Get Happy," and "Slam Slam Blues" (other "takes" of both "Congo" and "Slam Slam" were later issued as "Bird's Blues"). The contrast in the styles of the players is marked, and Bird and Diz stand out in bold relief. At the same time, the group is homogeneous, illustrating Gillespie's point about the similarity of the styles of the thirties and forties.

On "Slam Slam," a slow, "down home" blues, Parker shows his blues roots quite directly and foreshadows his famous "Parker's Mood." The faster "Congo" has no written opening line; the solos by Gillespie and Parker spring from interludes of Afro-Cuban rhythm into straight 4/4. (Incidentally, there has always been confusion over who the drummer is on the various tracks, Specs Powell or J. C. Heard. Heard told me, "I was doing a session in another studio in the same building. When I finished, I went to their studio to visit, and Dizzy asked me to sit in on 'Congo Blues' and 'Slam Slam Blues.'" Therefore, we can assume that Powell is on the other two.)

The other session took place on November 26 and still stands as a milestone in jazz history. It was the date for Savoy that included "Now's the Time," "Billie's Bounce," "Ko Ko," and "Thriving From a Riff." It was the first time that Parker was actually the leader on a record date, and on it he made two of his most durable masterpieces.

The simple blues riff "Now's the Time" later became a rhythm-and-blues hit under the title of "The Hucklebuck" (Parker did not get credit on the r&b version). Parker's solo combines the heritage of his Kansas City background with his longer-lined, more rhythmically complex flights. The naked beauty of this solo has stood up for twenty years without losing any of its impact as a piece of art.

The other blues line, "Billie's Bounce" (it should have read "Billy's Bounce" as it was named for booking agent Billy Shaw), is a more intricate theme; its rhythmic contours are as representative of the new music as "Now's the Time" is of the old.

The second masterpiece is the virtuoso performance by Parker on "Ko Ko," a whirlwind workout on the chords of "Cherokee." Parker had been featured on "Cherokee" with McShann and had made extensive use of it in jam sessions from that time on. Its difficult progressions in the middle section were a stumbling block for a great many musicians. Bird not only negotiated them but played inventively as he whipped along. Martin Williams wrote of this recording: "Ko Ko" may seem only a fast-tempo showpiece at first, but it is not. It is a precise, linear improvisation, for one thing, which has exceptional melodic content, and, incidentally, at times almost an atonality in its handling of the chord changes from "Cherokee." It is an almost perfect example of virtuosity *and* economy: following a pause, notes fall over and between this beat and that beat—breaking them asunder, robbing them of any vestige of monotony—rests fall where heavy beats once came, now heavy beats come between beats and on weak beats. It has been a source book of ideas for fifteen years and no wonder; now that its basic innovations are more familiar, it seems even more a great performance in itself."

Musicians have called the last break that Parker takes at the close of the piece a condensed history of bop. "He says it *all* in there," has been a typical comment.

"Warming Up a Riff," an incomplete, slower version of "Cherokee" recorded while the musicians were running through the number, does not match the brilliance of "Ko Ko" but it too is great and demonstrates the way Parker developed a solo—retaining, discarding, shaping with a spontaneity found only in the master players. "Meandering," a ballad improvisation on "Embraceable You" also cut with the musicians unaware, was not released until Savoy compiled an anthology of the entire date on an LP entitled *The Charlie Parker Story*. (This album is one of a series, issued after Parker's death, in which his entire output for the label, including incomplete takes, was issued.) Parker's ballad style, at least as of "Meandering," had not developed to the full extent of breaking up a melody line as he was to do later on his Dial recordings. "Thriving from a Riff" (originally issued as "Thriving on a Riff") is based on "I Got Rhythm." Its theme later became known as "Anthropology."

As a result of some liner notes by pianist John Mehegan on the back of the LP, confusion resulted concerning the correct personnel. Mehegan called the pianist Bud Powell and kept citing his introductions as "typical Bud intros," which they would not have been even if it had been Powell playing them. On the original 78-rpm issues, the label lists one Hen Gates as the pianist. It was assumed at the time that this was Dizzy Gillespie, and this is correct. (Later, a pianist from Philadelphia, Jimmy Foreman, used the same pseudonym in Gillespie's big band.) The evidence was corroborated in *The Jazz Review* by Sadik Hakim (known in the forties by his birth name, Argonne Thornton), who also revealed that he played on "Thriving" but that Gillespie was on piano for all other selections. A comparison of the piano solo on "Thriving" with Thornton's work on recordings with Eddie "Lockjaw" Davis, Dexter Gordon, and Lester Young substantiates his claim. His unique, dissonant, arpeggiated style is very recognizable.

Gillespie also plays the short trumpet passages on "Ko Ko." It is not he on "Thriving" as the notes suggest. Miles Davis just played a more organized solo than the ones he took on "Billie's Bounce" and "Now's the Time," but Davis' solos on these two numbers are not as "lugubrious and unswinging" as Mehegan says; they represent a young, nervous Miles, but nevertheless they have beauty. At that time, incidentally, Miles was heavily indebted to Freddie Webster.

In 1945, Parker also appeared on some recording dates as a sideman for the Continental label. Among his short solos and background comments are some unforgettable gems: the introduction and solo on "Mean to Me" with Sarah Vaughan; an obbligato to blues shouter Rubberlegs Williams "4-F Blues," a gorgeous melody statement and interpretation on "Dream of You" with trombonist Trummy Young; and a brilliant set of exchanges with Gillespie on Trummy's "Sorta Kinda."

Besides working with Gillespie on Fifty-second Street in 1945, Parker later led a group of his own in the fall of the year at the Spotlite, a club hosted by Clark Monroe of Uptown House fame. Sir Charles Thompson was a member of the group, and in September the pianist used Bird and a third man from the combo, Dexter Gordon, together with trumpeter Buck Clayton, on a date for Apollo that produced "Takin' Off," "If I Had You," "20th Century Blues," and "The Street Beat." Parker is in typically swift form on "The Street Beat" and "20th Century Blues" is a lovely vehicle for Bird's earthy expression.

At the very end of the year, Bird rejoined Dizzy, who had returned to a small group after an unsuccessful try at forming a big band. Together, they went to the West Coast for an engagement at Billy Berg's in Hollywood. California was not ready for them. Outside of a small circle of musicians and hip listeners, the reaction they received was hostile. Then, too, the price of heroin, according to Howard McGhee, was much higher than in New York. Parker did not always show up, and Gillespie had to hire tenor man Lucky Thompson to augment the band, which included Al Haig, Stan Levey, vibraphonist Milt Jackson, and bassist Ray Brown.

Ross Russell, who ran the Tempo Music Shop, a store that specialized in jazz, decided to form a record company and picked this group to do the first date. A rehearsal was scheduled, but the studio was overrun with visiting hipsters to the point of chaos. "Diggin' for Diz," an original (based on the chords of "Lover") by arranger-pianist George Handy, was committed to disc, however. According to Russell, Handy played piano on the date. Previously, Dodo Marmarosa was thought to be the pianist.

The actual session never came off as scheduled. When it came time to do the date, on February 7, neither Parker nor Handy was there. Gillespie and the rest of his group recorded five tunes, one of which was "Diggin' for Diz." Thus Russell's Dial label was born. The version with Parker and Handy was released many years later and is a rare item.

I remember hearing Bird, Dizzy, and their band on Rudy Vallee's weekly network radio program during this time. (Crooner Vallee, who also plays alto sax, was Parker's boyhood idol, the man who supposedly inspired him to take up the alto.) Singer-pianist Harry "The Hipster" Gibson was appearing with Vallee on a fairly regular basis, and he was instrumental in placing Bird and Diz on the show. The reaction at Berg's got no better, however, and Gillespie decided to return to New York in February. Parker remained. Gillespie has explained this with, "They wanted to know why I left him in California. I didn't. I gave him his fare and he spent it and stayed on."

Drummer Levey has told it more explicitly. "When the time came for the band to leave, I had all the plane tickets for the guys. But Charlie couldn't be found. He'd disappeared. For two hours that night, I took cabs all over town looking for him. Not a trace. I guess I must have spent $20 on cabfare. Finally, I gave up, rode out to Burbank airport, and took off for New York. Bird never made that plane."

This was the beginning of a slide that eventually put Parker in Camarillo. Bird was really scuffling. Howard McGhee tells of him coming to the club where McGhee was working in order to borrow money. Stories have it that he was living in a reconverted garage.

On March 28, close to two months after Gillespie's Dial date, Parker finally recorded for Russell. This was the session that included Gillespie's "A Night in Tunisia," with Parker's famous four-bar break, into which he poured another miniature history of modern jazz; "Ornithology," and two Parker compositions—the rhythmic "Moose the Mooche" and the melodic "Yardbird Suite." Miles Davis had come out to the Coast with Billy Eckstine and was on the date, along with Lucky Thompson, Dodo Marmarosa, and guitarist Arv Garrison, among others. Parker is mellower here than he was later on in his quintet days, except for the fantastic break and driving solo on "Tunisia." The relaxed delivery on "Yardbird Suite" and "Ornithology" (another master of this was released as "Bird Lore") shows his link to Lester Young in spirit if not in exact style.

From January to April, Bird also appeared at several of Norman Granz's Jazz at the Philharmonic bashes, some of which have been pre-served on record. JATP, as the series came to be known, was started by Granz, then a film editor at MGM studios, in July of 1944 at Los Angeles' Philharmonic Auditorium. His first tour with a JATP unit (through the Western states and Canada) was not too successful, but when albums recorded onstage at the Los Angeles concerts enjoyed wide sales, Granz was able to travel with a troupe all over the United States.

The basic unit usually consisted of a couple of trumpets, at least two tenor saxophones, a couple of altos, a trombone, and a rhythm section. Excitement, engendered by feverish solos backed by riffs from the other horns, was the main ingredient. In effect, JATP was a jam session moved from a smoky club to the concert stage. However, with the loss of the informality of jamming, there was an air of hokey emotionalism, although this was not so prevalent in the early years as later. Whatever shortcomings JATP had, there was always something of musical merit to hear, and often the excitement was genuine.

Parker's work in the 1946 concerts contains some raggedy passages and a number of reed squeaks, and the background riffs are sometimes as much against as with him, but nevertheless, he manages to spin a few classics. His solo on "Lady Be Good" is one of his grand statements; "After You've Gone" becomes a cyclonic wind in his swinging holler; and the twists and turns with which he negotiates "I Can't Get Started" contain a rare kind of acrid beauty.

One West Coast altoist, Sonny Criss, was strongly moved during the short time Bird spent playing in California. His sound and style were extremely reminiscent of the way Bird sounded in the JATP recordings.

The strained edge in Bird's playing was reflective of what he was feeling in California. Economically and mentally, things became worse for him. For a while he had a group with Miles Davis, Joe Albany, bassist Addison Farmer, and drummer Chuck Thompson at the Club Finale. He also sat in at an after-hours place called Lovejoy's. After receiving a bad write-up in a local paper, he told trumpeter Art Farmer, "Diz got away while the getting was good, and I'm catching everything."

Things came to a head on July 29, during a recording date for Dial with Howard McGhee, pianist Jimmy Bunn, bassist Bob "Dingbod" Kesterson, and drummer Roy Porter. Bird was in a state of anxiety that even a great quantity of straight whiskey could not alleviate. He never forgave Russell for later releasing the sides, but actually, although below his best, they are not quite so bad as they seemed to many listeners when first issued. McGhee recounts that "Bird was really disturbed. He was turning around and around, and his horn was shooting up in the air, but the sound came out fine. There were no wrong notes, and I feel that the records are beautiful."

Perhaps McGhee is a bit overzealous in his praise, for "Max Is Making Wax" is extremely chaotic, and Parker's short solo on "Bebop" clearly shows the tension he was under—he is in and out of the ensemble in an obviously unrehearsed manner. "The Gypsy" is played almost straight, but it is not incompetent; rather, it is more like a beginner who is content to just play his piece and risk no mistakes by being venturesome. The most famous of the four sides is "Lover Man." What seems to be halting playing here was just Bird's way of breaking up a melody line as he later showed with "Don't Blame Me" and "Embraceable You." It is a performance of rare beauty. Charlie Mingus once chose it when asked to name his favorite Parker recordings. "I like all," he said, "none more than the other, but I'd have to pick 'Lover Man' for the feeling he had then and his ability to express that feeling."

In all the numbers, you can hear tension and anguish in Parker's sound, for this is where a man's state of being is really bared. There is a pathetic air about "The Gypsy" and the little whimper at the end of "Bebop" is unnerving.

There have been many reports and many interpretations of what happened to Charlie Parker at the "Lover Man" session, but the most plausible comes from an eyewitness who says that Parker had been taking the stimulant Benzedrine for several days and was in shaky condition as the effects of its prolonged use began to tell. A young physician present at the date observed Parker's condition and, knowing of his heroin addiction, mistook his symptoms for heroin withdrawal. Accordingly, he gave Parker a stimulant, assuring him it would help. It was the last thing that the altoist's physical and mental condition could stand, and it pushed him over the brink he had been skirting for months.

After the date, back in his hotel, Parker set fire to his room, presumably by falling asleep with a cigarette in his hand, and then ran down to the lobby without his pants. The police were called, and eventually he was committed to Camarillo State Hospital. Elliott Grennard, who wrote the short story "Sparrow's Last Jump," based on the recording session and its attendant incidents, felt that Bird's breakdown was due to lack of drugs, because as soon as the doctor gave him a shot of morphine, he became rational again.

Parker spent six months at Camarillo, where he was given psychiatric treatment. Bird was released in Russell's custody after much effort, many visits, and the employment of a private psychiatrist. Some of the people active in West Coast jazz circles helped stage a benefit for Bird and raised between $600 and $900. With the money, he purchased some clothes and two plane tickets back to New York. The other ticket was for Doris Sydnor, a girl he had known since 1944, who was to become his third wife in 1948. She had traveled to California to visit him in the hospital.

Before leaving for New York, Parker did two dates for Dial. The first was for the purpose of recording singer Earl Coleman, at Bird's insistence. Russell figured that if he did this, he wouldn't have to use Coleman on a farewell date he had planned, one that would include McGhee and tenor saxophonist Wardell Gray.

Erroll Garner was in Los Angeles working as a single. He had headed a trio including bassist Red Callender and Drummer Doc West, but none of the clubs would pay him enough to maintain it. As Callender and West were still around, the trio was engaged to accompany Parker and Coleman. It was agreed that the trio would do two sides, and "Trio" and "Pastel" were recorded.

Coleman, a disciple of Billy Eckstine, took two hours and twenty minutes of the three-hour session to finish his numbers, but he was better than Russell had given him credit for. In fact, "This Is Always" sold extremely well as a single, and "Dark Shadows" is a moving blues. Parker blows concisely and beautifully in his solo space. Part of his solo from the original issue of "Dark Shadows" was transcribed for Woody Herman's saxophone section in the band's arrangement of "I've Got News for You." Bird's solos were new songs with melodies that were at once logical and disarming. Gillespie has recounted a story that illustrates the essence of this talent. "I saw something remarkable one time," said Diz. "He didn't show up for a dance he was supposed to play in Detroit. I was in town, and they asked me to play instead. I went up there, and we started playing. Then I heard this big roar, and Charlie Parker had come in and started playing. He'd play a phrase, and people might never have heard it before. But he'd start it, and the people would finish it with him, humming. It would be so lyrical and simple that it just seemed the most natural thing to play."

The quartet sides without Coleman are "Cool Blues" (one of the faster masters was released as "Hot Blues") and "Bird's Nest," an "I Got Rhythm" derivative. Parker and Garner are not ideally suited to each other, but there is no severe clash. To the contrary, the passage of time has been kind to their collaboration, and one finds much that is swinging and witty in spite of the variance of their time conceptions.

The Garner session was done on February 19. A week later, the septet date with McGhee, Gray, guitarist Barney Kessel, Marmarosa, and the rest took place. McGhee is credited with three tunes, "Cheers," "Stupendous," and "Carvin' the Bird," although the latter, a blues, later showed up as "Swedish Pastry," written by Kessel, on a recording by Swedish clarinetist Stan Hasselgard for Capitol. "Stupendous" is loosely based on Gershwin's "'S Wonderful" and has the uncommon AABC construction. On "Carvin' the Bird," Parker does the "carvin'," as he is anchor man in the three-horn exchanges. Once he has said it, it is the final word.

Bird's one written contribution, supposedly ready weeks before the date, was, according to Russell, "scribbled in a taxicab on the way out." This is "Relaxin' at Camarillo" a blues line, but one, like "Billie's

Bounce," that contains shifting accents quite unlike any blues from the past. At a rehearsal two days before the date, the entire time was spent, Russell once explained, "in everybody's trying to learn this sinuous twelve-bar line. Actually, they didn't get it down anywhere near cold by the end. I remember driving Dodo Marmarosa home later that night. He kept talking about this line. It was still bugging him. He hadn't been able to get it straight. It was only twelve bars, but he couldn't get it."

I remember talking with a young tenor saxophonist from Detroit in the summer of 1947. We had come from hearing Bird at the Onyx on Fifty-second Street. He hadn't played "Camarillo," but Ralph Diamond brought it up because he knew I had just begun to play alto. "If you can play "Camarillo" you've got the whole thing," he said. He wasn't implying that once you knew this tune you could use the licks interchangeably on any song and play bebop in six easy lessons. What he was saying made great sense: if one mastered this line, he would then have a grasp of the rhythmic nuances implicit in Bird's music that made it a new and vital force.

Kenny Clarke said of "Camarillo." "It shows exactly how Bird felt about the blues and the odd sets of progressions he'd devise to prove that he knows more about the blues than any living musician."

When Parker came back to New York in 1947, he began his most creative period, one in which he led his own quintet in clubs across the United States and on several trips to Europe. First of all, he surrounded himself with sidemen who were in complete rapport with him, musicians who understood his music and knew how to complement it. Miles Davis had not yet reached full maturity (the years with Parker helped him greatly toward this goal), but he had improved tremendously since 1945. His light, middle-register sound was a perfect foil for Bird; if his solos were not up to Parker's on the very fast numbers, his personal lines were refreshing at medium tempo, and his tender, sustained-note ballad performances were an apt contrast to Parker's darting, intricate interpretations of standards.

Although Bud Powell was on the Savoy session that produced "Donna Lee" (long credited to Parker but said by Gil Evans to have been written by Davis), "Buzzy," "Chasin' the Bird" and "Cheryl," the pianist who backed Bird most of the time in the rich years was Duke Jordan, a sensitive accompanist with a lyrical solo style. Together with bassist Tommy Potter and drummer Max Roach, Jordan helped form a rhythm section that was the ideal climate in which Parker could flourish. The recordings made for Dial and Savoy in 1947 and 1948 are the classic performances.

As a body of work, they represent the refinement of a musical philosophy and the quintessence of small-band playing in their era just as Louis Armstrong's Hot Five and Count Basie's Jones-Smith Inc. were definitive in theirs.

There were so many facets to Parker's giant talent, and each is well illustrated by the recordings of this period. Vibraphonist Teddy Charles, in naming his favorite Parker recordings, categorized several from the 1947–1948 period in a neat little itinerary: "Bird the Pioneer, showing disciples the way, founding settlements and schools. Swingtown—"Scrapple from the Apple," Bluesville—'Parker's Mood' and 'Cheryl.' Counterpoint—'Chasing the Bird' and 'Ah-Leu-Cha,' and Melodyburg— 'Embraceable You.' "

Blues, always vital to Parker, are found in abundant variety, from the elemental "Parker's Mood" and "Bluebird" through the Latin-flavored "Barbados" and "Bongo Bop" to the sophisticated "Cheryl" and the blithe, buoyant "Perhaps."

Another favorite jumping-off place for Parker was the "I Got Rhythm" chord pattern. As with the blues, he made his own variations, sometimes intermixing portions of "Honeysuckle Rose" and "I Got Rhythm"—as on "Scrapple from the Apple"—but, more importantly, interpreting these progressions in his own way. He made the multimeaning word "changes," the designation for chord progressions, seem especially appropriate. These numbers were usually driving, up-tempo outings with diamond-hard Parker, such as "Dexterity," "Crazeology," and the mercurial "Constellation." Nor did he limit his breakneck tempos to the "Rhythm" pattern—"Bird Gets the Worm" (on "Lover, Come Back to Me") and "Klaunstance" (on "The Way You Look Tonight") are virtuoso performances of the highest order. The remarks made by French clarinetist Hubert Rostaing are relevant here. He called Parker "an incredible improviser, who exploits his virtuosity but does so almost unconsciously, because he has something to say and not because he has worked up a chorus that is hard to play. His instrumental technique is extraordinary, but personal; he plays such and such a figure because he 'feels' it (though sometimes he plays bits of phrases that 'fall under his fingers'), and the most complicated one always has a typical stamp that is his alone."

The selections mentioned in the immediately preceding paragraphs are all by Parker, save "Crazeology." His compositions have the same clarity and spontaneity as his playing. Perhaps his best piece is "Confirmation." Martin Williams feels this way and has described it as "a most delightful and ingenious melody. For one thing," he wrote, "it is a continuous linear invention. Most pop songs and jazz pieces have two parts, a main strain and a bridge, or middle strain. The main strain is played twice before the bridge and once after it. 'Confirmation' skips along beautifully with no repeats (except for one very effective echo phrase) until the last eight bars, which are a kind of repeat in summary.

"Moreover, the bridge does not seem an interruption or an interlude that breaks up the flow of the piece but is a part of the continuously developing melody. Finally, if the chord sequence to 'Confirmation' preceded the melody, then the melody became so strong as Parker worked on it that it forced him to alter the chords to fit its developing contours."

Parker's ballad playing created yet another atmosphere—it is definitely "love" music. His way of sculpting a melody line was completely unique. André Hodeir compared it with Louis Armstrong's way. "Louis transfigures the original melody by subtly distorting it rhythmically and by adding some extra figures," writes the French critic. "Bird encloses it and leaves it merely implied in a musical context that is sometimes fairly complex."

Citing the classic performances of "Don't Blame Me" and "Embraceable You," he remarks, "Parker now and again lets the phrase-pretext put in a brief appearance, but at other times it can only be guessed at behind the garland of notes in which it is embedded and which, far from being useless embroidery, form by themselves a perfectly articulated musical discourse of which the theme, hidden or expressed, is merely one of the constituent elements."

The period 1947–1948 was the zenith of Charlie Parker's career and the time of his greatest influence. He shaped musicians of all instruments, but primarily this multifaceted player turned out hundreds of alto saxophonists for each of his sides. Every city had its "Bird." Most jazz fans have never heard of John Pierce (not the one who played with George Russell in the sixties), Art Whittecombe, Bill Spencer, Flaps Dungee, Bill Cannon, Johnny Carter, or Leo Douglas. Phil Woods, Charlie Mariano, Cannonball Adderley, Jackie McLean, and Charles McPherson are more familiar names. Each, in his own way, reflects Bird in general and in varying specifics. But no one has been able to get the whole man; each has had to be content with his own piece.

[. . .]

There was an alto saxophonist in the Gillespie band who also owed Bird, but perhaps not as much as most of his contemporary alto men. He was Ernie Henry, who, like both Parkers and Chaloff, failed to live out his thirties. Henry, who died at the age of 31 in December of 1957, first achieved recognition as a member of Tadd Dameron's group in 1947. He recorded with Dameron on both Savoy and Blue Note. "A Bebop Carol," "The Tadd Walk," "The Squirrel," "Dameronia," and "Our Delight" all feature his singing, upper-register swing. He had his own sound and style of phrasing even then. Other recordings of his during this period include "Doubletalk," "Boperation," and "The Skunk," with Howard McGhee and Fats Navarro on Blue Note.

In 1948 Henry joined Gillespie's orchestra and remained through 1949. He can be heard on the Victor recordings of "Duff Capers," "Swedish Suite," and, to especially good advantage, "Minor Walk."

In 1950 and 1951 Henry worked with Illinois Jacquet. Then he returned to Brooklyn and was not heard from, except for reports of an occasional jam session, for several years. In 1956, he worked and recorded with Thelonious Monk. He also recorded under his own name and with Kenny Dorham and Matthew Gee for Riverside in 1956 and 1957. At the time of his death, he had been back with the then re-formed Gillespie band for almost a year.

Some of Henry's most passionate, expressive work is with Monk on "Brilliant Corners" and "Ba-lue Bolivar Ba-lues-are" in the Riverside album *Brilliant Corners*. Several critics rapped his own LP's for out-of-tune playing and faulty fingering. If he had lived into the sixties, I wonder how he would have been judged by the supporters of the "new thing."

Although Charlie Mingus mistook Davey Schildkraut for Parker in a "Blindfold Test" [a column] it has most often been said that Sonny Stitt is "the closest thing to Bird." It is a cross he has had to bear throughout his career. At one point it turned him completely away from the alto to the tenor. Stitt has long insisted that he was playing his way before he had ever heard Parker. Miles Davis says he heard Sonny when Tiny Bradshaw's band came through St. Louis in 1942 and recalls that Stitt was playing in the same general style he employs today. Stitt himself says he did not hear the records Parker made with McShann until 1943. He was then 19 and was still with Bradshaw. He was anxious to meet Bird, and when the band's travels took him to Kansas City, he set out to find him. When he did, the two went to a club and jammed together for an hour. Stitt says that Parker then told him, "You sure sound like me."

The estimate is accurate if the word "sound" is emphasized. Sonny's sound and spirit are very close to Bird's, but there are some basic differences. Stitt attacks his notes differently. As Michael James has pointed out: "Even leaving aside structural differences—Stitt's style has been far more symmetrical, never so adventurous rhythmically . . . just as his choruses are much less complex than Bird's, so is the surface tension of his style considerably more uniform."

James's conclusion is also well-taken. "The material gleaned from Parker is not used to prop up some despicable piece of jerry-building but implements the basic structure of an edifice well designed in itself. That this is true in the earliest stages of his career is shown by his work on 1946 recordings such as 'Royal Roost' ('Rue Chaptal'), 'Epistrophy' and 'Fat Boy.' "

In 1946 Stitt also recorded excellent solos on "That's Earl Brother" and "Oop Bop Sh' Bam" with Dizzy Gillespie. In 1947, he was voted the new star on alto by the critics and musicians of a poll conducted by *Esquire* magazine. By this time, however, he was not around to receive the acclaim that went with this. He was in the Federal Narcotics Hospital in Lexington, Kentucky.

When he was released in late 1949, Sonny returned to the jazz scene on tenor saxophone. While he did not give up the alto completely, he certainly de-emphasized it. From 1950 to 1952 he co-led a small band with Gene Ammons. This unit recorded for Prestige, as did Stitt on his own. The tenor "battles" on "Blues Up and Down" and "Stringin' the Jug" with Ammons are creative as well as exciting. In the early sixties, Ammons and Stitt were reunited for a couple of club engagements and several records. By this time, however, Stitt was working on his own, but as a wanderer who would pick up a new rhythm section in each city he visited. Sonny also toured with JATP in 1958 and 1959, was reunited with Gillespie for three months in 1958, and played with Miles Davis in 1961.

In the sixties he was finally able to secure another cabaret card, the license that allows him to work in New York clubs. In a 1959 interview he told writer Dave Bittan, "I want to be in New York with my own combo. I'd like to get an apartment and make this city my headquarters. It was a long time ago when I got in trouble. I don't want to talk about it. It's a distasteful subject. I'm still paying for it. I was young. . . . I didn't know what it was all about. . . . My people were churchgoers and knew only the beautiful things in life. . . . They didn't tell me about the bad things."

Although born in Boston (in 1924), Sonny grew up in Saginaw, Michigan. His father, Edward Boatner, was a music teacher at Wylie and Sam Houston Colleges in Texas and led a one-thousand-voice choir at the New York World's Fair of 1939. He now teaches music in New York. Actor Clifton Webb once studied with him. Stitt's mother plays and teaches piano and organ. Sonny took the surname of her second husband, Robert Stitt. His brother Clifford, a concert pianist, and sister Adelaide, a singer, have kept the name Boatner.

In this musical family, young Edward (Sonny's given name) began to learn piano at the age of 7 but later switched to clarinet. Then came alto, tenor, and even baritone saxophone, on which he recorded some roaring solos in the early fifties. Now his playing time is divided between tenor and alto. He is equally adept on both, capable of high-velocity solos at medium and, especially, up tempos and of lyrical ballad expositions, although he does like to double-time on the latter. On tenor, his love of Lester Young shows through.

Stitt enjoys the challenge of a "cutting" session with another saxophonist, and he is a hard man to best in such horn-to-horn combat. Possessing a combination of stamina and inventiveness, he seldom loses. Those who were at the Half Note on a particular night in 1961 will attest that he fell before Zoot Sims on "Sweet Georgia Brown," but this is the exception rather than the rule. He has a justifiable pride in his talent. Fellow saxophonist Stan Getz has said of him, "With Stitt, you've gotta work. He doesn't let you rest. You've *got* to work or else you're left at the starting gate. It's hard for me to say which horn he's better on, alto or tenor."

Al Cohn tells of an incident involving Getz and Stitt that is as illustrative as it is amusing. "Stan was playing at the Red Hill in Camden, New Jersey, and Sonny came by to sit in. He called a very fast tempo and took the first solo. By the time Stan got to play, the bass player's hand was about to drop off. As soon as the number ended, Sonny packed up his horn and split. Stan said, 'And he didn't even give me a chance to get even with a ballad.' "

Most of Stitt's recording has been for Verve, although he has recorded for a variety of other labels in the sixties. In his days as a peripatetic leader, he was fortunate to have his peers accompany him when it came time to record. The complaint against the trios that backed him on his stops all over the map was that they were afraid of playing with him. By the time relaxation and confidence set in, he would be off to another town.

One of his best recordings on alto was done for Roost in the mid-fifties with a small ensemble and Quincy Jones arrangements. A blues, "Quince," and a heartfelt treatment of Tadd Dameron's "If You Could See Me Now" are not to be missed. "The Eternal Triangle," a long track in a Verve album with Dizzy Gillespie and Sonny Rollins, demonstrates the kind of tenor heat he can generate when confronted with such a formidable saxophonist as Rollins. Perhaps a better over-all picture of his talent can be gained by listening to *Personal Appearance*, a Verve album in which he plays both his horns in a group of selections typical of his repertory.

In 1962 Stitt recorded on alto with a string section, as Parker had done almost ten years before. He revealed here a talent for composing pretty melodies, reminiscent of "popular" music before the advent of rock 'n' roll. To some of these tunes, he has written lyrics, but they are as yet unrecorded as vocals.

One very good album from the sixties is *Stitt Plays Bird* on Atlantic. Today it takes something out of the ordinary to inspire Stitt to his full powers, and the Parker-based material is just that. And "Ko Ko," especially, is a performance of unrelenting drive that is thoughtful nevertheless.

An apocryphal story has it that several weeks before Parker's death, he met Stitt and told him, "Man, I'm not long for this life. You carry on. I'm leaving you the keys to the kingdom."

Several years later, Stitt's reaction to a magazine writer who tried to make him claim that he was the "new Bird" was one of hostility. "I'm no new Bird, man!" he cried. "And Cannonball Adderley isn't either! Nobody's Bird! *Bird died!*"

Parker's death occurred on March 12, 1955, but his physical decline had set in long before. In 1948 a doctor warned him about the dangerous condition of his health. As the forties became the fifties, however, he was still consistently in command of his powers. Kenny Dorham held the trumpet spot in his quintet after Davis, Al Haig replaced Duke Jordan, and Tommy Potter and Max Roach remained. In 1950 Red Rodney and Roy Haynes came in for Dorham and Roach; in 1951 it was Walter Bishop and Teddy Kotick who took over for Haig and Potter. On recording dates, the personnel was even more varied: Roach, Kenny Clarke, Davis, Rodney, and pianist John Lewis were among the sidemen.

This was the time that Parker began an association with Norman Granz, who was then affiliated with Mercury Records. Later, Granz formed his own companies, Clef and Norgran (these eventually became Verve), and continued to record Bird in a variety of formats. The most rewarding artistically was, as usual, the small group, which produced "Visa" and "Passport" in 1949 (although trombonist Tommy Turk intrudes heavily in "Visa"), "She Rote," and "Au Privave" in early 1951, and "Blues for Alice" and "Swedish Schnapps" in the summer of 1951. Then, too, there was the reunion with Gillespie in June of 1950.

For Granz, Parker first recorded some Afro-Cuban sides with

Machito's orchestra in December of 1948 and January of 1949. His solos on "Mango Manque," "Okiedoke," (it should have read *Okiedokie*, one of his favorite expressions), and "No Noise" (Flip Phillips is also on this one) show his marvelous ability to remain himself and still fit into an alien format. In December 1950, he and Phillips again played in front of Machito, this time in two sections of a Chico O'Farrill Afro-Cuban jazz suite. Both play separately on "Mambo," but in "Jazz," where the time is strictly 4/4, there are chase choruses in which Phillips, by preceding Parker, unwittingly helps demonstrate the pedestrian versus the sublime, as Bird makes silk purses out of sow's ears.

A Latin excursion of a different nature is the Parker LP *South of the Border*, recorded in two sessions (March, 1951, and January, 1952) with Benny Harris, Walter Bishop, and bongo and/or conga. The slight harmonic material and the clave combine to make this one of Parker's most earthbound sets, although he flies on "Tico Tico" and because he played "My Little Suede Shoes" it became a vehicle for fellow musicians, who otherwise might never have discovered it.

Bird again rises above the ordinary and the trite in the LP *Charlie Parker Big Band*, which includes standards like "What Is This Thing Called Love?," "Temptation," "Autumn in New York," and "Night and Day," arranged by Joe Lipman for conventional dance orchestra (March, 1952) plus string section (January, 1952). Included in this album are "Dancing in the Dark" and "Laura," two selections from a summer of 1950 *Bird with Strings* recording date. This ensemble, consisting of seven strings, oboe, French horn, harp, and rhythm section, was an amplification of a group used on a very successful album, the first *Bird with Strings* recording, made in November, 1949. In that one there were only four strings, harp, oboe, and/or English horn (played by Mitch Miller) in addition to the rhythm section.

The idea of casting Parker with strings came from "Repetition," recorded in the summer of 1949 and first issued in an album called *The Jazz Scene*. Neal Hefti had written the piece for big band with string section but with no soloist in mind. Parker happened to be in the studio and was included strictly as an afterthought, and at his own request, Granz wrote in the notes to the album: "Parker actually plays on top of the original arrangement; that it jells as well as it does is a tribute both to the flexible arrangement of Hefti and the inventive genius of Parker to adapt himself to any musical surrounding."

Dizzy Gillespie told of how "Yard used to come and play with my big band. He'd never heard the arrangements before, but you'd think he'd written them. The brass would play something and cut off, and bang! Charlie Parker was there, coming in right where he was supposed to. It's a shame that when he was making those records with strings that the music wasn't up to his standards. There should have been a whole symphony behind him."

The *Bird with Strings* albums consist of standards like "Summertime," "I Didn't Know What Time It Was," and "Everything Happens to Me," but the number most acclaimed is "Just Friends," a less obvious piece of material, wherein Parker departs much further from the melody than on the others. It is one of his classic performances, one of the few of his own recordings he admitted liking.

Many people felt that strings were Granz's idea, that their purpose was to make Parker more popular. Doris Parker claims that it was really Bird's desire to play with strings and that Granz was merely satisfying his wish. Admittedly, the surroundings are extremely conservative and bland, but you cannot argue with the beauty of Parker's playing. He is compelling even when just stating a melody.

As a result of these recordings, a wider audience did materialize, and Parker soon was booked into Birdland (the club that had been named for him) for sixteen weeks with the string ensemble. Tours followed, but often this necessitated hiring local string and rhythm sections that usually were not up to the standard Parker was used to in his accompanying units. A typical incident took place in Rochester, New York, in 1952. After playing the first set with a horrible house-band rhythm section, Bird bemoaned his predicament to jazz enthusiast Lon Flanigan. He told him and his friends, "I need a rhythm section like old people need soft shoes."

Flanigan recounted the outcome to writer Robert Reisner: "Luckily, this happened on a Tuesday night, when most of the good local musicians were not working. Enough of them were in the house to provide Bird with a decent beat for the rest of the night. Bird took the manager of the place aside, and, with some help from us, convinced him that the house band did not play an appropriate style for a bebop musician. The next day, Art Taylor and Walter Bishop arrived by plane to salvage the rest of the week."

How many times Parker was not rescued by his regulars we do not know, but it must have been a source of great annoyance for him to have to play with inferior musicians at a point in his career when he should have been enjoying his greatest success.

Strings were not the only accouterments that Bird was surrounded with in the fifties. In May, 1953, Granz recorded him backed by flute, oboe, bassoon, clarinet, French horn, rhythm, and a vocal group headed by Dave Lambert. Gil Evans did the arrangements. All this proved to be a bit rich as an overall musical diet, but Parker plays an idea-packed, kinetic solo on "In the Still of the Night," and just because he recorded "Old Folks"—like "My Little Suede Shoes"—his contemporaries also played it. A third number, "If I Love Again" finds him in a happy, skipping mood.

Granz also recorded Parker with JATP again, when Bird made the 1949 tour with Norman's troupe. These numbers are "The Opener," "Lester Leaps In," "Embraceable You," and "The Closer." Bird is particularly good on the last two.

A studio jam session of June, 1952, which also included Johnny Hodges, Benny Carter, and Ben Webster, produced sides containing some excellent Parker in a swing atmosphere. J. J. Johnson, writing of Bird's solo on "Funky Blues" (the title tune of the album), said: "As advanced as Charlie Parker played, he never lost sight of tradition and 'grass roots' in jazz. I suspect he enjoyed playing with Hodges and Webster and company." I'm sure he did. Bird had a love of and respect for good music of any kind. In a *Blindfold Test* conducted by Leonard Feather, he reacted to Ellington's "Passion Flower" with "a beatific grin as he recognized the alto soloist," wrote Feather.

"That was Duke," said Bird, "featuring Johnny Lily Pons Hodges! I always took my hat off to Johnny Hodges 'cause he can *sing* with the horn; oh, he's a beautiful person. That record deserves all the stars you can muster."

On the same occasion, Parker said of George Wettling's "Heebie Jeebies." "You want my honest opinion? Well, that's music—that's very good Dixieland." This was a period when the factions of jazz were at war, and Bird himself was subjected to some strong abuse from the "moldy figs," as the champions of modern jazz liked to call them.

Feather also played some classical music for Parker. Bird readily identified Stravinsky and said: "That's music at its best. I like all of Stravinsky—and Prokofiev, Hindemith, Ravel, Debussy and of course Wagner and Bach." Several years later he named Bartók as his favorite. In the forties, at the Roost, he would play the opening phrases of Hindemith's "Kleine Kammermusik" as a call to let his sidemen know that it was time for the next set. In the fifties, according to Bill Coss, "He never listened to jazz in his home. For that matter, he seldom listened to jazz anywhere unless he happened to be on a job. His main interest was in classical music, mostly the moderns. And when he was not devoting time to that he was watching Hopalong Cassidy or assorted other Westerners, or, when the Parkers lived on Tenth Street and Avenue B in New York, he was in the neighborhood bars, arguing for hours with Ukrainian laborers and their women. No one sat in on these occasions. It rather defies the imagination to think of Bird in such an atmosphere, but it seemed to give him a great deal of pleasure no matter the amount of actual communication that went on. That he really wanted that companionship could be seen in the fact that he entered a roundhouse brawl in one bar one day over a small point of honor and emerged beaten and battered but, finally, accepted by the group."

In July of 1950, Parker married his fourth wife, dancer Chan Richardson. They had two children, a daughter, Pree, born in 1951, and a son, Baird, born the following year. He also thought of Kim, Chan's daughter from a previous marriage, as his own. (Leon, his son from his first, teenage marriage, was born in 1937 and was raised by Bird's mother until he was 10.)

Parker's ill health, always lurking beneath the surface of his dissipation, hospitalized him in early 1951, just after he had returned from some European engagements. He had a peptic ulcer; it was to plague him, along with heart and liver trouble, through the last years of his life. He suffered much pain in the form of periodic attacks and seizures. Observed one night shortly before his death, he was eating codeine pills as if they were candy.

His daughter Pree became ill and died of pneumonia, and Parker's spirits were severely depressed during 1953 and 1954. Apparently he had given up heroin (Dr. Robert Freymann, who attended him at the time of his death, said that his eyes and used-up veins indicated that he wasn't using drugs), but he was drinking excessively. He took on weight, much of it bloat. Pictures taken in his last years show why people thought he was much older than he actually was.

Parker must have had a tremendous constitution to be able to abuse his body for as long as he did. His drinking was prodigious. Howard McGhee tells of Bird's polishing off eight double whiskeys before he started his first set at the Los Angeles club in which they were working. One night at the Magpie (as the little bar above Birdland was then called) in 1953, I saw him consume eight Manhattan cocktails in a half hour with no apparent ill effects.

Then there was the Prestige recording session of January, 1953, for which Miles Davis was flanked by the tenors of Sonny Rollins and Parker. (When the sides were finally released in the late fifties, as part of an LP called *Collector's Items*, Parker was billed as Charlie Chan, the pseudonym he first used on the *Jazz at Massey Hall* album.) I was the A&R man for the Davis recording, and as a callow youth who still placed his favorite musicians on pedestals, I had quite a task trying to serve as buffer between record company and musicians on the one hand and musicians and engineers on the other. Things were progressing in a relatively smooth manner, after Davis; late arrival, when the refreshments arrived. Bird had asked for gin, which I ordered, along with some beer. It was customary to have a bottle on hand in case someone wanted a drink, but I believe I did as many sessions with sandwiches and coffee as with alcohol.

There were six musicians on the date, and the likelihood of anyone really getting loaded was not great because there were several people to share one fifth of gin. I hadn't reckoned with Bird. He assumed command of the bottle and emptied most of its contents into his mouth before finally surrendering it. Then he fell asleep for a while. When he woke up he was moving slowly and rather deliberately. At the end of the session, Miles berated Bird for having gotten himself into such a condition on his record date and told Parker that he (Miles) had never done that to him. Parker, sobered and alert by then, said, "All right, Lily Pons," and offered him some deliberate clichés, including "To produce beauty, we must suffer pain—from the oyster comes the pearl."

(One thing might be cleared up here about the session. After his stumbling on the second "take" of "The Serpent's Tooth," Parker played a moving solo on "'Round Midnight," which I described in the notes to the album as being "full of the pain and disappointment he knew too well." But I also gave him credit for playing the bridges at the beginning and end of the song. It wasn't until Danish writer Erik Weidemann pointed out that it was Rollins that I realized my mistake. In the years that had elapsed between the recording and its release, I had forgotten something that I may have specifically asked for in the studio.)

It has been said that "some weeks before his death," Bird passed a blind accordionist on Broadway and, dropping some money in his cup, asked him to play "All the Things You Are." The event actually took place a week before the *Collector's Items* date. Bird had come over to Prestige to get an advance. Bob Weinstock had left a check for him, and Charlie wanted to know where he could cash it. Billie Wallington and I went over to the Colony Record Shop with him to facilitate matters. That is when we encountered the accordionist. When we left Colony, the accordionist was playing the song, and Bird praised the man for making the right changes. I don't remember whether Parker gave him any more money, but if he did, it was not "the last twenty-five cents in his old trousers," as one account of this incident has stated.

If he didn't wear old trousers, Bird often wore rumpled ones. The jazz musician has usually been known as a sharp dresser and often a style setter. Parker was the antithesis of this. In the late forties, his usual outfits were unpressed double-breasted pinstripe suits and loud floral-design ties. He paid a little more attention to clothes in the fifties—he was one of the first New Yorkers to wear a duffle coat—but clothes were never important to him.

Although he was not the natural clown that Gillespie is, Parker was a witty man. He used to introduce the trios that played opposite him at the Fifty-second Street clubs with an announcement that "put on" owner and audience at the same time. "The management has gone to grrrrrrreat expense," he would intone, "to bring you the next group. Let's bring them on with a rousing round of applause." The last line would be delivered with rapidity in a descending arc, it cadences amazingly like a Parker solo.

Once Gillespie was heading an all-star big band at Birdland that was billed as Dizzy Gillespie's Dream Band. Parker was not playing with the group, but he was standing nearby, between sets, when someone asked Diz, "How's your dream band?" When Gillespie replied, "You mean my *wet*-dream band," Bird with his resonant voice, affected a mock-professorial tone, which he did so well on occasion, and inquired loudly, "Are you referring to somnambulistic ejaculation?"

A stranger aspect of his humor was revealed one night at the Open Door in Greenwich Village. He and tenor man Brew Moore, after playing at each other's behinds as they walked slowly around the dance floor in a musical "goosing" session, finished up by playing to a large spot of old chewing gum stuck to the floor.

The sessions at the Open Door were Sunday evening affairs run by Bob Reisner, beginning in April, 1953, and continuing through 1954. Bird was featured many times, and although the quality of his performances varied, there were supreme moments. Once Parker brought in two corny singers who did "Route 66" in a near-hillbilly manner while he took an intermission. Any member of the audience who left played into Parker's hands. The purpose of his little experiment was to get a turnover. He had a percentage deal with Reisner, and there were people waiting outside to get in.

On another occasion, after taking a solo, he sat down on a chair in the middle of the floor (the group played right on the dance floor, as there was no bandstand) with a handkerchief held to his face, fell asleep, and couldn't be awakened.

Reisner summed up the situation when he wrote: "The Sunday sessions were full of suspense and drama. Would he show? Was he well? Would he hang around or wander off? One night he disappeared, and I found out later that he had played across the street at another place called The Savannah Club for free, or maybe a couple of drinks. He felt he could not be bought. When he played free or for a few friends, he was at his best. His performances were uneven, but what seemed bad temper and perverseness—like falling asleep on the stand—is understandable, considering that he had advanced ulcers, dropsy, bad heart, and with it all, he could play like a dream and could melt and cow people and fell a two-hundred-pound man with a blow. Bird was the supreme hipster. He made his own laws. His arrogance was enormous, his humility profound."

At the end of the summer of 1954, Parker was booked into Birdland with the strings. On the stand he called one tune and came in playing another. After chastising and firing the group, he went home and attempted suicide by drinking iodine. Later he claimed that the whole thing had been a ruse to get himself committed to the hospital so that he couldn't be legally held accountable for debts he had incurred. On September 1 he was admitted to Bellevue and remained there for nine more days. On September 28 he returned of his own accord. The hospital report stated: "The patient committed himself to the Psychiatric Pavilion, stating that he had been severely depressed since his previous discharge, that he was drinking again, and feared for his own safety." On October 15 he was "discharged in his own custody."

Fifteen days later, he was presented in concert in Town Hall by Reisner. Parker played as well as he ever had, thrilling the large crowd Unfortunately, the concert ended prematurely—it had started late, as many jazz concerts do—because of union regulations. The stagehands rang down the curtain while Bird was still playing. Leonard Feather has described Parker at the time of the concert: ". . . he looked healthy, talked sensibly, played magnificently and told me he was commuting daily between New Hope, Pa., where he and Chan had found a home, and Bellevue Hospital, where he was undergoing psychiatric treatment. He had dropped 20 pounds of unhealthy excess fat; he was like a new man, and New Hope seemed the right place for him to be living."

This happy state didn't last too long, however. Feather recounts meeting him at the bar above Birdland about a month before his death. He was "raggedly dressed. He said he had not been home to New Hope lately. The bloated fat was back. His eyes looked desperately sad."

Parker lived in Greenwich Village with friends in the last few months of 1954, occasionally traveling to nearby Eastern cities for short gigs. His last great recordings were a year behind him—sides made in August 1953, containing "Chi Chi," "I Remember You," "Now's the Time," and "Confirmation." These four feature a rhythm section of Al Haig, Percy Heath, and Max Roach. (The Verve LP *Now's the Time* lists these men for all eight selections, but actually Hank Jones and Teddy Kotick, along with Roach, are on the last four—"Laird Baird," "Kim," "Cosmic Rays," and "The Song Is You"—made in December, 1952.)

December, 1954, marked Parker's last record date. The two numbers taped were "Love for Sale" and "I Love Paris," eventually used to complete a *Charlie Parker Plays Cole Porter* album. It is worth listening to, as is anything else he did, but it is a tired Bird, and the exceptional moments are few.

His last public appearance was at Birdland. On occasion he had been barred from the club despite the fact that it had been named for him. The first night of the job, March 4, 1955, was also the last. With Parker were Kenny Dorham, Bud Powell, Charlie Mingus, and Art Blakey, a formidable array, to be sure. There was a good crowd early that evening at the club, drawn by the exciting prospect of hearing these five play together. What followed instead was chaotic and depressing. Parker had arrived early, in bedroom slippers, but left for something and returned late. Dorham has given this account: ". . . the trouble started right away. . . . He had words with Oscar Goodstein, and when Oscar said go and play, Bird, indicating Bud Powell, who was in no fit mental condition to, answered, 'What am I going to play when you give me this to play with?' Then Bud and Bird started to feud. Bud said 'What do you want to play, Daddy?' Bird said, 'Let's play some "Out of Nowhere."'

"Then Bud—that giant who was a shade below the caliber of Parker—asked Bird, who could play in any key and any time, 'What key you want it, Daddy?' Bird snarled back, 'S, Mother.' "

After this hassle, Parker played a few phrases and left the stand. He came back but refused to play. When Powell left the stand, Bird called his name repeatedly on the microphone. The troubles continued through the evening. Dorham did most of the soloing. Finally, Mingus grabbed the mike and told the audience that he didn't want to be associated with this and that these people were killing jazz. Bird got drunk and left the club. Someone saw him later at Basin Street, then located around the corner on Fifty-first Street, his face wet with tears.

Five days later, Parker stopped in at the apartment of his friend the Baroness Nica de Koenigswarter, called the Jazz Baroness, in the Hotel

Stanhope. He was to leave for a job in Boston that night but became ill and started vomiting blood shortly after he entered the room. Nica called her doctor, and he advised that Parker be taken to a hospital. When Bird refused, they decided that he could remain there. The Baroness and her daughter ministered to his needs, and Dr. Freymann visited him several times a day. On the third day, Saturday, Parker seemed much better. The doctor gave him permission to sit up and watch television. While laughing at a juggling act on the Dorsey brothers' show, he had a seizure. By the time the doctor arrived, minutes later, he was dead. The autopsy cited lobar pneumonia as the cause of death, but Freymann said it was a heart attack.

The Baroness has explained that she wanted to let Chan, from whom Parker had been separated, know about his death before she found out from the radio or newspapers. Therefore she did not notify anyone until Monday night, when "Chan was finally contacted." Yet when Chan called Bird's mother in Kansas City to tell her, Mrs. Parker already knew—Doris Parker had called and told her. Doris Parker has said that Art Blakey had phoned her in Chicago and informed her of Parker's death.

The Baroness, who went to the Open Door on the Sunday night immediately following Bird's death, certainly hid well the bad news she carried so fresh in her mind.

On Tuesday the story broke in all the New York papers. It was then that errors and discrepancies in the circumstances of Parker's death were noted. Parker's age was given as 53, but by whom? Later the date of his death on his tombstone was marked as March 23 instead of March 12. (Why?) And why did Doctor Freymann refuse to sign the death certificate? Why did the body lie unidentified in the morgue for two days? These questions have remained unanswered.

The funeral was held on a gray day of downpour in New York at Adam Clayton Powell's Abyssinian Baptist Church. Once the coffin was almost dropped. Then the body was sent to Kansas City, where Bird had requested that it not go, for burial. Some musicians, such as Gail Brockman, came from as far away as Chicago for the funeral services. Other New York-based musicians were conspicuous by their absence.

Soon after his death, the words "Bird Lives" began to appear on buildings, fences, and subway steps and walls—and through his music, he does live. But for all the sincerity found in these graffiti, they were also symbolic of his deification by beatniks, many of whom really knew little about his music.

His life inspired Bob Reisner to compile a documentary that is the source of many of the anecdotes and facts in this chapter. The book, *The Legend of Charlie Parker*, published in 1962, was adapted into play form in 1965. Bird-like musicians have also been the central characters in two novels, *The Sound* by Ross Russell and *Night Song* by John A. Williams. In 1965 a film version of the latter was produced, with Dick Gregory playing the part of Eagle.

Bird was a man who would try to shortchange his sidemen because he *needed* money but would back down when his bluff was called; a man who at the end was at the constricting mercy of his "judges," as he called his booking agents; a man who could pick up any old saxophone, fitted with a strange mouthpiece and a worn-out reed, and make music for eternity.

Charlie Parker's greatness is demonstrated by the body of his recorded art, but what made him great can be heard in even the abbreviated phrase of an individual solo. Listen, for example, only to the end of his first solo on the alternate take, initially unissued, of "Parker's Mood" on the LP *Charlie Parker Memorial* on Savoy. You'll hear the soul of a giant.

PART TWO

Now's the Time:

Charlie Parker in the Jazz Press

The most valuable articles about Charlie Parker written during his lifetime are the ones that reflect Parker's own feelings, observations, and goals. The jazz press didn't pay much attention to Parker when he was based in New York City in 1944 and 1945. But upon his return to that city in 1947, his presence in music magazines such as *Metronome* and *Down Beat* increased. Here are some of the best articles with Parker's voice in them, plus two articles written after his death.—CW

LEONARD FEATHER
YARDBIRD FLIES HOME (1947)

Metronome, August 1947

Perhaps in part because he was a musician, Leonard Feather was one of the early proponents of the music of Dizzy Gillespie and Charlie Parker. When Charlie Parker returned to New York City in April 1947 from his hospitalization in California for drug-withdrawal symptoms, Feather took the opportunity to interview the saxophonist. The result was the following, the first substantive article on Parker to incorporate his own views on life and music. As in the 1949 article "No Bop Roots in Jazz," in this profile Parker seems to differentiate between his music and jazz, and prefers to simply "call it music." (At this time, debate was raging in the jazz world as to whether there was a "true" or superior form of jazz. Proponents of New Orleans–derived jazz had touted that style over the big-band developments of the 1930s. When the music of Parker, Gillespie, and others emerged in the mid-1940s, New Orleans jazz fans expanded their criticism to include the new musical developments.) This article is also perhaps the first to document Charlie Parker's interest in Western classical music, an idiom that would fascinate him for the rest of his life. As always, Feather was sensitive to Parker's personal life. The "nervous breakdown" referred to was in fact drug- and alcohol-induced, and the "eleven-year panic" was Parker's addiction to heroin. Sadly, only the second half of Parker's goal to "get straight and produce some music!" was attained.—CW

Charlie "Yardbird" Parker is back in New York—and glad of it. The idol of thousands of musicians, most brilliantly modern of all alto sax men, he has come back to start a new career and a new life which will help to erase memories of the old.

Charlie came back late in April, to find that even some of his old friends barely recognized him. His weight was up from 127 to 192. He looked healthy and happy.

What was the story behind the regeneration of this great musician?

Hoping to find the answer, I met Bird one Saturday night up at Bob Bach's WNEW jam session, and after the program we walked over to a bar on Sixth Avenue near 52nd Street. Charlie was glad to have someone to talk to, he said—someone on whom he could unload a lot of things that were on his mind, without fear of being misunderstood.

Some of the confidences were off the record. He reminded me constantly not to make him sound like a moralizer or a reformer. He talked eloquently, sensibly, and without any of the jiving illiteracy and profanity that constitute the dialogue of less articulate musicians.

"It began on August 29, 1920," said Bird, "in Kansas City. . . . I went through the elementary school. Spent three years in high school and wound up a freshman. I played baritone horn in the school band. Started seriously on alto sax when my mother bought me one in 1935—I was around 15."

His career started early. Just after Jay McShann came to Kansas City in 1937, Charlie worked for him. Some of his other early jobs were with Lawrence Keyes and Harlan Leonard. He came to New York in 1939 for a while but did no steady work. The following year he was East again, playing with Jay McShann at the Savoy. With this band he made his first records, on Decca.

He was in the Earl Hines band playing tenor in 1942, along with Dizzy and Shadow Wilson, Eckstine and "Little Benny" Harris; but the recording ban kept this memorable group off wax. Later Charlie worked briefly with Cootie Williams and Andy Kirk, with the original Billy Eckstine band in '44, and then around 52nd street during the post-'45 era, with Ben Webster and with Dizzy and then with his own group, featuring Miles Davis, at the Three Deuces. He rejoined Dizzy to go to the Coast, stayed out there after Dizzy went back, and got into the spin which culminated in a complete nervous breakdown a year ago, followed by seven months at Camarillo State Hospital in California.

This is a brief career resume. To lead up to the last even again from a more intimate standpoint, we must go back to Bird's early days in Kansas City.

Charlie was around show people when he was very young. "It all came from being introduced too early to night life," he says now. "When you're not mature enough to know what's happening—well, you goof."

Charlie's dissipation began as early as 1932, taking a more serious turn in 1935 when an actor friend told him about a new kick. One morning, very soon afterwards, he woke up feeling sick and not knowing why. The panic, the eleven-year panic, was on. Eleven years torn out of his life like an irreplaceable chapter in a book.

"I didn't know what hit me . . . it was so sudden. I was a victim of circumstances," he recalls. "High school kids don't know any better. That way, you can miss the most important years of your life, the years of possible creation.

"I don't know how I made it through those years. I became bitter, hard, cold. I was always on a panic—couldn't buy clothes or a good place to live. Finally, out on the Coast last year, I didn't have *any* place to stay, until somebody put me up in a converted garage. The mental strain was getting worse all the time. What made it worst of all was that nobody understood our kind of music out on the Coast. They *hated* it, Leonard. I can't begin to tell you how I yearned for New York."

Things reached a climax one night after a recording session at which Charlie had showed alarming signs of unbalance. During the night he completely lost control. He doesn't remember anything about the next few days. Ross Russell, the Dial recording man, whose help he recalls with gratitude, spoke up for him, and the authorities had Yardbird sent to Camarillo, where, after a while, he was given physical work to do and his mind and body were built up to a point they had never reached since childhood.

When he was well enough to leave the hospital, Charlie's first thought was to get to New York. "As I left the coast they had a band at Billy Berg's with somebody playing a bass sax and a drummer playing on the temple blocks and ching-ching-ching-ching cymbals—one of those real New Orleans style bands, that *ancient* jazz—and the people liked it! That was the kind of thing that had helped to crack my wig."

Charlie today is charged with an enthusiasm and ambition such as he never knew in the bad old days. He declares (and every great musician admits it sooner or later) that he plays best when he is under the influence of nothing at all. He feels sorry for the kids who think: "So-and-so plays great, and he does such-and-such; therefore I should do like he does and then I'll blow great too."

He has found friendships that make life seem more important, too. When you ask him about Billy Shaw, the agent who has just signed him up and who has proved a good friend as well as a good manager, he can't find words to describe his gratitude. "Just the greatest, that's all," he says.

Charlie was married twice during the panic years and has a nine-year-old son by his first wife domiciled with Charlie's mother in Kansas City. He is separated from his second wife. His mother, states Charlie, is the most wonderful person—"not in show business . . . she's just my mom and she really is a mom." His father is deceased. Charlie's childhood home life was not unhappy and had nothing to do with his flying off at a tangent so young.

As this was written, Charlie was preparing for several weeks out at a farm: he was hoping to persuade two other members of the frantic 52nd Street clique to come along with him, drummer Max Roach and pianist Bud Powell, both fine musicians who had had similar experiences. The farm is Powell's mother's place in Willow Grove, Pa., a suburb of Philadelphia. When he comes back, Bird will have a small band and play concerts. "Big bands are limited—you can do so much more with a combo."

He cited a non-jazz parallel: "Have you heard that album of music by Schönberg with just five instruments playing while an actress recites some poetry, in German? It's a wonderful thing—I think it's called *Protée*."

And speaking of classical music—"have you heard *The Children's Corner* by Debussy? Oh, that's so much music! . . . Debussy and Stravinsky are my favorites; but I like Shostakovitch . . . Beethoven too. . . . You know, it used to be so cruel to the musicians, just the way it is today—they say that when Beethoven was on his deathbed he shook his fist at the world; they just didn't understand. Nobody in his own time really dug anything he wrote. But that's music."

In the jazz field, Charlie pays his respects to Thelonious Monk as the man responsible for many of the harmonic changes that came to be a part of what's now called bebop music. But, says Bird: "let's not call it bebop.

Let's call it music. People get so used to hearing jazz for so many years, finally somebody said 'Let's have something different' and some new ideas began to evolve. Then people brand it 'bebop' and try to crush it. If it should ever become completely accepted, people should remember it's in just the same position jazz was. It's just another style. I don't think any one person invented it. I was playing the same style years before I came to New York. I never consciously changed by style."

Of those playing in this style today, he selects as outstanding exponents Sonny Stitt, Fats Navarro, and Miles Davis. And he points out that Curley Russell, Chocolate (the bass player), Bud Powell and Monk are among the "originals."

His favorite arranger? "Jimmy Mundy . . . Calvin Jackson, who writes for MGM . . . and he can play, too! . . . Ralph Burns; anybody who's writing for Dizzy's big band; and of course Dizzy himself."

Regarding his own records, Charlie says, "I still haven't produced any that completely satisfied me: I hope to some day." He made two Dial dates before returning to New York: one was with a group of musicians unfamiliar to him, and he wasn't too happy about it, but the other was a trio date with Erroll Garner which he believes was great.

Charlie, at twenty-six, feels that the new life offers him great opportunities. Before anything else he wants to do a lot of manual labor at the farm because "all this extra weight I'm carrying is too much for me." After that, he'll have only one thought in mind, a thought that may well permeate the minds of all the great musicians who have been inspired by him in the past, and may be guided by him in the future:

"Let's get *straight* and produce some music!"

LEONARD FEATHER

A BIRD'S-EAR VIEW OF MUSIC (1948)
Nobody gets the bird from bird as broadminded parker takes the blindfold test

Metronome, August 1948

In this, his only "blindfold test," Parker shows a wide appreciation for many styles and forms of music, and once again makes the case for not labeling music according to style. Interestingly,

Leonard Feather chose to play one of Parker's earliest solos, on the 1942 Jay McShann recording of "Sepian Stomp" (aka "Sepian Bounce"); Parker calls his own his solo "nowhere." Note that Parker correctly identified one of his favorite composers, Igor Stravinsky.

Note: The list of recordings reviewed by Parker, originally spread over two pages, will be found at the end of the article.—CW

CHARLIE PARKER likes music!

This statement has more significance than you might think—especially if you read it in the light of the narrow, one-track-minded opinions of most bop fans and many bop musicians. Charlie sees music as a whole, instead of looking only along the particular channel through which he has found his personal outlet.

It took six months of reminders and broken appointments to get Bird to take the test, which was finally conducted at this writer's apartment at 1 A.M., between sets at the Royal Roost. In a subsequent chat, Bird made it clear that his high ratings of the records played were in no way based on a desire to avoid offending anyone. They represent his honest opinion, and they should give pause to many of his most ardent admirers.

The Records

1. I like this. Very weird—marvelous idea. Is it Woody Herman? Stan Kenton? I don't know what to say about it—it's such a shock. Give it four stars, definitely.
2. That was some real marvelous alto work. I think I liked that better than the last record. Four stars.
3. That's typical Goodman. Is that an octet? I liked the piano; fine guitar; good drums, good vibes—Red Norvo. And Benny's always superb, that's natural. He's one of the few that never retards. I don't agree with people who think Benny's old fashioned. Three stars.
4. I liked that one too. It was Bud Powell on piano, wasn't it? I didn't recognize the alto man but he played good. Fine trumpet work too. I have to give that three stars.
5. Sure, I recognize that—"Sepian Stomp." It sounds dated, antiquated. It's all right, but you couldn't judge it by what's going on now; I mean, it's another phase altogether. I guess *then* it might have been

okay, but now . . . ! How do I sound to myself? Nowhere—I should say not! Give it two stars.

6. You want my honest opinion? Okay. Well, that's music—that's very good Dixieland. Baby Dodds on drums, right? I forget the clarinet player's name, but I've played with him on a couple of occasions and I like him, and the trumpet player too, I mean as far as Dixieland goes. I like Dixieland, in a way; I mean, I can listen to it—it's still music. There's a status of appreciation you can reach if you listen for it. Three stars.

7. Is it by Stravinsky? That's music at its best. I like all of Stravinsky—and Prokofiev, Hindemith, Ravel, Debussy . . . and, of course, Wagner and Bach. Give that all the stars you've got!

8. Ha! That's something you rarely hear nowadays, you know? That's what you call *swing!* Real swing! Who was it, Earl Hines? Roy? Lips? Alto was real nice; I liked the tenor player too. You've got to appreciate swing; music graduates, it goes from ragtime to jazz and from jazz to swing and from swing to . . . rebop. (*sic*) I give it four stars, in its category.

9. I'd say that's his majesty the Count, right? That's another brand of music altogether; he gets a sound and emotion out of that band I don't think *nobody* gets. I'll always appreciate what that band pro-duces (*laughing*). Basie plays some weird piano. And then when the band comes in they get a . . . they get something—how would you describe the emotion they get out of that band? They get a groove out of that band—all the sections melt into that rhythm section . . . that's of course four stars, you know that!

10. That was Barnet. I like Barnet's band; I like his style of music. I like Barnet as a person, though I don't know him—never have met him, in fact—but what I've seen of him I like. His ideas and taste are excel-lent. And he's got good *musical* ideas, too. Arrangement was real fine. I'll give it three stars, for one reason: this is something that was done by Duke, and it's on the order of Duke's record. Had it been a deriva-tive of Barnet's mind, I'd give it four, five, six, seven stars; as it is, it deserves every bit of the three stars.

11. Dizzy Gillespie . . . the other half of my heartbeat; sure! Dizzy and the baritone did a very good job; the band sounded good, big, full, but the performance sounded a bit strained. It was kind of tense and taut. Three stars.

12. (*Charlie's face lit up in a beatific grin as he recognized the alto soloist.*) That was Duke—featuring Johnny Lily Pons Hodges! I

always took off my hat to Johnny Hodges 'cause he can *sing* with the horn; oh, he's a beautiful person. That record deserves all the stars you can muster.

Afterthoughts by Bird

You're surprised how much I liked . . . well, mine is a very natural, normal reaction. That's *music*, Leonard. Music, if it's presented right, is music, whether it be Dixieland, jazz, swing, or what have you. There's no way in the world you can turn your back on it; it's got to have a class and a place.

Of everything you played, I think I enjoyed Stan's record best—the second one, featuring the alto. Kenton is the closest thing to classical music there is in the jazz field, if you want to call it jazz; I mean, as far as I'm concerned, there's no such thing; you can't classify music in words—jazz, swing, Dixieland, et cetera; it's just forms of music; people have different conceptions and different ways of presenting things. Personally, *I* just like to call it music, and music is what I like.

Records Reviewed by Bird

Charlie Parker was given no information whatever, either before or during the blindfold test, about the records played for him.

1. Stan Kenton. "Monotony" (Capitol). Arr. Pete Rugolo.
2. Stan Kenton. "Elegy For Alto" (Capitol). Arr. Pete Rugolo.
3. Benny Goodman Sextet. "Nagasaki" (Capitol). Goodman, clarinet; Red Norvo, vibes; Mel Powell, piano; Al Hendrickson, guitar; Louis Bellson, drums.
4. Sonny Stitt Quintette. "Seven-Up" (Savoy). Stitt, alto; Kenny Dorham, trumpet; Bud Powell, piano.
5. Jay McShann. "Sepian Stomp" (Decca, c. 1941). Charlie Parker, alto.
6. George Wettling. "Heebie Jeebies" (Commodore). Wettling, drums; Billy Butterfield, trumpet; Ed Hall, clarinet; Wilbur de Paris, trombone; Dave Bowman, piano.
7. Eugene Goossens, Cincinnati Symphony. Stravinsky: *The Song of the Nightingale* (Part I) (Victor).
8. Oran "Hot Lips" Page and his Band. "Lafayette" (Decca, c. 1940). Page, trumpet; Don Stovall, alto; Don Byas, tenor; Pete Johnson, piano.

9. Count Basie. "House Rent Boogie" (Victor, 1947). Arr. Buster Harding. Basie, piano.
10. Charlie Barnet. "The Gal from Joe's" (Apollo, 1947). Barnet, alto.
11. Dizzy Gillespie. "Stay on It" (Victor). Gillespie, trumpet; Cecil Payne, baritone. Arr. Tadd Dameron.
12. Johnny Hodges. "Passion Flower" (Victor). Hodges, alto; Duke Ellington, piano.

MICHAEL LEVIN AND JOHN S. WILSON
NO BOP ROOTS IN JAZZ: PARKER (1949)

Down Beat, September 9, 1949

This often-quoted but seldom-reprinted article begins provocatively with Charlie Parker's statement, "Bebop is no love-child of jazz." As in the last article, he differentiates between jazz and bop, a distinction that is seldom made today; artists from Louis Armstrong to Duke Ellington to Charlie Parker to Ornette Coleman are usually considered part of the same lineage. The writers characterize themselves as pushing Parker to define bop, and he is clearly uncomfortable doing so. Parker had recently returned from France where he played at the May 1949 International Festival of Jazz. Reportedly, he had met French classical saxophone virtuoso Marcel Mule while in Paris. This article may be the first to quote Parker's intention to return to France to study classical music, a plan that he never carried out. Importantly, Parker makes it clear that while he may gain some inspiration from European classical music, the music that he envisions will also have significant traits that he does not associate with the European concert music tradition. This article is also the source of the legendary story of Parker's 1939 musical breakthrough in Harlem. Note that in this original version, the account is largely told by paraphrasing Parker. In later books and articles, those paraphrases were presented as direct quotes of Parker, but it is unknown whether those alterations were based on Parker's actual statements (possibly tape-recorded) or if they were journalistic license.

Note: Parker's birth year, reported here as 1921, was actually 1920.

His first Decca recordings with McShann were made in 1941, not 1940. The Hindemith piece Parker had in mind was probably the Duet for Viola and Cello.

Parker's reference to the Academy of Music in Paris is unclear; he may have meant the Conservatoire National de Musique.—CW

"Bop is no love-child of jazz," says Charlie Parker. The creator of bop, in a series of interviews that took more than two weeks, told us he felt that "bop is something entirely separate and apart" from the older tradition; that it drew little from jazz, has no roots in it. The chubby little alto man, who has made himself an international music name in the last five years, added that bop, for the most part, had to be played by small bands.

"Gillespie's playing has changed from being stuck in front of a big band. Anybody's does. He's a fine musician. The leopard coats and the wild hats are just another part of the managers' routines to make him box office. The same thing happened a couple of years ago when they stuck his name on some tune of mine to give him a better commercial reputation."

Asked to define bop, after several evenings of arguing, Charlie still was not precise in his definition.

"It's just music," he said. "It trying to play clean and looking for the pretty notes."

Pushed further, he said that a distinctive feature of bop is its strong feeling for beat.

"The beat in a bop band is with the music, against it, behind it," Charlie said. "It pushes it. It helps it. Help is the big thing. It has no continuity of beat, no steady chug chug. Jazz has, and that's why bop is— more flexible."

He admits the music eventually may be atonal. Parker himself is a devout admirer of Paul Hindemith, the German neoclassicist, raves about his *Kammermusik* and *Sonata for Viola and Cello*. He insists, however, that bop is not moving in the same direction as modern classical. He feels that it will be more flexible, more emotional, more colorful.

He reiterates constantly that bop is only just beginning to form as a school, that it can barely label its present trends, much less make prognostications about the future.

The closest Parker will come to an exact, technical description of what may happen is to say that he would like to emulate the precise complex harmonic structures of Hindemith, but with an emotional coloring and dynamic shading that he feels modern classical lacks.

Parker's indifference to the revered jazz tradition certainly will leave some of his own devotees in a state of surprise. But, actually, he himself has no roots in traditional jazz. During the few years he worked with traditional jazzmen he wandered like a lost soul. In his formative years he never heard any of the music which is traditionally supposed to inspire young jazzists—no Louis, no Bix, no Hawk, no Benny, no nothing. His first musical idol, the musician who so moved and inspired him that he went out and bought his first saxophone at the age of 11, was Rudy Vallee.

Tossed into the jazz world of the mid-'30s with this kind of background, he had no familiar ground on which to stand. For three years he fumbled unhappily until he suddenly stumbled on the music which appealed to him, which had meaning to him. For Charlie insists, "Music is your own experience, your thoughts, your wisdom. If you don't live it, it won't come out of your horn."

Charlie's horn first came alive in a chili house on Seventh avenue between 139th Street and 140th Street in December, 1939. He was jamming there with a guitarist named Biddy Fleet. At the time, Charlie says, he was bored with the stereotyped changes being used then.

"I kept thinking there's bound to be something else," he recalls. "I could hear it sometimes but I couldn't play it."

Working over "Cherokee" with Fleet, Charlie suddenly found that by using higher intervals of a chord as a melody line and backing them with appropriately related changes, he could play this thing he had been "hearing." Fleet picked it up behind him and bop was born.

Or, at least, it is reasonable to assume, that this was the birth of bop. All available facts indicate this is true. But Parker, an unassuming character who carries self-effacement to fantastic lengths, will not say this in so many words. The closest he will come to such a statement is, "I'm accused of having been one of the pioneers."

But inescapable facts pin him down. He says he always has tried to play in more or less the same way he does now. His earliest records, which were cut with Jay McShann in 1940 (on Decca) back him up on this. They reveal a style which is rudimentary compared to his present work, but definitely along the same lines: light, vibratoless tone; running phrases, perkily turned; complex rhythmic and harmonic structures.

From 1939 to 1942, Charlie worked on his discovery. He admits he thought he was playing differently from other jazzmen during this period. Indicative of his queasiness about saying who did what before with which to whom, is his answer to our query: Did Dizzy also play differently from the rest during the same period?

"I don't think so," Charlie replied. Then, after a moment, he added, "I don't know. He could have been. Quote me as saying, 'Yeah.'"

Dizzy himself has said that he wasn't aware of playing bop changes before 1942.

Whether he'll admit it or not, the calendar shows that Charlie inaugurated what has come to be known as bop. In some circles he is considered to be the world's only legitimate boppist.

"There's only one man really plays bop," one New York reed musician said recently. "That's Charlie Parker. All the others who say they're playing bop are only trying to imitate him."

Despite his unwillingness to put anybody down, a slight note of irritation creeps into Charlie's usually bland mien when he considers the things which have been done by others in an attempt to give his music a flamboyant, commercial appeal. The fact that Dizzy Gillespie's extroversion led the commercially minded to his door irks Charlie in more ways than one. As part of Dizzy's build-up, he was forced to add his name to several of Charlie's numbers, among them "Anthropology," "Confirmation," and "Shaw 'Nuff." Dizzy had nothing to do with any of them, according to Charlie.

As for the accompanying gimmicks which, to many people, represent bop, Charlie views them with a cynical eye.

"Some guys said, 'Here's bop,'" he explains. "Wham! They said, 'Here's something we can make money on.' Wham! 'Here's a comedian.' Wham! 'Here's a guy who talks funny talk.'" Charlie shakes his head sadly.

Charlie himself has stayed away from a big band because the proper place for bop, he feels, is a small group. Big bands tend to get over-scored, he says, and bop goes out the window. The only big band that managed to play bop in 1944, in Charlie's estimation, was Billy Eckstine's. Dizzy's present band, he says, plays bop, could be better with more settling down and less personnel shifting.

"That big band is a bad thing for Diz," he says. "A big band slows anybody down because you don't get a chance to play enough. Diz has an awful lot of ideas when he wants to, but if he stays with the big band he'll forget everything he ever played. He isn't repeating notes yet, but he is repeating patterns."

The only possibility for a big band, he feels, is to get really big, practically on a symphonic scale with loads of strings.

"This has more chance than the standard jazz instrumentation," he says. "You can pull away some of the harshness with the strings and get a variety of coloration."

Born in Kansas City, Kan., in 1921, to a family which was in relatively comfortable circumstances at the time, Charlie moved with his parents to Olive Street, in Kansas City, Mo., when he was seven. There were no musicians in his family, but Charlie got into his high school band playing baritone horn and clarinet. He had a special fondness for the baritone horn because it helped him win medals awarded to outstanding musicians in the band. Not that he played the horn particularly well, but it was loud and boisterous and dominated the band so much the judges scarcely could ignore it.

In 1931, Charlie discovered jazz, heavily disguised as Rudy Vallee. So that he could emulate Rudy, his mother bought him an alto for $45. Charlie settled on the alto because he felt the C Melody wasn't stylish and a tenor didn't look good. His interest in the alto was short-lived, however, for a sax-playing friend in high school borrowed it and kept it for two years. Charlie forgot all about it until he was out of school and needed it to earn a living.

It was back in his school days, he says, that his name started going through a series of mutations which finally resulted in Bird. As Charlie reconstructs it, it went from Charlie to Yarlie to Yarl to Yard to Yardbird to Bird.

After his brief exhilaration over Vallee, Charlie heard no music which interested him, outside of boogie-woogie records, until he quit high school in 1935 and went out to make a living with his alto horn at the age of 14. As has been mentioned, he was under the influence of none of the jazz greats. He had never heard them. He was influenced only by the necessity of making a living and he chose music because it seemed glamorous, looked easy, and there was nothing else around.

This primary lack of influence continued as the years went by. The sax men he listened to and admired—Herschel Evans, Johnny Hodges, Willie Smith, Ben Webster, Don Byas, Budd Johnson—all played with a pronounced vibrato, but no semblance of a vibrato ever crept into Charlie's style.

"I never cared for vibrato," he says, "because they used to get a chin vibrato in Kansas City (opposed to the hand vibrato popular with white bands) and I didn't like it. I don't think I'll ever use vibrato."

The only reed man on Charlie's list of favorites who approached the Bird's vibratoless style was Lester Young.

"I was crazy about Lester," he says. "He played so clean and beautiful. But I wasn't influenced by Lester. Our ideas ran on differently."

When Charlie first ventured onto the music scene in Kansas City, the joints were running full blast from 9 p.m. to 5 a.m. Usual pay was $1.25 a night, although somebody special like Count Basie could command $1.50. There were about fifteen bands in town, with Pete Johnson's crew at the Sunset cafe one of the most popular. Harlan Leonard was in town then, along with George Lee's and Bus Moten's little bands. Lester Young, Herschel Evans, and Eddie Barefield were playing around. Top local pianists were Roselle Claxton, Mary Lou Williams, Edith Williams, and Basie.

Charlie spent several months picking up on his alto. On Thanksgiving night, 1935, he got his first chance to play for pay when he was rounded up with a small group of others to do a gig in Eldon, Mo. He was offered $7 for the night, not because he was any good but because practically every musician in Kansas City was working that night and the guy who hired him was going crazy trying to find men to fill the date. Driving to Eldon, they had a crackup. Two of the men were killed and Charlie got out of it with three broken ribs and a broken horn. The man who had hired him paid his medical expenses and bought him a new horn.

In February, 1936, Charlie started out for Eldon again with another group and this time he made it. The rest of the combo was a shade older than Charlie. J. K. Williams, the bass player, was 72. The rest were in their 30s and 40s. Charlie was 15. But, as the baby of the group, he got a lot of attention and advice. He had taken guitar, piano, and sax books with him and set about learning to read seriously. The pianist, Carrie Powell, played for him and taught him simple major, minor, seventh, and diminished chords.

By the end of the Eldon job, in April, he could read fairly well but not quickly. He went back to Kansas City and got his first club job at 18th and Lydia at either the Panama or the Florida Blossom (he can't remember which). It paid him 75 cents a night.

"The main idea of the job," Charlie recalls, "was to be there and hold a note."

Soon after this, he tried jamming for the first time at the High Hat, at 22nd and Vine. He knew a little of "Lazy River" and "Honeysuckle

Rose" and played what he could. He didn't find it difficult to hear the changes because the numbers were easy and the reed men set a riff only for the brass, never behind a reed man. No two horns jammed at the same time.

"I was doing all right until I tried doing double tempo on 'Body and Soul,'" Charlie says. "Everybody fell out laughing. I went home and cried and didn't play again for three months."

In 1937 he joined Jay McShann's band, but left after two weeks. Later he was arrested for refusing to pay a cab fare. His mother, who didn't approve of his conduct then, wouldn't help him out and he was jugged for 22 days. When he got out, he left his saxophone behind and bummed his way to New York.

For three months he washed dishes in Jimmy's Chicken Shack in Harlem. This was at the time Art Tatum was spellbinding late hour Shack habitués. Charlie got $9 a week and meals. Then he quit and bummed around a while, sleeping where he could.

"I didn't have any trouble with cops," he recalls, "I was lucky. I guess it was because I looked so young." He was 17.

After he had been in New York for eight months, some guys at a jam session bought him a horn. With it he got a job in Kew Gardens which lasted for four months, even though he hadn't touched a horn for $1\frac{1}{2}$ years. Then he moved into Monroe's Uptown House with Ebenezer Paul on drums, Dave Riddick on trumpet, and two or three other guys. There was no scale at Monroe's. Sometimes Charlie got 40 or 50 cents a night. If business was good, he might get up to $6.

"Nobody paid me much more then except Bobby Moore, one of Count Basie's trumpet players," Charlie says. "He liked me. Everybody else was trying to get me to sound like Benny Carter."

Around this time, the middle of 1939, he heard some Bach and Beethoven for the first time. He was impressed with Bach's patterns.

"I found out that what the guys were jamming then already had been put down and, in most cases, a lot better."

At the end of 1939, shortly after his chili house session with Bid Fleet, he went to Annapolis to play a hotel job with Banjo Burney [Bernie?]. Then his father died and he went back to Kansas City, where he rejoined McShann.

Charlie cut his first record in Dallas, in the summer of 1940, with McShann. His first sides were "Confessin'," "Hootie Blues" (which he wrote), "Swingmatism," and "Vine Street Boogie."

His solos with McShann are on "Hootie," "Swingmatism," "Sepian

Bounce," "Lonely Boy Blues," and "Jumpin' Blues." He tried doing a little arranging then but he didn't know much about it.

"I used to end up with the reeds blowin' above the trumpets," he explains.

The McShann band went from Texas, to the Carolinas, to Chicago, back to Kansas City, headed east through Indiana, and then New York and the Savoy. Charlie drove the instrument truck all the way from Kansas City. While they were at the Savoy, Charlie doubled into Monroe's where he played with Allen Terry, piano, George Treadwell (Sarah Vaughan's husband) and Victor Coulsen, trumpets; Ebenezer Paul, bass; and Mole, drums.

He left McShann at the end of 1941 and joined Earl Hines in New York early in 1942. This was the Hines band which also had Dizzy, Billy Eckstine, and Sarah Vaughan. Charlie had known Dizzy vaguely before this and it was about this time they both started getting into the sessions at Minton's.

It was on this visit to New York, in late 1942 after he had worked out his basic approach to complex harmony, that Charlie heard Stravinsky for the first time when Ziggy Kelly played *Firebird* for him.

Charlie played tenor for the 10 months he was with Hines. He started out getting more money than he had ever seen before—$105 a week. With McShann he had gotten $55 to $60. But the band was sent on an army camp tour in a *Pabst Blue Ribbon Salute* package put together by Ralph Cooper and their salaries started going down. This, with booking hassels, eventually broke up the band. Charlie dropped out in Washington, in 1943, and joined Sir Charles Thompson ("Robbins Nest" composer) at the Crystal Caverns.

Later he came back to New York and cut his first sides since the McShann discs—the Tiny Grimes "Red Cross" and "Romance without Finance" session for Savoy. Charlie worked off and on around New York during 1943 and 1944. In the spring of 1944 he was playing the Spotlite on 52nd Street, managed by Clark Monroe of Monroe's, and on the site of the old Famous Door, when Doris Sydnor, the hatcheck girl there, raised an interested eye at him. Charlie, according to Doris, didn't notice it.

"He ignored me very coldly," she reports.

But Doris was a persistent girl. She didn't even know what instrument Charlie played when she first met him, but she stacked records by the Bird and Lester Young on her phonograph and listened and listened until she caught on to what they were doing. She and Charlie were married on Nov. 18, 1945, in New York.

Right after his wedding, Charlie went out to the coast with Dizzy to play at Billy Berg's. He stayed there after the Berg's date was finished.

On the coast he started cutting sides for Ross Russell's Dial label until his physical breakdown in August, 1946, landed him in a hospital. His opinion of these Dial discs is low.

"'Bird Lore' and 'Lover Man' should be stomped into the ground," he says. "I made them the day before I went to the hospital. I had to drink a quart of whiskey to make the date."

Charlie stayed in the hospital until January, 1947. Russell, who had hired a psychiatrist and a lawyer, got him released then in his custody and staged a benefit for the Bird which produced some cash and two plane tickets back east.

But Parker is bitter about Russell's role in this. He says that Charlie Emge of *Down Beat* was equally helpful, that Russell refused to sign the papers releasing him unless he, Parker, renewed his contract with Dial. Later, Parker claims, he found that he had needed no outside help to get out.

When he originally signed with Russell, Charlie was already under contract to Herman Lubinsky, of Savoy records. Before leaving New York, he had signed with Lubinsky to cut some 30 sides. Four of these were done before he went to the coast—"Ko-Ko," "Billie's Bounce," "Now's the Time," and "Anthropology." Lubinsky bought all four tunes from Charlie for $50 apiece.

Today Charlie has come full cycle. As he did in 1939, when he kicked off bop in the Seventh avenue chili house, he's beginning to think there's bound to be something more. He's hearing things again, things that he can't play yet. Just what these new things are, Charlie isn't sure yet. But from the direction of his present musical interests—Hindemith, etc.—it seems likely he's heading toward atonality. Charlie protests when he is mentioned in the same sentence with Hindemith, but, despite their vastly different starting points, he admits he might be working toward the same end.

This doesn't mean Charlie is through with bop. He thinks bop still is far from perfection, [and] looks on any further steps he may take as further developments of bop.

"They teach you there's a boundary line to music," he says, "but, man, there's no boundary line to art."

For the future, he'd like to go to the Academy of Music in Paris for a couple of years, then relax for a while and then write. The things he writes all will be concentrated toward one point: warmth. While he's writing, he also wants to play experimentally with small groups. Ideally, he'd like to spend six months a year in France and six months here.

"You've got to do it that way," he explains. "You've got to be here for the commercial things and in France for relaxing facilities."

Relaxation is something Charlie constantly has missed. Lack of relaxation, he thinks, has spoiled most of the records he has made. To hear him tell it, he has never cut a good side. Some of the things he did on the Continental label he considers more relaxed than the rest. But every record he has made could stand improvement, he says. We tried to pin him down, to get him to name a few sides that were at least better than the rest.

"Suppose a guy came up to us," we said, "and said, 'I've got four bucks and I want to buy three Charlie Parker records. What'll I buy?' What should we tell him?"

Charlie laughed.

"Tell him to keep his money," he said.

* * *

Coda

We both were tremendously impressed by the cogency and clarity of Parker's thinking about music. Musicians, classical or jazz, are traditionally unanalytical about the things they create. Parker, however, has a definite idea of where he wants to go and what he wants to do, though he is properly vague as to the results.

His insistent vagueness as to exactly what bop is to him is no pose. Parker is a musician fighting for his proper mode of expression, a vastly talented man who hasn't the schooling yet to expand as completely and properly as his musical instincts would have him do.

If we understand his crypticisms correctly, Parker feels that traditional jazz has strongly lacked variety and economy of form as well as the wealth of discipline and control of ideas to be found in modern formalistic music. On the other hand, he feels the symphonic score of today lacks drive (contained, perhaps, in his concept of dynamics) and warmth, and that his group of musicians will help inject these aspects traditional to the jazz scene.

Parker's insistence that bop has no connection with jazz is interesting as an example of a younger musician bursting forms which he finds constricting and which he feels have outlived their usefulness. We suspect his position might be difficult to maintain.

He undoubtedly is seriously searching for a synthesis of the best in formalistic and folk music. If he can achieve it, he will pull off a feat seldom before accomplished in music. Many composers have utilized folk themes and folk feeling, but none has completely integrated the colors and emotional patterns into scored music.

He is, like all good musicians, inordinately impressed with technique. He has a fondness for lush string tones that, as he uses more of it, will settle more into balance as will his taste for such technical musicians as Jimmy Dorsey.

Parker feels very strongly on the subject of dope in all its forms. He told us that while he was still a young boy in Kansas City he was offered some in a men's room by a stranger when he hardly knew what it was. He continued to use it off and on for years until his crackup in 1946, and says bitterly that people who prey on kids this way should be shot.

Parker told us flatly: "Any musician who says he is playing better either on tea, the needle, or when he is juiced, is a plain, straight liar. When I get too much to drink, I can't even finger well, let alone play decent ideas. And in the days when I was on the stuff, I may have *thought* I was playing better, but listening to some of the records now, I know I wasn't. Some of these smart kids who think you have to be completely knocked out to be a good hornman are just plain crazy. It isn't true. I know, believe me."

Parker struck us as being direct, honest, and searching. He is constantly dissatisfied with his own work and with the music he hears around him. What will come of it, where his quite prodigious talent will take him, even he doesn't know at this stage.

But his ceaseless efforts to find out, to correct, to improve, only bode well for himself and that elderly progenitor, jazz.

NAT HENTOFF

COUNTERPOINT (1953)

Down Beat, January 20, 1953

As of this book's publication, Nat Hentoff is in his fifth decade of writing intelligent and sympathetic articles about jazz musicians and their art. Hentoff wisely chose to build this article around

*Charlie Parker's actual words rather than paraphrasing his opin-
ions and observations. Once again, Parker expresses his admiration for Western classical music and describes his plan to record a
Paul Hindemith–inspired piece combining a jazz rhythm section
with instruments associated with classical music. That desire was
only partially realized later in May when Parker recorded three
pieces featuring a jazz rhythm section, woodwind quintet, and jazz
vocal group. (For more discussion of this session, see Phil Schaap's
"The Verve Sessions," page 225, and Barry Ulanov's* Metronome
*review, page 246. Parker's reaction to the way the session turned
out can be inferred from the 1953 radio interview with John Fitch.
All three articles are included in this anthology.)—CW*

"When I recorded with strings," said Charlie Parker, "some of my friends
said, 'Oh, Bird is getting commercial.' That wasn't it at all. I was looking
for new ways of saying things musically. New sound combinations.

"Why, I asked for strings as far back as 1941 and then, a year later, when
I went with Norman [Granz], he okayed it. I liked Joe Lipman's fine arrangements on the second session and I think they didn't turn out too badly.

"Now," said the always far-ranging Bird, "I'd like to do a session with
five or six woodwinds, a harp, a choral group, and a rhythm section.
Something on the line of Hindemith's *Kleine Kammermusik*. Not a copy
or anything like that. I don't want ever to copy. But that sort of thing."

Charlie is really in love with the classics and unlike a number of people who say they are, Charlie knows them intimately. "I first began listening seven or eight years ago. First I heard Stravinsky's *Firebird Suite*. In the
vernacular of the streets, I flipped. I guess Bartók has become my favorite.
I dig all the moderns. And also the classical men, Bach, Beethoven, etc.

"It's a funny thing, listening to music, any kind," Bird went on. "What
you hear depends on so many things in yourself. Like I heard Bartók's
Second Piano Concerto over here and later, I heard it again in France. I
was more acclimated to life, then, and I heard things in it I never heard
before. You never know what's going to happen when you listen to music.
All kinds of things can suddenly open up."

Charlie doesn't feel, as some musicians do, that modern jazz and classical music are becoming too closely interrelated. "They're different ways
of saying things musically, and don't forget, classical music has that long
tradition. But in 50 or 75 years, the contributions of present-day jazz will
be taken as seriously as classical music. You wait and see."

The Bird went on to talk about some of the men in contemporary jazz he especially admires. "As long as I live, I'll appreciate the accomplishments of Thelonious Monk. And Bud Powell plays so much.

"As for Lennie Tristano, I'd like to go on record as saying I endorse his work in every particular. They say he's cold. They're wrong, He has a big heart and it's in his music. Obviously, he also has tremendous technical ability and you know, he can play anywhere with anybody. He's a tremendous musician. I call him the great acclimatizor.

"And I like Brubeck. He's a perfectionist as I try to be. I'm very moved by his altoist, Paul Desmond."

Talk of perfectionism led Charlie to ruminate about his records. "Every time I hear a record I've made, I hear all kinds of things I could improve on, things I should have done. There's always so much more to be done in music. It's so vast. And that's why I'm always trying to develop, to find new and better ways of saying things musically."

And that is also why Charlie Parker has become so respected here and abroad as one of the focal figures in the evolutionary history of jazz.

LEONARD FEATHER

PARKER FINALLY FINDS PEACE (1955)

Down Beat, April 20, 1955

Here, Leonard Feather harkens back to his previous Parker articles and brings Parker's story up to date. Feather gives a brief first-hand account of Parker's final and tragic engagement at Birdland, about a week before the saxophonist's death on March 12, 1955.—CW

The agony of living is over for Charlie (Yardbird) Parker. It was an agony he had been ever more reluctant to face during the past year. Those of us who were fortunate enough to know Bird as a friend had the bitter experience of watching him disintegrate, of knowing that it was too late to help him because he no longer cared to be helped or to help himself.

Those who came to hear Charlie in the great years saw only the fingers and heard only the incredible sounds of his horn. Knowing nothing of his inward struggle as a human being, they talked carelessly, and sometimes a little too loud, about his history of narcotics addiction, his personality quirks, and the legends that had enveloped him.

Behind this facade that they saw and heard was an intelligent, articulate, and intensely warm human being. It was when he first came back to New York in 1947, after the months in California's Camarillo State hospital following his first breakdown, that Charlie presented his real inner self to the writer, talking frankly of how dope had taken 11 years out of his life (he was then 27).

"It all came from being introduced too early to night club life," he said. "When you're not mature enough to know what's happening—you goof." The heroin habit had him in its grip not long after he started on it in 1935, and the all-too-familiar pattern of increasing dependence, of cures and gradual relapses was repeated time and again.

"I don't know how I made it through those years," he told me "I became bitter, hard, cold . . . what made it worst of all was that nobody understood our kind of music out on the coast. They *hated* it. Leonard, I can't begin to tell you how I yearned for New York."

For quite a while, New York seemed to have the regenerative qualities he sought. And it had Doris Parker, the tall, kind-hearted girl who towered over him physically as she looked up to him mentally and musically. There was a period of normal living when even a trip to the beach together, for Charlie and me and our wives, seemed typical of the simple pleasures he could enjoy like anyone else.

But it didn't last. Soon the search for Nirvana resumed and the moments off the bandstand seemed dedicated to the pursuit of oblivion; if it wasn't narcotics it was alcohol. Looking up from a hospital bed, recovering from an ulcer siege, Bird said to me: "The doctor told me if I don't quit drinking I'll die. I've had my last drink."

How many years ago was that—four, five, six? No matter—there were so many times afterward that he forgot. And there were the times that he remembered again, too; when Doris left and he seemed to have found happiness with Chan, a beautiful little brunette. Charlie became a loving stepfather to Kim and an adoring father to Pree and Laird, the two children Chan bore him.

But the multiple strains of living soberly after a whole adult lifetime of dissipation, of being a Negro in a white society, of adjusting himself to the lack of understanding of his personality and his music, gradually told on Charlie again. Then, a year ago, his little daughter Pree died of pneumonia. This was perhaps the breaking point that led to the pattern of self-immolation, to the tragic evening last September when, after a pitiful performance at Birdland, he stumbled out of the club that had been named for him, went home to Chan, and swallowed iodine.

I saw Charlie three times after that. The first time, playing a Town Hall concert, he looked healthy, talked sensibly, played magnificently and told me he was commuting daily between New Hope, Pa., where he and Chan had found a home, and Bellevue hospital, where he was undergoing psychiatric treatment. He had dropped 20 pounds of unhealthy excess fat; he was like a new man, and New Hope seemed the right place for him to be living.

The second time, a month ago, he was standing in a bar over Birdland, raggedly dressed. He said he had not been home to New Hope lately. The bloated fat was back. His eyes looked desperately sad.

The final night, Charlie was playing at Birdland for two nights only, with Bud Powell, Kenny Dorham, Art Blakey, and Charlie Mingus. One set was too much for anyone who had known and respected this man. He refused to take the stand, quarreled with Powell, stalked off after playing a few desultory bars, and a few minutes later was seen by a friend around the corner at Basin Street, with tears streaming down his face.

"You'll kill yourself if you go on like this," said Mingus, who loved Charlie and was mortified at the spectacle of his imminent self-destruction.

A week later, Charlie Parker was dead.

What can all the verbal post-mortems do? Charlie Parker has gone, and we can console ourselves only with the thought that his tormented soul has finally found peace.

As Gerry Mulligan commented, standing outside Birdland with a group of silent friends the day the news broke, "For a man that put so much into his life, Charlie certainly got precious little out of it."

And as another musician said, "Perhaps, after all he'd gone through and was going through, this was the only thing left for him—maybe the best."

Amen, and rest in peace.

LEONARD FEATHER
A FIST AT THE WORLD (1965)

Down Beat, March 11, 1965

This personal remembrance again included some of Leonard Feather's earlier writings about Charlie Parker [omitted here], but the new material stemming from the writer's acquaintance with Parker is what makes this article valuable. The circumstances of Parker's death described here are the ones most commonly reported. Rumors that Parker may have died from injuries sustained in a fight have long circulated but have never been proven.—CW

It takes a little adjustment, when you are of Charlie Parker's generation, to accept the fact that 10 years have passed since the headline on the front page of the late and unlamented New York *Daily Mirror* screamed Bop King Dies In Heiress' Flat.

It takes even more adjustment to accept with equanimity the fact that Parker is as misunderstood in death as he was in life. When he and Dizzy Gillespie were creating a new spirit and a new form in jazz, their whole bebop movement was roundly and mercilessly denounced by almost every one of the men who could have done the most to help them: the critics. And only recently one of these men, in the worst chapter of the worst book on jazz ever written, devoted 11 pages to a tasteless, venomous attack on Parker's memory.

Reading this vitriol, I wondered how those who loved Parker might feel if ever they should see this desecration.

Perhaps they would take it all in stride, because during Parker's lifetime the obloquy and viciousness were an inescapable part of his scene. Nor was there relief when he died; even then, the fact that Bird was in the home of Lord Rothschild's sister at the time of his death was much more important to the headline writers than the loss of an artist whom most of his contemporaries had called the greatest jazz figure of our generation.

In the last 10 years, Parker has become the subject of a morbid, James Dean–like reverence on the part of many who had little time for him or perhaps barely knew of him alive. Yet as the filth in the aforementioned book makes clear, others, who failed to understand his music, are determined to denigrate his personality.

Obviously, Parker was a man not easily understood. The many conflicts of evidence were made clear in Bob Reisner's *Bird: The Legend of Charlie Parker,* a compilation of statements by those who knew Parker, published in 1962 by Citadel Press. All I can add to the huge bulk of testimony will be a few observations of Charlie as I knew him. (Incidentally, I never heard him call himself Bird. To me it was always Charlie or, occasionally in jest on the telephone, "Leonard? This is Yardbird.")

Not being familiar with any of the medical or pathological evidence about Parker's condition, I cannot throw around any impressive words like dichotomy or schizophrenia. Certainly, though, the Parker revealed in many pages of Reisner's book is a man strangely different from the one I most frequently saw. Perhaps I was fortunate in seeing only the happier side—and in the almost total lack of any business relationship. To me he was just a friend—and an idol.

My pleasantest and most vivid memories go back to the two or three years after his release from Camarillo State Hospital in California and return to New York City. During most of this time he seemed healthy. There were periods of dissipation, mostly alcoholic as far as one could discern, but if he was addicted to narcotics during this time, it was evident neither to me, a friend who saw him only intermittently . . . nor even to Doris.

Doris Sydnor Parker, who is still my friend, is a lanky, good-hearted girl whom Charlie had met when she was a hat-check girl in one of the 52nd St. clubs where he worked. She was taller than he by several inches.

Charlie and I originally got to know one another slightly through his combo work with Gillespie, and through just one record date he made for me—a Sarah Vaughan session, for which he showed up so late that we cut only three somewhat ragged sides, with Dizzy, Flip Phillips, and a rhythm section. He kept in the background for the ballads but took a superb solo on "Mean to Me." This was May 25, 1945.

At that time most of us in jazz knew little or nothing about hard narcotics. Marijuana was in common use, but heroin, cocaine, and opium were just commodities we had read about in sensationalist books or seen dealt with in B movies. We had never heard such terms as "busted" for arrested, "fuzz" for police, and all the other jargon that came into common use in bop circles after a vast clique of junkies had fanned out from Bird. (Even the word junkie was unfamiliar.) Perhaps for this reason, it was not unusual for some of his admirers to observe Bird with a mixture of reverence for his music and morbid revulsion at what they had heard about his addiction.

By the time Parker had gone to California on the disastrous trip that ended with the "Lover Man" recording date, his breakdown, and the seven months in Camarillo, we knew a great deal more about the curse that had struck our profession. We had seen the headlines about Charlie and knew of the agony he had endured. But in April, 1947, he came back to New York, and some of his friends scarcely recognized him. His weight had bounced from a pathetic 127 to a rotund and happy 192.

Hoping to find the story behind this regeneration, I met him one night at one of Bob Bach's WNEW jam sessions. After the show we walked over to a bar on Sixth Ave. near 52nd St. Charlie said he was glad to be with somebody with whom he could talk freely, without the fear of being misunderstood. He talked partially off the record; these confidences, now as then, cannot be violated. Whatever comments he made for the record were accompanied by urgent pleas not to make him sound like a moralizer or reformer.

Charlie talked freely and eloquently. When not surrounded by jive-talkers, he was the most articulate of men; his English was flawless, his use of hip terms only occasional. His diction and the timbre of his speaking voice could have earned him a career on radio.

[. . .]

At 26, Charlie felt that the new life now opening up to him offered great opportunities. Before anything else, he told me, he wanted to do plenty of manual labor at the farm "because all the extra weight I'm carrying is too much for me." After that his only ambition, he said, could be expressed in one simple phrase: "Let's get *straight* and produce some music!"

The road to hell, then as now, was paved with good intentions. The temptations were too close and too constant; yet in the next few years there were many good stretches. There were the days when Charlie and Doris found a normal, bourgeois happiness in conventional ways.

When my wife and I went to Long Island with them for a day at the beach, Charlie was content to eat hot dogs and drink a glass of beer while we chatted about music, politics, and mutual friends. For a while it seemed as though he had adjusted to a life he had never known before. But that was the basic problem: the normal was abnormal for Bird.

His deepest instincts, as I observed them, were grounded in the desire to love and be loved, to maintain a fruitful relationship with his art and society. His humanity and kindness were always in evidence. When my wife and I were immobilized by a serious auto accident, at a period when Charlie probably had trouble finding the cab fare, he took the long trip from his apartment to the hospital not once but several times. During those visits he found common ground for amiable conversations with my father, an Englishman in his 60s whose world was totally removed from Charlie's.

But my starkest recollection goes back to the time when it was Charlie who was in the hospital. He had suffered a violent ulcer siege. When I uttered some platitude about taking better care of himself, he sat up in the bed and said, "I can't afford not to. The doctor told me if I don't quit drinking, I'll die. I've had my last drink."

Three or four years and several thousand drinks later, he made one last effort to come to terms with reality. At a Town Hall concert in the fall of 1954 he looked well, talked well, and played superbly. He told me: "I have a new life. I come in every day from Pennsylvania to take psychiatric treatment at Bellevue." He had gone through a series of changes in his private life: the breakup with Doris, the new life with Chan, the pride of fatherhood when Laird and Pree were born to Chan; and then, early in 1954, the death of Pree from pneumonia.

To most observers the loss of his infant daughter, more than any other factor, seemed to hasten the pattern of self-destruction.

One night at Basin Street, soon after Pree's death, I was watching the show when I felt a tugging at my pants leg. I turned to find Charlie squatting at the side of the table. He refused to get up, take a seat, or move from this awkward spot. He mumbled for a while about the need to talk to someone, about the tragedy of Pree, the cruelty of life. After a while, he edged away.

It was after Pree's death, though, that Charlie made the final attempt to straighten himself out. Had he moved away entirely from the environment of jazz and the night-club world and the pushers, perhaps he would be alive today. But he might have found such a life too demanding, too constricted to be worth living.

A few months after the Town Hall concert, early in 1955, I received a letter from Chan.

"We've moved to New Hope, Pa.," it read in part. "It's in Bucks County, and the nicest. We're on nine acres—two horses and a sheep. I adore it, and Bird is playing the commuter. 4:30 to Trenton and I pick him up at the station. Let's hear from you."

In March, 1955, I saw Charlie again. He was standing in a bar located above Birdland, raggedly dressed.

"New Hope?" he asked. "No, I haven't been back there lately." The name of the town now seemed to take on an ironic and paradoxical symbolism. Charlie's eyes looked very sad, and the bloated excess fat had returned.

There was the final weekend of work, when Birdland changed its managerial mind and put him in for two nights with Bud Powell, Kenny Dorham, Art Blakey, and Charlie Mingus. It was a dismal sight. Bird quarreled with Powell, walked off the stand after playing a few bars, and within minutes was around the corner at Basin Street (then on 51st near Broadway). Tears were streaming down his face. He begged a couple of old friends to come over to Birdland and see him.

A few days later, before leaving for a booking in Boston, he stopped off at the home of his friend Baroness Nica de Koenigswarter. The rest is known—at least almost all of it.

One detail will never be known, however. Reflecting on those last moments, on the final torture of those 35 years, I sometimes wonder whether, at least in his mind's eye, Charlie Parker shook his fist at the world.

PART THREE

Parker's Mood(s):

Interviews wit

Charlie Parker

These interviews present Charlie Parker's views on many subjects without the coloring of journalists. Of course, the interviewers have their own interests and viewpoints that shape their questions, and the interviewers vary in sensitivity and listening skills. In my new transcriptions, I have tried to make the text as accurate as possible within reason (I've edited out some verbal false starts and repetitions, and most occurrences of "uh"). Words or phrases in brackets are meant to clarify and explain aspects of the interview. Words or phrases in parentheses are semi-intelligible and are my best guesses. Whenever a passage is truly unintelligible, I have marked it as such, rather than guess what was meant. In a few cases, some non-Parker topics hae been edited out (marked by three asterisks).—CW

TRANSCRIBED BY CARL WOIDECK

INTERVIEW: CHARLIE PARKER, MARSHALL STEARNS, JOHN MAHER, AND CHAN PARKER (1950)

New York, New York, c. May 1, 1950

This interview is our best source for Parker's own reminiscences of his youth and early musical experiences. Parker's story about his early jam session humiliation is touching and his account of his January 4, 1945, session with singer Rubberlegs Williams is hilarious. Parker also mentions some more recent events and his desire to study music in Paris.

This taped interview with Charlie Parker has been transcribed in several forms and published several times, for example in Jazz Journal *(May 1964) and in the book* Bird's Diary *(Ken Vail, Castle Communications, 1996). It is also available in audio form on CD (see the Discography). A few moments of the tape that are not relevant to Parker and his music have been edited out.—CW*

[The interview begins in progress.]

Marshall Stearns: Now, at seventeen years old, you were on an automobile trip.

Charlie Parker: Yeah.

Marshall Stearns: And you got in an accident.

Charlie Parker: Yeah.

Marshall Stearns: And that was in Kansas City?

Charlie Parker: That was going—that was between Kansas City and Jefferson City, Missouri.

Marshall Stearns: Oh. Playing a gig or something?

Charlie Parker: Yeah. I was going on a Thanksgiving gig.

Marshall Stearns: And what happened? You broke how many ribs?

Charlie Parker: I broke three ribs and had a spinal fracture.

Marshall Stearns: That's an awful thing to happen to you at that age, you know?.

Charlie Parker: Oh yeah, it was. I mean, everybody was so afraid that I wouldn't walk erect no more. But everything was all right.

Marshall Stearns: Well look, what happened? You say then you got a job.

Charlie Parker: Yeah.

Marshall Stearns: *And you studied.*

Charlie Parker: In Jefferson City, yeah. I got a job in this place where he owned, but prior to that, this was when they were laughing at me. I knew how to play—I'd figured—I'd learned the scale and—I'd learned to play two tunes in, in a certain key, in the key of D for your [alto] saxophone, F concert?

Marshall Stearns: *Yeah.*

Charlie Parker: I'd learned how to play the first eight bars of "[Up a] Lazy River," and I knew the complete tune to "Honeysuckle Rose." I didn't never stop to think about there was other keys or nothin' like that. [*Laughter.*] So I took my horn out to this joint where the guys—a bunch of guys I had seen around were—and the first thing they started playing was "Body and Soul," long beat [implied double-time] you know, like this. [*Demonstrates.*]

Marshall Stearns: *Oh, yeah.*

Charlie Parker: So I go to playin' my "Honeysuckle Rose" and [unintelligible], I mean, ain't no form of conglomeration [unintelligible]. They laughed me right off the bandstand. They laughed so hard [unintelligible].

Marshall Stearns: *How old were you then?*

Charlie Parker: Oh, this was along about the same time: Sixteen, seventeen.

Marshall Stearns: *Before the accident?*

Charlie Parker: About a year before the accident.

Marshall Stearns: *Where did you get your sax, then?*

Charlie Parker: Well, my mother bought me a horn for—oh—years before that, but I wasn't interested. I wasn't ready for it then. I didn't get interested in a horn until I got interested in baritone horn when I was in high school. But I'd had the saxophone for a few years.

John Maher: Where did you go to high school, Charlie?

Charlie Parker: Kansas City, Missouri. I went to Lincoln.

John Maher: Did you play in the high school marching band?

Charlie Parker: Mm hm.

John Maher: Did you—oh, did you play in that? Did they have a symphony band in high school?

Charlie Parker: They had a—what they called a symphony band, yes.

John Maher: Did you play in that too?

Charlie Parker: Yeah.

John Maher: Baritone?

Charlie Parker: Baritone horn, that's right.

Marshall Stearns: And you'd learned "Honeysuckle Rose" and you'd learned the first eight bars of—which tune was it?

Charlie Parker: "Up a Lazy River." [*Laughter.*]

Marshall Stearns: "Lazy River." And you were just innocent enough so that when you walked in—

Charlie Parker: I never thought about that there were other keys, you know?

Marshall Stearns: You played it all in—what key was it?

Charlie Parker: F.

Marshall Stearns: In F.

Charlie Parker: D for the saxophone.

Marshall Stearns: In D for the saxophone. Oh, what a story!

John Maher: What a slaughter of the innocent! [Laughter.]

Charlie Parker: They murdered that, too. Oh, boy!

Marshall Stearns: Who did you play with? I mean, what band did you walk in on with that?

Charlie Parker: Oh, it was a band working in a joint. There was a bunch of young fellows that had a band around Kansas City. It was Jimmy Keith's band then, so, Keith and a piano player and Robert Wilson and James Ross and [unintelligible; sounds something like "Shibley Gavan"]. That's the fellows' names that were working at this club in Kansas City. [Unintelligible.]

Marshall Stearns: Well, so after that, you decided, "I'm going home and work it out?"

Charlie Parker: Yeah, that's it. I knew I had [unintelligible] out then, yeah. [*Laughter.*] I knew then it must be figured out some kind of way. That was it.

Marshall Stearns: And then you went back, and it was only—what? Two or three months, then, that you—

Charlie Parker: Yeah, I was away about two or three months.

Marshall Stearns: And where did you go when you say you "were away?" Were you in—outside of Kansas City?

Charlie Parker: Yeah, actually I was on this job. I was down there. The name of the town was Eldon, Missouri. It's about thirty-five miles from Jefferson City.

Marshall Stearns: *Oh, I see. And you—did you play a job there? Or was it—*

Charlie Parker: Yeah, it was a job. It's a resort, a summer resort. [Unintelligible.] During the summer months from about June [unintelligible] summertime.

John Maher: *And that was where you had the chance to study while you were playing?*

Charlie Parker: Yeah.

Chan Richardson Parker: *Bird bought his son [Leon] a horn for Christmas.*

Charlie Parker: Yeah. Yeah, he got an alto, same as mine.

John Maher: *How old is he now?*

Charlie Parker: Fourteen.

Marshall Stearns: *Does he play with it now?*

Charlie Parker: He—he didn't have one before I bought him that one, you know? We made him bring it to the dance. He sat around and listened to me. [*Laughter.*] It sure is a lot of fun having a son that old, you know? A child [unintelligible].

Marshall Stearns: *[Unintelligible] only twelve years old. It's a lot of fun. She [Stearns's daughter?] plays a C-melody one when I'm not looking. [Laughter.] They never had any C-melody saxes, did they, when you were (a kid)?*

Charlie Parker: Yeah. In fact, they were more popular than alto.

Marshall Stearns: *Were they?*

Charlie Parker: Sure. [19] '32, '33. 'Cause Guy Lombardo was just getting popular then. That's what he was using.

Marshall Stearns: Frankie Trumbauer was playing a C-melody.

Charlie Parker: Yeah.

* * *

Chan Richardson Parker: Are you going to put [unintelligible; possibly "Leon"] in school, in music school, in France?

Charlie Parker: Sure. Right away.

Chan Richardson Parker: With you?

Charlie Parker: In fact, we can go back to school together. I'm going to take him to France when [Unintelligible.] go to school together, music school, Academie de Musicale [possibly the Conservatoire National de Musique in Paris].

Marshall Stearns: Charlie, what do you remember of your father? Was he around when you were growing up?

Charlie Parker: Some of the time. He died when I was uh—oh, about—when I was married and the baby was born.

Marshall Stearns: What sort of work was he in? What was he doing?

Charlie Parker: He was like a—in his active years, he was a waiter on this train. Santa Fe. Runs from Kansas City to Chicago. Los Angeles and back. Florida and back. Texas and back.

Marshall Stearns: I see.

Charlie Parker: He sure was a well-tutored guy. He spoke two, three languages.

Marshall Stearns: He did?

Charlie Parker: Yeah.

Marshall Stearns: Did he play any instruments?

Charlie Parker: No. He was a dancer in his real young years.

Marshall Stearns: Really?

Charlie Parker: Circus—in the circus on the TOB line. Ringling Brothers. [*Laughter.*]

John Maher: What was he on? Was he on TOBA [Theater Owners' Booking Association]?

Charlie Parker: Yeah, that was the circus, yeah.

John Maher: Some years ago, I heard about that—

Charlie Parker: Yeah.

John Maher: —during the old Keith-Orpheum circuit days.

Charlie Parker: Yeah.

John Maher: [It was] dying out then. Late '20s.

Marshall Stearns: And he met your mother in Kansas City?

Charlie Parker: Yeah, they met in Kansas City.

Marshall Stearns: And how's your mother now? She's still alive, isn't she?

Charlie Parker: Yeah. She's *very* much alive! [*Laughs.*]

Marshall Stearns: Is she?

Charlie Parker: Fine, yeah.

Marshall Stearns: She got a lot of energy?

Charlie Parker: [Unintelligible] yeah. She just graduated from nurses' school a couple of months ago.

Marshall Stearns: No!

Chan Richardson Parker: No kidding.

Charlie Parker: Yeah. [Unintelligible] invitation. I sent her a watch.

Chan Richardson Parker: How old is she, Bird?

Charlie Parker: Boy, I'd say sixty-two.

John Maher: Wonderful.

Charlie Parker: And graduated from nurses' school. [*Laughter.*]

Marshall Stearns: Hey, that's marvelous.

Charlie Parker: She's active as can be, man. She don't look or act it, you know? I mean she's spryer than me, you know. She's very seldom ill. You know? She lives in that good climate in [the] country. She takes good care of herself. She owns her own home. She's got twice [unintelligible]. She's pretty well situated.

Marshall Stearns: Do you have any brothers and sisters, Charlie?

Charlie Parker: I got a brother.

Marshall Stearns: Older or younger?

Charlie Parker: Older.

Marshall Stearns: Did he ever play any instruments?

Charlie Parker: No. He's a mail inspector at the post office in Kansas City.

Marshall Stearns: Uh huh. And no sisters. [To Chan Parker's daughter, Kim:] Hi, darlin'. [To Charlie Parker:] So, your mother is a very, very energetic, lively person, huh? See, in a way, that's where you got your spirit and—[Laughter] [unintelligible] You know?

Charlie Parker: I guess so.

Marshall Stearns: Your dad was a dancer, you see, that has the rhythm, so, that could explain part of that, you know?

Charlie Parker: Yeah, he could dance, all right.

John Maher: The first rhythms you ever played, though, on the baritone horn, were they marching band rhythms, were they 4/4—

Charlie Parker: Mm hm.

John Maher: —pretty much?

Charlie Parker: This is what it was: When I first went to high school, I was interested in music, you know. So they gave me one of these, um, alto horns, you know? [*Imitates alto horn.*] Coop, coop. Coop, coop. Coop, coop. Coop, coop.

John Maher: Brass? Steel?

Charlie Parker: Coop, coop. So then I liked the baritone horn. When my successor [*sic*] graduated, I went right in, you know? I mean, when what's-her-name graduated. When, uh, when the baritone player before me graduated, I took the horn.

Marshall Stearns: Is that a big brass horn that goes—not like a tuba?

Charlie Parker: No, it isn't as big as a tuba. It's got three valves. It's between a tuba and an alto horn. (It's) pretty big. You hold it, you know, like this. [*Laughter.*] Wow.

Marshall Stearns: I can't figure you playing that! When did you get on reeds? When your mother gave you the saxophone, huh?

Charlie Parker: Yeah, well, I mean, she—I had the—I had the saxophone then, but it was loaned out.

Marshall Stearns: Oh.

Charlie Parker: A friend of mine was playing saxophone at the time. He had a band, so he borrowed the horn. He kept it over two years, too. He kept it maybe a year after I got out of high school. I got out of high school in '35. And, uh—

John Maher: The year after I did.

Charlie Parker: Yeah. And, uh—oh, a gang of things happened that year. I got the horn, I got married.

Marshall Stearns: Let's see, you—when were you born? What was your—you were born in what? 19—

Charlie Parker: '20.

Marshall Stearns: —'20. Boy, you're awful recent! [Laughter.]

John Maher: I was born in 1918.

Charlie Parker: A whole lot of speed [unintelligible]. Wow!

Marshall Stearns: What happened in '36? You graduated from high school. You were playing saxophone by then, weren't you?

Charlie Parker: Mm hm. I got married.

Marshall Stearns: Married.

Charlie Parker: Did a gang of things that year.

Marshall Stearns: And this was all in Kansas City, huh?

Charlie Parker: Mm hm.

Marshall Stearns: I was out through Kansas City in about '40, and I caught Harlan Leonard and Jay McShann out there, and I don't know, maybe you were with McShann then. And I've been kicking myself ever since [laughs], you know. I didn't—

Charlie Parker: Yeah, I was with McShann's band over there [unintelligible].

Marshall Stearns: I came out with George Avakian. He was—

Charlie Parker: McShann didn't have a big band then, did he?

Marshall Stearns: No, it was a little seven- or eight-piece.

Charlie Parker: Yeah, I was in that band.

Marshall Stearns: You were?

Charlie Parker: It was at the Plaza, way out of Kansas City?

Marshall Stearns: Yes, we had to go outside of town to catch that band. And I heard that and I didn't—

* * *

Marshall Stearns: I want to ask you about some of those recording dates, what happened on them, you know. [Long pause.] What a story about that Rubberlegs Williams!

Charlie Parker: [*Laughs.*] He sure did that. The coffees got confused some kind of way and I was looking for the coffee that I had because I'd marked the container, you know?

Marshall Stearns: Well, you had the coffee in a—

Charlie Parker: It was all in containers. They sent out for coffee and sandwiches in a container. It was all in containers, you know? Everybody was eating the sandwiches. So I set my cup down beside the chair and dropped a Benzedrine in it, you know.

Marshall Stearns: Yeah.

Charlie Parker: And I was just waiting for it to dissolve [unintelligible]. Somehow or another, Rubberlegs gets hungry and he goes [to] collect his coffee and he got it mixed up with mine. And about twenty minutes later, he was all over the place. You've never seen anything—he don't do *nothing* the way he [unintelligible]. Rubberlegs really got busy, you know what I mean? [*Laughter.*] It was a funny thing.

Marshall Stearns: Well, he was really singing seriously, was he? He wasn't trying to kid, was he?

Charlie Parker: No, he wasn't, not a bit. And ordinarily, if it hadn't been for that, I mean, he would—he'd have sang a different style altogether.

Marshall Stearns: He would've?

Charlie Parker: Yeah. You never heard none of his records when he wasn't like that?

Marshall Stearns: No, no.

Charlie Parker: He's got records out when, you know, [he] was normal, you know?

Marshall Stearns: He'd sing much smoother and—

Charlie Parker: *Much* smoother.

* * *

Marshall Stearns: These records you made with—Trummy Young was on some of them.

Charlie Parker: Yeah?

Marshall Stearns: Remember? And with [Clyde Hart's] All Stars? And some came out on Manor, some came out—

Charlie Parker: Continental.

Chan Richardson Parker: Isn't that the one that Dizzy?—

Charlie Parker: Some came out on the Continental label.

Chan Richardson Parker: "I Can't Get Started," that was made that day, wasn't it?

Charlie Parker: No.

Chan Richardson Parker: It wasn't?

Charlie Parker: "Dream of You," "Seventh Avenue."

Marshall Stearns: Yeah.

Charlie Parker: Two other sides were made that day.

Marshall Stearns: Was that all for the same company, made that day? And then they just got them out on different—

Charlie Parker: Oh, that date was made for Continental, yeah, but I have seen some of those records out on the Manor label, I think.

Marshall Stearns: I guess Manor bought from the [Continental?].

* * *

Marshall Stearns: Was it more fun playing with the [Earl] Hines band or the [Billy] Eckstine band, those big bands? Which—

Charlie Parker: I think it was more fun playing with the Eckstine band. But the Hines band was much smoother.

Marshall Stearns: Billy makes a very easygoing leader, and everybody's having a ball. [Unintelligible.]

Chan Richardson Parker: Oh, it was a wonderful band.

Marshall Stearns: You heard it?

Charlie Parker: The greatest band ever, I think, yeah.

Marshall Stearns: Why I couldn't have heard that. This Tiny Grimes date. You made "Red Cross" [unintelligible] and "Tiny's Tempo." They since put it out with your name on it.

Charlie Parker: They did?

Marshall Stearns: Yeah. They figured it would sell more records, you see. Came out under Tiny's name.

Chan Richardson Parker: They're not allowed to do that, are they?

Marshall Stearns: I don't know.

Charlie Parker: No.

Marshall Stearns: Reissued under Parker's name.

Charlie Parker: They're not supposed to do that, but I mean, Herman Lubinsky [owner of the Savoy label] does a gang of things he ain't supposed to do. [*Laughs.*] That don't mean anything!

John Maher: All guys do. It's the old, old story. You can't—you can copyright a label, but you can't copyright a performance and once you sell your time that day, you're—

Chan Richardson Parker: I heard he has eleven sets of books. Whoever wants to see the books—[laughs]

Marshall Stearns: Oh, dear.

John Maher: Not like the old Irving Mills organization.

Charlie Parker: [*Laughs.*]

Marshall Stearns: Well, Charlie, is it true that "Mop Mop" was your idea originally? Leonard [Feather] says here that "Mop Mop" was one *of the things you threw off and then, finally, I don't know who, somebody else—*

Charlie Parker: It could have been, 'cause we used to do that a long time ago in Kansas City.

Marshall Stearns: You did "Mop Mop" in Kansas City?

Charlie Parker: Years ago. That was just putting drum beats in there just for the "bum, bum," we'd just play, when we'd get to the channel [the song's "B" section], you know, just play sometimes [sings a melody, then says:] "bomp, bomp," you know, just put them—just put it in.

Chan Richardson Parker: Oh, would you like to see these [photographs]?

Marshall Stearns: [possibly referring to the earlier topic:] That's a crazy mixture.

Chan Richardson Parker: Did you hear about Gene Roland's band?

Marshall Stearns: No.

Chan Richardson Parker: Tell him about it, Bird. It had eight reeds.

Charlie Parker: Oh, yeah. Twenty-seven-piece band rehearsing.

Marshall Stearns: How long ago was this?

Charlie Parker: A month, three weeks ago.

Chan Richardson Parker: A month ago.

Charlie Parker: A month ago.

Chan Richardson Parker: Do you know all those people?

Marshall Stearns: No.

Charlie Parker: Eight reeds, six trombones, and eight brass.

Chan Richardson Parker: [Possibly to Kim:] If you like.

Marshall Stearns: But, who—what label did they record for?

Chan Richardson Parker: They're not. They just rehearsed.

Charlie Parker: Didn't record. Just rehearsed.

Chan Richardson Parker: [Referring to the photographs:] This is Sonny Rich, Don Lanphere, and that's Eddie Bert, Zoot Sims and John Simmons, Al Cohn, Buddy Jones. This is Gene, it's his band. And the trumpet section, at first—every day at rehearsal, they had different people. Jon Nielson, Sonny Rich, Marty Bell, Red [Rodney], Al Porcino. And here, this is Gene. Don and Zoot and Al Cohn, Bird, Joe Maini.

Marshall Stearns: Wow.

John Maher: Look at that reed section. What a—

Charlie Parker: Eight saxophones.

Marshall Stearns: Well, how did it sound?

Chan Richardson Parker: Wonderful.

Charlie Parker: It was sounding [pause] *wild.*

Chan Richardson Parker: They had three drummers.

Marshall Stearns: Who was doing the arrangements?

Chan Richardson Parker: Gene.

Charlie Parker: Gene Roland.

John Maher: Well, you did record them, didn't you?

Charlie Parker: On this tape recorder.

Marshall Stearns: Just tape.

Charlie Parker: That's something. [Unintelligible.]

Marshall Stearns: Who has the tape? Do you have it?

Charlie Parker: Made one recording. No, I don't have it. Made one—made one master—

Chan Richardson Parker: Gene has it.

Charlie Parker: —but it was—but the balance was bad.

Marshall Stearns: Oh. Where were they made?

Charlie Parker: It was made in Nola's.

Marshall Stearns: Nola's?

Charlie Parker: Gene has all those, doesn't he? He was recording all the time up there.

Marshall Stearns: It's awful hard to record a big sound in New York because there are so few rooms that are—

Charlie Parker: It sure is. You know, at first the theory was that they must have a very toned-down room, something with a lot of soft things in it—

Marshall Stearns: Really dead. Absolutely dead.

Charlie Parker: —[Unintelligible] dead acoustics. That's wrong, man.

Marshall Stearns: Yeah.

Charlie Parker: Because in Europe, they have much better balance on records than we do here. And they record in old temples and old cathedrals and old churches and backyards fenced in and everything, you know. With *no acoustics whatsoever*. Just nothing but a chamber. An echo chamber. And the records come out with a great big sound.

John Maher: You know, in these small rooms they get, particularly in the high register, the sound, everything compresses, it gets squeezed. *[Tape ends with unintelligible voices.]*

TRANSCRIBED BY CARL WOIDECK

INTERVIEW: CHARLIE PARKER AND JOHN T. FITCH (RADIO NAME: JOHN MCLELLAN) (1953)

WHDH, Boston, Massachusetts, probably June 13, 1953

This interview with Charlie Parker was broadcast on WHDH radio in Boston and tape-recorded. Parker was in town working as a "single" with a local backup group. John Fitch remembers picking up Parker at a rooming house and having to wake the saxophonist up. Fitch feels he had a difficult time getting thoughtful responses from Parker and thinks that Parker had become accustomed to more of the superficial questions that most radio interviewers preferred. When played a selection by Bartók, he shows real familiarity with the composer, and had already elsewhere expressed interest in studying Western classical music. Nevertheless, Parker is very clear that the music that he, Dizzy Gillespie, Thelonious Monk, and others created in the 1940s was not influenced by classical music. When the topic comes up, Parker is adamant that he and his peers where not dissatisfied with earlier jazz styles but that their music was just their conception of where the music should go. As Parker mentions, he had just recorded the May 25, 1953, session with winds, voices, and rhythm section whose inspiration is discussed in Nat Hentoff's "Counterpoint" article (see page 79). Parker's feelings about the way that the difficult recording session turned out can be surmised in his pause in evaluating the record date. The session is also discussed here in Phil Schaap's survey of Parker's Verve-group recordings and is reviewed by Barry Ulanov in Part Six of this anthology (see page 246).

This interview is available in audio form (see the Discography). —CW

John Fitch: Welcome to Boston, Charlie, and more particularly, to our show.

Charlie Parker: Thank you, John. It's a pleasure to be on your show.

John Fitch: We thought that, with an unusual guest, perhaps we'd try a few unusual things this evening. And so, I've given you practically no indication of the sort of questions I'm going to ask you, or for that matter, of the type of music that I'm going to play for you, although of course in discussing it briefly last night over at the Hi-Hat where you're appearing, incidentally, through when?

Charlie Parker: Through Sunday.

John Fitch: Sunday night, and you have an afternoon session, too—

Charlie Parker: Yes, there's an afternoon session there running from 4 until 8.

John Fitch: Well, I'm sure that many of our listeners will want to drop in and catch you, either tonight, tomorrow afternoon, or tomorrow evening at the Hi-Hat at Columbus and Massachusetts Avenue, because I know they'll be in for a very good show. Well, as I started to say, in the brief talk we did have a chance to have last night, I did find out a few of the artists that Charlie Parker, himself, listens to, including some of the music of a different nature. It may surprise some of our listeners. So, if you're game, I'm set to play something for you to get the ball rolling. You set to listen?

Charlie Parker: All right, Johnny, go ahead.

John Fitch: All right, let's try this.

[*Music for Strings, Percussion, and Celesta* by Béla Bartók is played]

John Fitch: Um, I don't know quite what to ask you about that selection. Are you familiar with it?

Charlie Parker: Yes, it's one of Bartók's works. I forget the name, but Bartók is my favorite, you know.

John Fitch: Well, that was one of the things I picked up yesterday in the brief chance we had to get together, that in particular was just a very small fragment from the—from one of my favorite works, incidentally, the Concerto *for, um—no, no, it's not a concerto, it's* Music for Stringed Instruments, Percussion and Celesta *[sic].*

Charlie Parker: Yeah.

John Fitch: Well, the reason I chose that particular little portion of it, was because of its violent rhythmic ideas that he brings out in that. And so, if you'd like to say a few words about your favorite composer, why, go right ahead.

Charlie Parker: Well, there's—I mean, as far as his history is concerned, I mean, I read that he was Hungarian-born, he died in American exile in Manhattan General Hospital [actually, West Side Hospital] in New York in 1945. At that time, I was just becoming introduced to modern classics, contemporary and otherwise, you know? And, to my misfortune, he was deceased before I had the pleasure to meet the man [unintelligible]. As far as I'm concerned, he is one—beyond a doubt, one of the most finished and accomplished musicians that ever lived.

John Fitch: Well, now, you made a very interesting point, then, when you said that you heard him in 1945.

Charlie Parker: Yeah.

John Fitch: Because, this brings up a—a question that I've—I'd like to ask you, and if some of these questions sound as though I wrote them out ahead of time, I did. At a certain point in our musical history, prior to 1945, as a matter of fact, you and a group of others evidently became dissatisfied with the stereotyped form in which music had settled. So, you altered the rhythm, the melody, and the harmony, rather violently, as a matter of fact. Now, how much of this change that you were responsible for, you feel was spontaneous experimentation with your own ideas, and how much was the adaptation of the ideas of, your classical predecessors, for example, as in Bartók?

Charlie Parker: Well, it was 100 percent spontaneous. A hundred percent. Nothin'—not a bit of the idiom in which music travels today, known as progressive music, was adapted or even inspired by the older composers.

John Fitch: Well it—

Charlie Parker: Our predecessors.

John Fitch: It is rather strange, we have this, almost a progressive series of, not, not coincidences, but, where one follows the other. For example, after Debussy, considerably after, you have piano players like Erroll Garner, who—

Charlie Parker: Yes.

John Fitch: —is respected by, of course, by a great many people. But— and even earlier than that, the trumpet playing of Bix Beiderbecke, and his piano composition, were so largely taken, I mean, from the Debussy form.

Charlie Parker: Mm hm.

John Fitch: Very impressionistic, lush, rippling chords and clusters of chords, and even the titles of things like "In a Mist" and "Clouds" ["Clouds" is not by Beiderbecke; Fitch could have been referring to the Django Reinhardt composition, "Nuages."]

Charlie Parker: Yeah.

John Fitch: —remind you of, of Debussy. And I just wondered whether, in this case, it was, partly the same thing, or whether this was actually spontaneous.

Charlie Parker: Well, I'm not fam—too familiar with the Beiderbecke school of music, but the thing that's going—happening now known as "progressive music" or by the trade name "bebop," not a bit of it was inspired or adapted from the music of our predecessors: Bach, Brahms, Beethoven, Chopin, Ravel, Debussy, Shostakovich, Stravinsky, et cetera.

John Fitch: Then, whom do you feel were the really important persons, besides yourself, who evidently were dissatisfied with music as it was, and started to experiment?

Charlie Parker: Well, let me make a correction here, please. It wasn't that we were dissatisfied with it, it was just that another conception came along, and this was just the way *we* thought it should go. But, during that time, this happened in 1938, just a little bit before '45—

John Fitch: That's why I say—

Charlie Parker: It was—

John Fitch: —it was interesting that you commented.

Charlie Parker: —Dizzy Gillespie, Thelonious Monk, Kenny Clarke. It was Charlie Christian, '37, I guess. There was Bud Powell, Don Byas, Ben Webster, yours truly.

John Fitch: Mm hm. The storybook names, the ones that we read about in the—in our history—musical history books of the—of that time. Well, now, I know that it's difficult to, sort of, categorize musicians and schools of music, but, in thinking this over, I did, sort of, group what we hear today into about seven different categories. Now, I'd like to ask you what you feel, not only about the music, but about the future of each of these forms. For example, taking the earliest, just straight Dixieland, I mean, you do hear that today.

Charlie Parker: Yes.

John Fitch: It's featured in a lot of clubs. Now, do the musicians who play it merely satisfy the demand of the college crowd, or whoever it is that particularly wants to hear that, or, do they honestly want to play that?

Charlie Parker: Well, I'd rather say that they honestly want to play that. That's their conception, that's their idea, that's the way they think it should go, so they render, you know, likewise.

John Fitch: And how often and how long will they continue to play "High Society" and "When the Saints Go Marching In"?

Charlie Parker: There's no—there's no way in the world it can be—that you can tell how long it'll—it'll go on, you know?

John Fitch: Mm hm. With the same—roughly the same solos and—

Charlie Parker: Yeah, roughly the same ideas—well, that's—that's the skeleton, that's the way that music was set up, you know, with certain, I guess you'd call them "choruses," little ad-lib choruses that were remembered and handed down from person to person, and they just respected the solos of the older age, you know—

John Fitch: Mm hm.

Charlie Parker: —rather than the improvisation of spontaneous improvisation, that is—

John Fitch: But as I can probably gather—

Charlie Parker: "Ad lib," (in) other words.

John Fitch: —you have no interest in, in that subject at all.

Charlie Parker: Well, I like Dixieland, I like good Dixieland, it's all right, you know, but I just don't, I don't play it because I most likely wouldn't make a good job at it anyway, I just think it should go another way.

John Fitch: Uh huh. Now, what about the musicians who don't play "bebop," as you refer to it, and who also have grown tired of the Dixieland clichés. I don't even know what to call their music, but I—I mean people like Vic Dickenson, Doc Cheatham, Rex Stewart, many fine musicians who are not particularly Dixieland addicts, but who play, well, I just don't know what to call it.

Charlie Parker: Well, that came along during the Swing Era, say for instance, Dixieland, I think, was introduced in '14 or '15, and then the

Swing Era came in about 1928, and lasted until 1935, '36. I guess you'd put them, say, like, if you just had to categorize, you'd say that was Swing Era, you know?

John Fitch: Of course, there are a lot of them still around, and many of them, as Nat Hentoff has pointed out recently in Down Beat, *are finding it pretty tough to work, because people are, that is, the, the audiences are pretty violently split between Dixieland and cool—*

Charlie Parker: Mmm.

John Fitch: —music, and there seems to be no room for these middle-of-the road Swing musicians.

Charlie Parker: Well, I'd like to differ, I beg to differ, in fact. There's always room for musicians, you know. There's no such thing as the middle of the road. It—It'll be one thing or the other, either good music or otherwise, you know?

John Fitch: Mm hm.

Charlie Parker: And, it doesn't make any difference which idiom it might be in, Swing, "bebop" as you want to call it, or Dixieland. If it's good, it'll be heard.

John Fitch: Mm hm. What about the musicians who were in on the growth of bebop, but who quickly standardized a few clichés, and, and now cater exclusively to the "go-go-go" crowd? Is that just a fad, or are we going to have that with us for some time?

Charlie Parker: That, I wouldn't know either, since I don't cater to that particular thing. I wouldn't know, but, I mean, as far as I'm concerned, I think it's just rather more or less the way a man feels when he plays his instrument, to me, and if he feels that, it will stay. If he's just trying to commercialize on it, then most likely it'll vary from one thing to another.

John Fitch: Another group might be the experimenters and, [laughs] I dreamed up my own term, Classical Jazz, those who are well-schooled and have adapted a number of things they've been taught into their music. Um, I'm speaking particularly of Dave Brubeck and Gerry Mulligan, Gerry Mulligan who is devoted almost entirely to a real contrapuntal music without even having a piano to lend any homophony to the—to the things he plays. What about—what do you feel about them?

Charlie Parker: Well, the two men you mentioned, bein' extremely good friends of mine, even if they weren't friends of mine, I'd find their music very, very interesting. Not only from an intellectual standpoint, it's very intelligent music, and it's very well played. It's got a lot of feeling, and it isn't missing anything. It's definitely music, 100 percent.

John Fitch: Would you feel, yourself fitting into a group like that if you, I mean, played with them?

Charlie Parker: Oh, I imagine I could become acclimated, yes, I would like something like that.

John Fitch: Um, another group might be called the avant-garde, as primarily exemplified by Lennie Tristano.

Charlie Parker: Mm hm.

John Fitch: There we have—what they try to do occasionally, complete collective improvisation with no theme, no chorus, no chord changes on which to work. Just six men, or whatever it may be, improvising together. Is that—it's always struck me as being extremely difficult to understand how it's possible in the first place.

Charlie Parker: Oh, no, see [see?], those are just like you said, mostly improvisations, you know, and, uh, if you listen close enough, you can find the melody traveling along with any chord str—any series of chord structures, you know? And, uh, rather than to make the melody predominant in, in the style of music that Lennie and them present, it's more or less heard or felt. [This and the next answer from Parker have been left unedited to reflect the halting nature of his responses as he tries to understand the nature of Fitch's question.]

John Fitch: Well, I refer more particularly to—they made one record called "Intuition," and I've heard them do it in concert, in which they start off with no key, no basic set of chord changes or anything.

Charlie Parker: Uh huh. There must be a buildup to—to the r—to the—to the, um, both the key signature and the, uh, the chord structure that tends to create the melody.

John Fitch: As they go along.

Charlie Parker: Yes.

John Fitch: Then there is sort of a field apart, including, well, they're mostly individuals who—who stick out, like Duke Ellington, Ralph Burns writing for Woody Herman and Stan Kenton, whom you expressed an interest in.

Charlie Parker: Yes.

John Fitch: I think before we go any further, I'd like to get your comments on a particular Stan Kenton record, if you'd like to listen to one now.

Charlie Parker: Mmm.

["My Lady" by Stan Kenton is played]

John Fitch: There you have Stan Kenton. Oh, I guess that's rather obvious, but I'll turn to Charlie Parker for the rest of the—at least the featured soloist on that.

Charlie Parker: Yeah, that was Lee Konitz. Some very fine alto work on that record, too. I hadn't heard that one before, Johnny, what was the name of that?

John Fitch: It's called "My Lady."

Charlie Parker: Very beautiful.

John Fitch: *I'm not sure, but I think perhaps Lee wrote it himself. ["My Lady" was composed and arranged by Bill Russo.] I'm not—I'm not sure of that.*

Charlie Parker: It's a beautiful tune. Very well done, too.

John Fitch: *Well, now, I've given you an opportunity to speak of Stan Kenton.*

Charlie Parker: Yeah. Well, just I—as I was going on to say, Stan holds my definite interest, I mean, lots of ways. He's pioneered quite a bit in this progressive style of music. One particular record, though, I was asking you about a few minutes ago. Have you paid any attention, particular attention to (the) "House of Strings"?

John Fitch: *We haven't played "House of Strings." We did play "City of Glass" not too long ago, and we had a very interesting discussion here with Nat Hentoff and Rudoph Elie, the music critic of the* Herald and Traveler. *But, adding a little more to that, I would like just to mention an article in this current issue of* Down Beat *magazine written by Leonard Bernstein in which in the course of discussing a number of things, he mentions this. And I'd just like to read this to you for your, for your comments. [Leonard Bernstein, "The Jazz Scene Today,"* Down Beat, *June 7, 1953, p. 6.]*

Charlie Parker: All right.

John Fitch: *"Pretentiousness means calling attention to oneself. It means the guy is saying 'look at me, I'm modern!' And I think that's about the most old-fashioned attitude anyone can assume. I've found that about Kenton. It's modernistic, like old-fashioned modern furniture, which is just unbearable. It's moderne! Composition is an important word—it means that somebody has to make [sic "has made"] a piece which is a work, which hangs together from beginning to end." Now, I think in particular, he's referring to things of that nature, "House of Strings," "City of Glass," which are completely scored with, perhaps, little opening for improvisation by any soloist.*

Charlie Parker: No, well, you had two factors moving there. You say Nat wrote that?

John Fitch: No, this is—it was written by Leonard Bernstein.

Charlie Parker: Anyway, Leonard Bernstein, yeah. I can understand how he meant when he says a fellow would say, "look at me, I'm modern." That's strictly from the public—from the publicity agent's mouth, you know. Stan never has made such a statement, I know he hasn't. Most likely never will. But, he's still done many things, many good things toward the pioneering of this music: introducing of strings, different instrumentations, different chord structures, and just pioneering in general. A definite asset to the music.

John Fitch: What do you feel about a longer piece of music which is completely scored, which doesn't leave any opening for improvisation. Is that still jazz? [Unintelligible.]

Charlie Parker: Well, it depends how it's written; it could be, yes.

John Fitch: I see. Well, what about your own group, the people you work with, the other musicians who started with you—I've noticed that, for example, you play "Anthropology" and "52nd Street Theme," perhaps, but they were written a long time ago. What is to take their place and be the basis for your future?*

Charlie Parker: Hm. That's hard to tell, too, John. See, like, your ideas change as you grow older. Most people fail to realize that most of the things that they hear, either coming out of a man's horn ad lib, or else things that are written, you know, say, original things, I mean, they're just experiences. The way you feel, the beauty of the weather, the nice look of a mountain, maybe a nice fresh cool breath of air. I mean, all those things you can never tell what you'll be thinking tomorrow, but I definitely can say that music won't stop. It'll be—keep going forward.

John Fitch: And you feel that you, yourself, change continuously.

Charlie Parker: I do feel that way, yes.

John Fitch: And in listening to your earlier recordings, you become dissatisfied with them? Do you feel that—

Charlie Parker: Well, I still think that the best record is yet to be made, if that's what you mean.

John Fitch: That's about what I mean, and—

Charlie Parker: [Unintelligible.]

John Fitch: —I understand that you have something new in the offing.

Charlie Parker: Yes, we—the other day, two weeks ago Monday, with twelve voices, clarinet, flute, oboe, bassoon, French horn, and three rhythm. I have hopes that they might sound [pause] okay.

John Fitch: Well, we'll be very, very much interested in hearing them when they do come out. In the concluding moments of our show, I would like to play something else that I'm reasonably sure you haven't heard. Which might be considered a salute to you. We won't have time to hear it all, but I'm sure you'll be interested in at least hearing a bit of Stan Getz and his "Parker 51."

["Parker 51" by Stan Getz is played]

John Fitch: And there we have about all we have time to hear of "Parker 51" by Stan Getz from his Jazz at Storyville album, an obvious salute to you. [Jimmy Raney, the composer, has stated that the piece's title comes from the signature on a painting by artist Raymond Parker.] Is that the first time you've heard that?

Charlie Parker: Yes, that's the first time I have heard that, John.

John Fitch: Do you feel that he captured some of your own mood?

Charlie Parker: Oh, yes, it's—he's really too much. I sure liked that tune. That was "Cherokee," that was a satire on "Cherokee."

John Fitch: Uh huh. [Laughs.] Well, I'm afraid that our time has about run out. I certainly want to wish you a continuing good stay at the Hi-Hat. I did get a chance to hear you twice, and I enjoyed it thoroughly. I feel, if possible, you're playing better than ever before.

Charlie Parker: [*Laughs.*] Oh, thank you, John.

John Fitch: You have a wonderful group with Bernie Griggs on bass, and our own Herb Pomeroy on trumpet, both of whom are playing very, very well. And I hope that many of our listeners will take the opportunity to hear you either tonight or tomorrow afternoon at 3, or for your last night, Sunday night. And Charlie, may I thank you very much for being with us on The Top Shelf *this evening.*

Charlie Parker: Thank you John, it's always a pleasure to be on your show.

John Fitch: Thank you, and now, this is John McLellan speaking for Dan Leary, hoping you've enjoyed tonight's program of recorded music, and hoping, too, that you'll join us next Saturday at 7 with more music from The Top Shelf.

TRANSCRIBED BY CARL WOIDECK

INTERVIEW: CHARLIE PARKER, PAUL DESMOND, AND JOHN T. FITCH (RADIO NAME: JOHN MCLELLAN) (1954)

WHDH, Boston, Massachusetts, January 1954 [Broadcast between January 17 and January 23, 1954]

This is the only known taped interview between Parker and a well-known musician. In the preceding interview, Parker seemed uncomfortable answering some of John Fitch's questions. For this later interview, Fitch sets Parker more at ease by including saxophonist Paul Desmond, then playing with Dave Brubeck's quartet. The two musicians establish a rapport and have a good time joking with one another, and Parker's comment that his saxophone technique was acquired by studying and not "done by mirrors" is hilarious. Along the way, Parker mentions meeting composer Edgard Varèse in New York and talks of going to Paris to study Western classical composition and saxophone technique. Many of the dates that Parker gives are incorrect; more accurate ones are in parentheses.

This interview is available in audio form (see the Discography).
—CW

[Tape of interview begins in progress.]

Paul Desmond: . . . because there's many good people playing on that record, but the style of the alto is so different from anything else that's on the record or that went before. Did you realize at that time what effect you were going to have on jazz, that you were going to change the entire scene in the next ten years?

Charlie Parker: Well, let's put it like this: No, I had no idea that it was that much different. [*Laughs.*]

Paul Desmond: Well . . .

John Fitch: I'd like to stick in a question, if I may. I'd like to know why there was this violent change, really after all, up until this time the way to play the alto sax was the way that Johnny Hodges and Benny Carter played alto, and this seems to be an entirely different conception, not just of how to play that particular horn, but music in general.

Paul Desmond: Yeah, how to play any horn.

Charlie Parker: I'd [?]—that—I don't think there's any answer to—

John Fitch: The fact that—[unintelligible—overlaps with below]

Charlie Parker: —the way you're speaking, John. Yeah, that—that's what I said when I first started talking. That's my first conception, man, that's the way I thought it should go. And I still do. I mean, of course, it could stand much improvement. Most likely in another twenty-five or maybe fifty years, some youngster will come along and take the style and really do something with it, you know? But, I mean, ever since I've ever heard music, I thought it should be very clean, very precise, as clean as possible anyway, you know? And, more or less to the people, you know, something they could understand, something that was beautiful, you know? There's definitely—there's stories and stories and stories that can be told in the musical idiom, you know? You wouldn't say idiom, either, it's—it's so hard to describe music other than the basic way to describe it: music is basically melody, harmony, and rhythm. But I mean, people can do much more with music than that—it can be very descriptive in all kinds of ways, you know? All walks of life. Don't you agree, Paul?

Paul Desmond: Yeah, and you do always have a story to tell. It's one of the most impressive things about everything I've ever heard of yours.

Charlie Parker: Well that's more or less the object; that's the way I thought it should be.

Paul Desmond: Uh huh. Another thing that's been a major factor in your playing is this fantastic technique that nobody's quite equaled. I always wondered about that, too; whether there was, whether that came behind practicing or whether that was just from—from playing, whether it evolved gradually.

Charlie Parker: Well, um, you make it so hard for me to—answer, you know, because, I can't see where there's anything fantastic about it at all. I put quite a bit of study into the horn, that's true. In fact, the neighbors threatened to ask my mother to move once, you know. [*Laughter.*] When I was living out west, I mean, they said I was driving 'em crazy with the horn. I used to put in at least eleven, eleven to fifteen hours a day .

Paul Desmond: Yeah, that's, that's what I wondered.

Charlie Parker: (Well) that's true, yes. I did that for over a period of three or four years.

Paul Desmond: Oh. Yeah. I guess that's the answer.

Charlie Parker: That's the facts, anyway. [*Laughs.*]

Paul Desmond: I heard a record of yours a couple of months ago that somehow I had missed up to date, and I heard a little, 'bout a two-bar quote, from the Klosé book that was like an echo from home.

Charlie Parker: Oh.

[Desmond sings the opening bars of exercise 23 from *25 Daily Exercises for Saxophone* by Hyacinthe Eleonor Klosé.]

Charlie Parker: Yeah, yeah. Well, that was all done with books, you know. Naturally, it wasn't done with mirrors this time, it was done with books.

Paul Desmond: Now that's, that's very reassuring to hear, because somehow I got the idea that you were just sort of born with that technique, and you never had to worry too much about, 'bout keeping it working.

John Fitch: Y'know, I'm pretty glad that he's bringing up this point because I think a lot of young musicians tend to think that—

Paul Desmond: Yeah, they do, they just go out—

John Fitch: —that it isn't necessary to do this.

Paul Desmond: —go out and make those sessions and live the life, but they don't put in that eleven hours a day with any of the books.

Charlie Parker: Oh, definitely. Study is absolutely necessary in all forms. It's just like any talent that's born within somebody, it's just like a good pair of shoes when you put a shine on it, you know? It's like schooling brings out the polish, you know, of any talent that happens anywhere in the world. Einstein had schooling, but he has a definite genius, you know, within himself. Schooling's one of the most wonderful things there has ever been, you know.

John Fitch: I'm glad to hear you say this.

Charlie Parker: That's absolutely right.

Paul Desmond: Yeah.

Charlie Parker: Well?

John Fitch: (How) 'bout another record?

Charlie Parker: Yeah. Which one should we take this time?

John Fitch: Want to skip a little while, and—and we have—Charlie picked out "Night and Day"—

Paul Desmond: Okay—

John Fitch: —as one of his records. Is this with a band, or with strings?

Charlie Parker: No, this is just with the large band, this I think there's about nineteen pieces on this.

John Fitch: Why don't we listen to it, and then talk about it?

Paul Desmond: Bells. [An expression of approval, usually considered as being coined by saxophonist Lester Young.]

John Fitch: Okay.
["Night and Day" is played]

John Fitch: "Night and Day." Charlie Parker with a big band.

Paul Desmond: Charlie, this brings us kind of up to where you and Diz started joining forces, the next record we have coming up. When did you first meet Dizzy Gillespie?

Charlie Parker: Well, the first time, our official meeting I might say, was on the bandstand (of) Savoy Ballroom in New York City in 1939 [the band opened at the Savoy in February 1942] when McShann's band first came to New York [probably late 1941]. I'd been to New York previously, but I went back West and rejoined the band and came back to New York with 'em. Dizzy came by one night, I think at the time he was working with Cab Calloway's band, and he sat in the band. I was quite fascinated with the fellow and we became very good friends, and until this day we are, you know?

Paul Desmond: Mm hm.

Charlie Parker: But that was the first time I ever had the pleasure to meet Dizzy Gillespie.

Paul Desmond: Well, was he playing the same way before he played with you?

Charlie Parker: I don't remember precisely, I just know that he was playing a, oh, what you might call in the vernacular of the streets, a *beaucoup* [pronounced "boo-koo"] of horn, you know?

Paul Desmond: Beaucoup [Boo-koo]?

Charlie Parker: Yeah.

Paul Desmond: Okay.

Charlie Parker: You know, just like all of the horn packed up in once, you know?

Paul Desmond: Uh huh.

Charlie Parker: And we used to go around to different places and jam together, and we had quite a bit of fun in those days and shortly after (the) McShann band went West again I went out with them and I came back to New York again. I found Dizzy again in the Earl Hines organization in 1941 [reportedly December 1942] and I joined the band with him. It was in New York and I—we both stayed on the band about a year. It was Earl Hines, Dizzy Gillespie, Sarah Vaughan, Billy Eckstine, Gail Brockman, Thomas Crump. Oh there was Shadow Wilson, quite a few names that you'd recognize in the music world today, you know, were in that band.

Paul Desmond: It's quite a collection.

Charlie Parker: And, um, that band broke up in '41 [Parker actually left around August 1943]. In '42 [1945], Dizzy was in New York, he formed his own little combination in (the) Three Deuces (in) New York City, and I joined his band there. That's when these records you're about to play now, we made these in '42 [1945] in New York.

Paul Desmond: Yeah. I guess the first time I heard that group was, you came out to Billy Berg's—

Charlie Parker: Oh yes, but that was '45 [correct]. That was later. We'll get to that. [*Laughs.*]

Paul Desmond: Okay. I'm just illustrating how far I was behind all this.

Charlie Parker: Oh, don't be that way.

Paul Desmond: Okay.

Charlie Parker: Modesty will get you nowhere.

Paul Desmond: I'm hip [all laugh].

John Fitch: Shall we, shall we spin this 1942 [1945] one?

Paul Desmond: Yeah.

John Fitch: Okay, this is "Groovin' High" with Dizzy and Charlie. ["Groovin' High" is played]

John Fitch: "Groovin' High," 1942 [1945], with Charlie Parker and Dizzy Gillespie and some others.

Charlie Parker: Yes.

John Fitch: I guess, was it Slam Stewart and Remo Palmieri, I guess—

Charlie Parker: Yes.

John Fitch: —although I don't know who was on piano.

Charlie Parker: Uh, I think that was Clyde Hart—

John Fitch: Yes, I think so.

Charlie Parker: —and Big Sid Catlett, deceased now.

Paul Desmond: You said at that time New York was jumpin', in '42.

Charlie Parker: Yeah, New York was—well those were the what you might call "the good old days," you know, Paul? Gay youth.

Paul Desmond: Tell me about it.

Charlie Parker: Well, descriptively, just like I was going to say: gay youth, lack of funds.

Paul Desmond: Listen at Grandfather Parker talking here.

Charlie Parker: There was nothing to do *but* play, you know, and we had a lot of fun trying to play, you know? I did. Plenty of jam sessions, meant much late hours, pretty good food, nice clean living, you know, but basically speaking, much poverty. [*Laughs.*]

Paul Desmond: That's always good, too: no worries.

Charlie Parker: It has its place, definitely, in life.

Paul Desmond: Uh huh. Uh, would you like that sort of situation to have continued indefinitely?

Charlie Parker: Well, whether I liked it or not, it really did, Paul. I'm glad it finally blew over, of a sort, and I do mean of a sort.

Paul Desmond: Oh. [Laughs.]

Charlie Parker: Yeah, I enjoy this a little much—much more, in fact. (To) have the pleasure to work with the same guys of a sort, and I've met, and I've met other young fellows, you know, that come along. I enjoy working with them when I have the pleasure to, (and) if I might say, *you*, yourself, Paul.

Paul Desmond: Oh, thanks, Charlie.

Charlie Parker: Sure, I've had lots of fun working with you, man, it's a pleasure to know you (and) David, Dave Brubeck, David Brubeck.

Paul Desmond: [Laughs.]

Charlie Parker: (And) lots of other fellows (have) come along, you know, since that era, that particular era, that [really?] makes you feel that everything you did wasn't for naught, you know, that you really tried to prove something and—

Paul Desmond: Well, man, you really proved it.

Charlie Parker: Well—[*chuckles*].

Paul Desmond: I think you did more than anybody in the last ten years to leave a decisive mark on the history of jazz.

Charlie Parker: Well, not yet, Paul, but I intend to. I'd like to study some more; I'm not quite through yet. I'm not quite—I don't consider myself too old to learn.

Paul Desmond: No, I know many people are watching you at the moment with the greatest of interest to see what you're going to come up with next in the next few years, myself among the—the front row of them, and, well, what have you got in mind? (What) are you going to be doing?

Charlie Parker: Well, seriously speaking, I mean, I'm going to try to, um, go to Europe to study. I had the pleasure to meet one Edgard Varèse in New York City, he's a classical composer from Europe. He's a Frenchman, a very nice fellow, and he wants to teach me, in fact, he wants to write [radio static] for me some things for me for a—you know, more or less on a serious basis, you know?

Paul Desmond: Mm hm.

Charlie Parker: And, if he takes me over, I mean, after he finishes with me, I might have a chance to go to Academie de Musicale [perhaps the Conservatoire National de Musique] in Paris itself and study, you know. And, well, the principal—the prime—my prime interest still is learning to play music, you know. [Unintelligible.]

Paul Desmond: Would you study playing, or composition, or every-thing?

Charlie Parker: I would study both. I never want to lose my horn.

Paul Desmond: Yeah, you never should; that would be (a) catastrophe.

Charlie Parker: Never want to do that. That wouldn't work.

Paul Desmond: Uh huh. Well, we're—we're kind of getting ahead of the record sequence here, but it's been most fascinating. Uh, you want to say something about Miles Davis?

Charlie Parker: Yeah, well, I'll tell you how I met Miles. In 1944, Billy Eckstine formed his own organization. Dizzy was on that band also, Lucky Thompson, and it was Art Blakey—

Paul Desmond: Oh, yeah.

Charlie Parker: —Tommy Potter, and a lot of other fellows, and last and least, yours truly. And—

Paul Desmond: Modesty will get you nowhere, Charlie. [Both laugh.]

Charlie Parker: I had the pleasure to meet Miles for the first time in St. Louis when he was a youngster, he was still going to school. Later on, he came to New York, he finished Julliard [Davis did not], Miles did, he graduated from Julliard, and at the time, I was just beginning to get my band together, you know, five pieces here, and five pieces there and so I formed a band and took it into the Three Deuces for maybe seven [to] eight weeks, and at the time Dizzy had—Dizzy was—after the Billy Eckstine organization broke up, Dizzy was about to form his own band. There were so many things taking place then, I mean, it's hard to describe—describe it because it happened in a matter of months. Nevertheless, I went to California in 1945 with Dizzy, after I broke up my band, the first band I had, and I came back again to New York in '47, the early part of '47, and that's when I decided to have a band of my own permanently. And Miles was in my original band. I had Miles, I had Max [Roach], I had Tommy Potter and Al Haig in my band.

Paul Desmond: Mm hm.

Charlie Parker: Another band I had, I had Stan Levey, I had Curley Russell, I had Miles and George Wallington.

Paul Desmond: Yeah.

Charlie Parker: But, I think you have a record out there that—one of the records that we made with Max and Miles, I think, and yours truly—

Paul Desmond: Uh huh.

Charlie Parker: —Tommy [Potter], Duke Jordan. What is it, I think it's "Perhaps." Is it (not) that side? Well, came along in the years of, say, '47. '46, '47. These particular sides were made in New York City, at WNEW, 1440 Broadway. And this is the beginning of my career as a bandleader.

Paul Desmond: Okay, well let's—

John Fitch: Let's listen to "Perhaps."

["Perhaps" is played]

John Fitch: And so, because our time has run out, and there's still much more to discuss. We shall continue this transcribed interview with Charlie Parker by Paul Desmond next Saturday at 7. I'd like to remind you to avail yourself of the opportunity sometime tonight or tomorrow to hear Charlie Parker with his own group at the Hi-Hat, and Paul Desmond with the Dave Brubeck Quartet at Storyville. Now, this is John McLellan hoping you'll join me next Saturday at 7 for part two of the Parker story, and more recorded music from The Top Shelf.

Y a r
S u i
R e m
C h a

Parker's friends and colleagues have shared their memories of him in many articles and books. Here is a sampling of those reminiscences. The Gene Ramey and Dizzy Gillespie articles are particularly fond and articulate. Many more memories of Charlie Parker can be found in Robert Reisner's *Bird: The Legend of Charlie Parker.*—CW

MY MEMORIES OF BIRD PARKER (1955)

Melody Maker, May 28, 1955

This memoir by one of Charlie Parker's oldest friends and colleagues was published only two months after Parker's death. Seven years Parker's senior, Gene Ramey was already a professional musician when the two musicians first met in the mid-1930s. Their paths continued to cross, and Ramey was there when Parker experienced his now-legendary jam session humiliation at the hands of drummer Jo Jones. Parker and Ramey eventually joined Jay McShann's Kansas City band, and Ramey was in an ideal position to track Parker's rapid progress into musical maturity. In later years, when Parker and Ramey were both based in New York City, Ramey sometimes had to aid Parker when times got tough. In the 1950s, Gene Ramey's loyalty to his friend was so great that he offered to leave his musical job to go on the road in support of Charlie Parker.—CW

I first met Bird in 1934.

At the time, I was playing with a band from the Kansas side of Kansas City; Bird was with a band from the other side of the State line, in Kansas City, Missouri.

The leader of Bird's band was a pianist and singer named Lawrence "88" Keyes, who later became well known in the East. It was the first band Bird had ever worked in, and he seemed to me then like just a happy-go-lucky kid. In fact, the whole outfit was a school band, and Bird was hardly fully grown at that time—he was barely fourteen years old!

Bird wasn't doing anything, musically speaking, at that period. In fact, he was the saddest thing in the band, and the other members gave him something of a hard time.

Humiliation

About a year later I saw Charlie again. We were about two blocks down the street from Count Basie at the Reno Club, and Duke Ellington was at the Green Leaf, on the other side of the street. All of us had a regular habit of running from one club to another during intermissions. When I saw Bird during that time, he was a little bit downhearted, because everybody would be holding jam sessions—and he was one of the few musicians who was *never* allowed to sit in.

In particular, I remember one night when we were to jam with Basie. Jo Jones waited until Bird started to play and then, as an expression of his feeling, took his cymbal off and threw it almost the complete distance of the dance floor. It fell with a tremendous crash, and Bird, humiliated, just packed up his horn and walked out.

However, this gave him a big determination to play. "I'll fix these cats," he used to say. "Everybody's laughing at me now, but just you wait and see!"

At that time, George E. Lee, another bandleader in the area, would take his outfit up to a summer resort in the mountains every year. Well, Bird went up in the mountains, and when he came back, only two or three months later, the difference was unbelievable.

The Cycles

I think it was a guitarist named Efferge Ware who helped to straighten Bird out on the cycles—the relationship of the chords and how to weave melodies into them. Ware was a great chord specialist, although he did no solo work. He had lots of patience and explained everything to Bird, after which of course, Bird expanded on his own.

Naturally, after this sudden development in his style, Bird began to get lots of work. He was always an aggressive youngster with lots of ideas and suggestions. At that time, there were lots of jam sessions going on in night clubs and in various private houses. One night Bird suggested that we go out to Paseo Park—so after that, every once in a while, all the cats would get out there in the middle of the park and we'd play all night. The cops very seldom bothered us; in fact, they used to come out there to enjoy the music themselves!

The Jay McShann band, in which Bird and I worked together for so long, was the only band I've ever known that seemed to spend all its spare time jamming or rehearsing. We used to jam on trains and buses, and as soon as we got into a town, we'd try to find somebody's house where we could hold a session.

All this was inspired by Bird, because the new ideas he was bringing to the band made everybody anxious to play.

We were at a club in New Orleans on one occasion, playing a one-nighter, when we were informed by Decca that we were due for a record session in a couple of weeks. McShann suggested that we get together and do something real quick.

Real Warm!

It was one of those real warm days in New Orleans, but we got together and had a little session, and the ideas came across. I guess in about 45 minutes we had "Jumpin' Blues" ready. This arrangement was all a "head" put together by Bird, and the record featured one of his first great solos on wax.

Bird was one of the reasons it was such a happy-go-lucky band. He used to say: "If you come on a band tense you're going to play tense. If you come a little bit foolish, act just a little bit foolish, and let yourself go, better ideas will come."

Everything had a musical significance for him. He'd hear dogs barking, for instance, and he would say it was a conversation—and if he was blowing his horn he would have something to play that would portray that thought to us. When we were riding in the car between jobs we might pass down a country lane and see the trees and some leaves, and he'd have some sound for that.

And maybe some girl would walk past on the dance floor while he was playing, and something she might have would give him an idea for something to play on his solo. As soon as he would do that, we were all so close we'd all understand just what he meant. He might be looking another way, but as soon as he played that little phrase, everybody would look up and get the message.

In his solo on "Jumpin' Blues," I can't recall just what it was Bird was saying, but I remember we all used to make a joke about that first four bars. This was a phrase he had used before, which later became famous as "Ornithology."

Bird was also responsible for the invention of something that became a catchphrase with the band. There was a comical picture that used to appear in the papers quite often, of a guy who looked kind of hungry and sad. He was so expressive that Bird used to look at the picture and say, "Huh—*me* worry!" So after that, any time if we didn't get paid, or if somebody would be looking gloomy, or if someone would get drunk on the bandstand, we would all use this phrase—"*Me* worry!"

Now that I look back on it, Bird was so far ahead of his time that nobody really appreciated just how radical his ideas were. For instance, we used to jam "Cherokee" a lot, and Bird had a way of starting on a B natural against the B flat chord, and he would run a cycle against that— and probably it would only be two or three bars before we got to the channel [middle part] that he would come back to the basic changes.

Reserved Seats

In those days we used to call it "running out of key." Bird used to sit and try to explain to us what he was doing. I am sure that at that time nobody else in the band could even play, for example, the channel to "Cherokee." So Bird used to play a series of "Tea for Two" phrases against that channel, and since this was a melody that could easily be remembered, it gave the other guys something to play during those bars.

Bird left the band for some time in 1939, but returned later and remained with McShann until 1942, at which time the whole personnel began to disintegrate. In 1941, of course, we were at the Savoy Ballroom in New York for quite a while, and during that period Dizzy Gillespie practically worked with the band.

We always kept a seat on the bandstand for him, as well as a place for Chubby Jackson and Big Sid Catlett, and they would be there almost every night, any time they were in town.

Most of the members of that band are scattered far and wide today. Gus Johnson, the drummer, was with Basie's band until a few months ago;

McShann and a few others are still around Kansas City. Al Hibbler, who was our ballad singer, is now a big star in his own right; while Walter Brown, who made our hit blues vocal record, "Confessin' the Blues," has been out of circulation lately.

But I think it will be a long time before those of us who were a part of that scene will forget the spirit and freshness of the Jay McShann orchestra and the great inspiration that was lent to it by the immortal Charlie Parker.

BART BECKER
JAY MCSHANN: INTERVIEW (1979)

Excerpted from Cadence, September and October 1979

For this article, Bart Becker did both the interview and the transcription. Jay McShann met Parker in 1937, soon after the saxophonist returned from his first major breakthrough in the Ozark mountains. McShann led both Charlie Parker and Gene Ramey in McShann's band, which is often called the last great jazz band to leave Kansas City in the 1940s. McShann has told many times his version of how Charlie Parker got his nickname, Yardbird, which was later shortened to Bird. According to McShann, his band was on his way to a college job in Lincoln, Nebraska, when one of the band cars ran over a chicken in the road. Parker insisted on going back to pick up the "yardbird" to be cooked later for dinner. The band teased him about it and the name stuck. Parker's version of how he got his nickname can be found in Michael Levin and John S. Wilson's article (see page 69).—CW

Jay McShann: But I was always telling guys that, you know, we have Charlie Parker. Ask me what did he do, I tell them he played the blues. And if you listen closely, well, anything that Bird played . . . if it was a ballad he gave you the ballad sound, but Bird played the blues. Regardless how much technique he had. He played the blues. And I've had guys, oh they have great arguments about it, 'cause they said no. Because they was guys that came along and they couldn't see that Bird played the blues. Bird was one of the greatest blues musicians in the world. And he learned that from me and some of the others up 12th street.

Because he got his stuff together. He would run it up and down and back. I mean he knew his instrument backwards. Every time you would see him he would have his horn on his arm and probably have the book you know. Exercise book. And in jamming he was permanent stuff. But exercises really weren't saying too much. But finally he got his exercises down and he would run one chord into the other and put a meaning with it, you know. When he got that wasn't no stopping Bird. 'Cause by having that, knowing his horn backwards and then by having a little blues experience that he had heard practically all his life.

* * *

Cadence: Can you tell us about the first time you met Charlie Parker?

Jay McShann: Well the first time I heard Charlie Parker it was right after I had gone to work with Hop. See, I thought I had heard everybody in town and during that time you could pass by a club and you could hear the music out there see because it was piped out there. So I happened to be comin' by this particular club called The Barley Duke one night and I heard this horn blowin' and I said, "Boy, I've never heard that horn before." I was gonna go on home but I stopped in to see who it was. The guys got through playing and I walked over there to 'em and I said, "Hey man, what's your name?" He told me, "Charlie, Charlie Parker." I said, "I haven't heard you in town. I thought I had heard everybody. Where have you been?" "Oh I've been down in the Ozarks workin' with George Lee's band and I just got back. I wanted to go down there to woodshed." So that's when I first met him. See, it was hard to get musicians to go down to the Ozarks because you know they want to be around where the action is. And Bird said he went down there with George because it gave him a chance to get his things together. Of course I wasn't around K.C. I had heard some of the musicians talk about him when Bird used to come sit in everybody would pick up their horn and leave. They said he didn't have himself together. Those cats would say, "Oh, here's that cat here again." They'd pick up their horn, you know what I mean. So he told me that's why he went down there with George, but when he came back he was together, because I had never heard anybody blow like that before. Nobody was blowin' like Bird. And it's just like when we got to New York, Ben Webster went down and told all the saxophone players down on 52nd Street. He said, "All you guys who think that you can play saxophone, you'd better go up there and there's this little saxophone player up there with Jay McShann's band, a new band in town from Kansas City. All you guys better go up there and go to school." And I didn't know it then but Benny Webster told us about it later. He told us that he would hide, he didn't want nobody to see him y'know. (*Laughter.*) After he went down and told the rest of the guys down on the street he said he'd come on by and they'd run into each other hidin' from each other. (*Laughter.*) He said they'd have a big laugh about it. But you see nobody had heard nothing like that, really. Well we had heard it before in Kansas City, there were guys there and now even in the band you see everybody didn't try to play like Bird. You know we had a lot of individuals in that band. Just like Buddy [Bernard "Step Buddy" Anderson] he didn't try to play like Bird but Buddy was an individual. Both of 'em were real modern. I used to get so mad because Jimmy Forrest was in the band he would . . . Listen, Bird would blow everything there was to play on "Body and Soul" and Jimmy Forrest would come right back behind him and upstage Bird. The crowd would just scream and carry on. Bird was doin' all that stuff he did . . . I don't know why we set up the arrangement like that but we had it set up that way y'know, tenor would follow the alto solo. But you see, the people wasn't with the sound. See it was 25 years later before the audience got hip to that sound.

Cadence: When was the last time you saw Bird?

Jay McShann: Well, the last time I saw Bird was let's see . . . I think when I came out of the army. See I went in the army in 1944—I came out about '45 or '46. I think Bird was playing on 52nd St. I went down there to listen to Bird and he and Ben Webster was working together I think then. So Ben says, "well he works here but he plays down the street." (*Laughter.*) They'd take intermission and Bird would take his horn down across the street and blow with these cats over there y'know. Then is he gets carried away and he likes it he'll stay there y'know, he don't come back to his gig. (*Laughter.*) But right funny, I remember Earl Hines told me, "Man, I heard the group the other night. I tell you what, I want three men out of your group, now you know I'll get them. Why don't we just sit down and talk this thing over. How much money do they owe you and I'll straighten up with you whatever it is and y'know you'll get your money back because I'm gonna get them anyway because I know money will get them." So he wanted Bird and a couple of other cats. I said, "Well okay." And I told him what they owed me so he gave me the money. He said, "You know what, I'll tell you something. I don't think you know how to handle this guy Charlie Parker. You all are a bunch of kids. I'm gonna take him and make a man out of him. Now you don't know how to handle him." I said, "Well all right, okay." Well next time I saw Earl Hines he said, "Come get this madman. Listen this guy owes everybody in the band and every loan shark in town." (*Laughter.*) He also bought him a brand new horn see. Well quite naturally, if Parker wanted something, it didn't make no difference to him he'd just go hawk [hock] the horn so he could get what he wanted at the time. He was just a guy that just . . . that whole group was sorta happy-go-lucky. And if it was something he wanted, he got it y'know. Because he lived for today, he did, he lived for today. Bird could do anything. Here's what I mean, I'm speaking of over all music, you know what I mean. Whatever group he's with if they wanted to do it that way he could do it that way. But when Bird did it his way you knew it because you heard it.

CHRIS GODDARD
JAZZ ORAL HISTORY PROJECT: BUSTER SMITH (1981)
January 13, 1981

This interview is an excerpt from an interview conducted for the National Endowment for the Arts Jazz Oral History Project, administered by the Institute of Jazz Studies at Rutgers University. Chris Goddard is the interviewer.

Although Charlie Parker was strongly influenced by the recordings of tenor saxophonist Lester Young, Parker's primary alto saxophone influence was Henry "Buster" Smith. Young left Parker's home town of Kansas City in 1936, but Smith stayed in the city until 1938 and was available to Parker as a mentor and an early band leader. Parker modeled his style in part on Smith, and Parker got to the point at which he could play anything Smith could. In the video Celebrating Bird *(Gary Giddins, Sony Video Software Co., 1987), pianist Jay McShann recalled how close Parker came to his mentor's style: "I remember I heard a broadcast one night, during the time Bird was working with Prof ['Professor' Smith], and so I told Prof, I said 'Prof,' I says, 'you sure did sound good last night.' He says, 'What do you mean "sound good last night,"' he says, 'I didn't play last night. . . . That was Charlie Parker you heard last night.'"*

After Smith moved to New York City in 1938, Parker followed in 1939 and stayed at Smith's apartment temporarily. Smith left New York in the 1940s and lived in Dallas, Texas, where he recorded his only LP, The Legendary Buster Smith, *in 1959.*

Although Buster Smith suggests that Dizzy Gillespie might have known and worked with Charlie Parker on the East coast in 1939, they evidently first met in Kansas City; the year was probably 1940.—CW

Chris Goddard: *Before we go on with your story, I want to go on with Charlie Parker again. Do you have any idea why it was that Bird became such a wildly unstable character? Why was it necessary for him to get off on drugs and all that kind of thing?*

Buster Smith: I don't know anything about it, because he didn't smoke, didn't drink, didn't do anything when he was around me.

Chris Goddard: *You have no idea who started him?*

Buster Smith: No. I think he was playing down at the Atlas Club. Down there in Kansas City in them packing houses, the man had a big club down there. It was kind of like a dance hall, a beer tavern, kind of like a [unintelligible], but it was a big place. He was a White man. And Odell was playing with me—Odell and Charlie Parker, and several of the boys. All of them was Kansas City boys. But Neal would come down there and sit in. And I think I saw him one night give Charlie one of them cigarettes.

Chris Goddard: *Marijuana.*

Buster Smith: Yeah. But they tried to keep things hid from me, because they thought I would try to be clean with things, and Charlie gave me the respect that [unintelligible]. Then when Dee Stewart had the band down in the Continental Club down there, he would smoke one. Yeah, he drank heavy. And I think one or two other boys in there would smoke one. We'd take an intermission . . . We were working from 8 to 5 in the morning, and we took 15 minutes off every hour. And I think one or two, I don't know [unintelligible] and Odell. Anyway, there was one or two of the boys that were foolin' with one of them sticks down there, and then Dee himself. Yeah, they smoked one now and then. And he got to me and said, "Buster, you take a puff off of one of them." I said, "Oh man, I wouldn't fool with that stuff." "Oh man, go ahead. It will make the music sound better." I said, "Well, let me see." Then I took me two or three draws off of the thing. That thing made me . . . It got so that I had to be directing the band, and I'd look around there and it looked like the band was playing too slow, and I just got clean off-balance, when we got off that morning, and when I got home the wife said she had to fan me all the rest of the morning—the [unintelligible] on my head big as the end of your thumb. So I quit. I ain't never smoked another since.

Chris Goddard: But is there anything to suggest in Charlie Parker's sort of youth, when you first met him . . . Did he seem to be an unstable kind of guy?

Buster Smith: No. He was a normal man, normal boy. Good boy.

Chris Goddard: Because his behavior really became very peculiar later on.

Buster Smith: Yeah, he was a good boy. He was like that with me down in Kansas City. A good boy, good to get along with, agreeable with anything you wanted to do—it was all right with him. He changed after he got foolin' with that [unintelligible] around that big company. Because Lester Young didn't smoke, he didn't drink. He didn't do nothin' like that. He didn't fool with that stuff.

Chris Goddard: There's that little story you told me, which is funny, about how you'd be sleeping in the bed with your wife and you let Charlie sleep during the day when you were [unintelligible].

Buster Smith: Yes.

Chris Goddard: But what kind of guy was it who would use your bed, use your hospitality, but sleep in his bed leaving his shoes on? That wasn't a very nice thing to do.

Buster Smith: No. He must have been gettin' off then. But I didn't pay no attention to him because I'd hardly ever see him. I was busy writing music and be gone. And he had to be there all by himself all day. And he just wouldn't pull his shoes off. My wife got to grumbling about it, because she was working herself. She was working in the restaurant. I was off at the Woodside writing music, and she'd be down there at Andy Kirk's restaurant, waiting tables. And she'd come home sometimes, and she'd see him laying up there with his shoes on. Clothes on, too. So she got to squawkin'. So I had to get after him about it. So it wasn't long before he left there.

Chris Goddard: I mean, he preferred to leave rather than take his shoes off. He didn't see reason about it.

Buster Smith: Well, his old lady got to talkin', and she didn't want him there in the first place. She said, "Charlie, get you a room, so we don't have to [unintelligible] in sin. Try to get you a room somewhere." It was, I think, the next couple of days, that Diz and them made him a little [unintelligible] and took it over to Philadelphia and played a show there for about a week. They stayed about a week, and when they got through with it, McShann sent for him to come back to Kansas City.

Chris Goddard: Was this before he was ever with McShann? Or had he been with McShann and left, and then gone back again?

Buster Smith: Let me see. I forget . . . To be correct . . . I don't know where he was with McShann and left . . . I don't think so.

Chris Goddard: Because that would mean that he and Dizzy played together as early as 1938 or 1939 . . .

Buster Smith: Yeah.

Chris Goddard: Which is very early.

Buster Smith: Well, he come down there . . . When he first came there, he came and sat in with Dizzy and them, and they was working . . . Yeah, that's when he ended up taking him on over to Philly with him.

Chris Goddard: He had a band.

Buster Smith: Yeah. He was a good get-off man. And somebody made up a little show, and Dizzy got the job, and then he went over with him.

Chris Goddard: By this stage, was Charlie able to read?

Buster Smith: Read? Yeah, he read, but he wouldn't read fast. He didn't like to play none of them reed choruses; they was too stiff. Everything that was augmented quarter-note, half-note, whole note, something like that, but all them sixteenth and all that syncopation stuff like that, he didn't care about foolin' with too much. He'd go along with it as long as he got somebody else playing the lead—the lead in the section. He'd go along. He'd stay right in there with them. He didn't want you puttin' nothin' off on him by himself to lead nothin'. No. Just solos to ornament. He could do that.

Chris Goddard: Did he ever talk to you, when you and he were together a lot, about who he liked to listen to?

Buster Smith: No.

Chris Goddard: Who really influenced him?

Buster Smith: No.

Chris Goddard: Who he liked.

Buster Smith: No, no. He always told me, "Prof, you the king." I said, "Man, go ahead." "*You* the king."

* * *

Chris Goddard: Now, when Charlie Parker was with you in the little band that you had in '38, what was the name of the club you were working at?

Buster Smith: Lucia's Paradise.

Chris Goddard: Was he literally modeling himself on you? He'd try to do these double-time things that you would do?

Buster Smith: Yeah. Mmm-hmm.

Chris Goddard: And in between gigs or in between sets, would he ever ask and say, "What is it exactly you're doing here?" Would you show him things?

Buster Smith: No, not that way. He just listened, and come up behind me and do the same thing I do.

Chris Goddard: He had such great ears he could just do it like that?

Buster Smith: Yeah! He'd pick up on . . . He'd react that way. He didn't ask you to show him nothin'. You make it, he'll make it too. Yeah, he was just a natural-born alto player. Yeah. He didn't jam too much down there at them big clubs where all them cats were down . . .

Chris Goddard: He did not?

Buster Smith: No.

Chris Goddard: Why?

Buster Smith: Not too much. Well, I don't know. He just sat around and listened at 'em. But he'd go to one of them bigger clubs where Pete Johnson and them was all playing and goin' on, and there wasn't many over there, he'd go there and sit in and play.

Chris Goddard: Do you think that he was in any way scared to get into the Ben Websters, the Lester Youngs, the Coleman Hawkinses at that time?

Buster Smith: No. He wasn't scared.

Chris Goddard: I wonder why he didn't go and sit in with them?

Buster Smith: Well, he figured they was a little bit too big for him. They were a little too high for him. And he was around . . . Before he got with me, he was around with them a little bit on the scatter-rag bands, playing the way they want to play and it didn't make no difference if you didn't have no arrangements or nothin' like that—just every man for himself. But them big boys, like Lester Young and Ben Webster and all of them, man, he come around and listened at 'em, but he wouldn't sit in and jam with 'em. They wouldn't jam with . . . Sometimes two or three of them would be over there with Pete at the Lone Star, and he'd sit in and jam with 'em, play a few pieces. But mostly he jammed with the [unintelligible] and the White boys when they'd come around town there, and go find some highway place—they'd be over there jamming. He'd get into that.

Chris Goddard: He'd jam with White guys?

Buster Smith: Mmm-hmm. Yeah.

Chris Goddard: Who? Do you know?

Buster Smith: Some of them bands would come in town. Henry Busse and them, and some of them other hotel bands come down there, and then them boys come out there and listen, so the musicians would play and they'd go around somewhere there ain't too many in there, some of them small places, and they'd go in there and they'd set 'em up with a little jam session, jammin' until daylight or something like that. He used to go in some of them good-time houses, with a piano player . . .

Chris Goddard: Those boarding houses?

Buster Smith: Yeah. Where they can play all them tough numbers like "Body and Soul" and stuff like that, and "Cherokee" . . . That's really how you learn how to play the horn, change all them chords and keys, and playing one key and moving a half-tone up and all that kind of stuff. They liked that. And Lester Young liked that.

Chris Goddard: Are you suggesting that these White guys could do all that?

Buster Smith: Sure, they did. Yeah.

Chris Goddard: *Did you get the impression that Charlie practiced all the things on alto that you didn't practice? Did he do scales and arpeggios and all the exercises?*

Buster Smith: I don't think so. I never heard him doing it. He never would pick up his horn . . . that I'd know of. Now, at home, he was always walking with that horn up under his arm, going somewhere, up and down the street. If he ain't goin' nowhere to play, he'd have that horn up under his arm. A little old case with a zipper on it.

Chris Goddard: *So he was a really dedicated musician?*

Buster Smith: Yes.

Chris Goddard: *Was he so dedicated at that stage that he wasn't taking any interest in girls or anything else at all?*

Buster Smith: No. No, no! He wasn't seen with no girls. No, he didn't talk to no girl, no one. He just seemed to be always studying music. Lester Young was that way. Yeah. He didn't speak (?) to no girl or nothin'. No. Partying and goin' on, sitting down at a table and partyin' and goin' on. No, you wouldn't see them doing that. Both of them was on the same key. They didn't think about anything but playing with their horn. Yeah. He was just that peculiar. He hadn't been smokin' nothin', didn't drink nothin', so I guess they were taking that for granted, too. They didn't party, they didn't think about no women. All they wanted to do was somebody to set up a little jamming going on, and they'd get right in the middle of it. Lester would get right in there. He was playing. If the piano player was any good, he'd get right in the middle of it.

Chris Goddard: *He really liked to jam?*

Buster Smith: Yeah. Little ole Bird here, he just kind of listened at 'em awhile . . .

Chris Goddard: *Is that because he reckoned he'd learn more by listening than playing?*

Buster Smith: Yeah. And getting some ideas.

Chris Goddard: Was he shy?

Buster Smith: No!

Chris Goddard: Did you get the impression at that stage that he had any idea that he was going to revolutionize music?

Buster Smith: Yeah, I kind of thought it, because he was too crazy about his horn. And I know he had to be . . . He had to be outstanding one day. I knew he was going to be. And after he got rid of the old horn, I knew he was going . . . He played a solo, they had some number there and he played a solo in it, and then all them cats in New York were there, and they said, "Who was that alto player?" and I said, "That's Charlie Parker." They said, "That cat sure played a beautiful solo there." I said, "He's a devil of an alto player. They call him the Bird. Yardbird."

Chris Goddard: How did he get that name?

Buster Smith: He got the name from . . . When he'd get off of work at night, he said, "I'm goin' home and knock over me one of them yardbirds." So the boys would ask him, I even asked him, "What do you mean, yardbird?" "I'm going to get me one of them chickens."

Chris Goddard: He liked to eat chicken?

Buster Smith: Yeah, yeah. He'd go catch one of these chickens and kill 'em. I guess he was staying with his parents, and he'd have them cook him a chicken. Middle of the night, didn't make no difference to him. And so them boys got to callin' him Yardbird, and that's the way he [unintelligible].

Chris Goddard: I get it.

Buster Smith: Yeah. They couldn't call him "Charlie." "Yardbird!" He'd look out, "Yeah!"

Chris Goddard: Did you get the impression that he was very ambitious? That he really was determined that he was going to be better than anybody else?

Buster Smith: No, he didn't have that idea. He always said that horn, "This is my baby. This is my baby, and I'm gonna stay with this baby." And he'd sleep with the horn on the pillow. Every night.

Chris Goddard: Why was he so obsessed with it?

Buster Smith: Yeah! You find some musicians just obsessively like that. Yeah, he slept with it on his pillow.

JAZZ ORAL HISTORY PROJECT: HOWARD MCGHEE (1982)

November 23, 1982

This interview is an excerpt from an interview conducted for the National Endowment for the Arts Jazz Oral History Project, administered by the Institute of Jazz Studies at Rutgers University. Ira Gitler is the interviewer.

Howard McGhee met Charlie Parker in 1942 or 1943 and played with him extensively in 1946 and 1947 when they were both based in Los Angeles. Like Dizzy Gillespie, Howard McGhee was strongly influenced by Roy Eldridge, and like Gillespie, McGhee was interested in exploring new directions in jazz. McGhee's excellent trumpet facility and his forward-looking attitude made him a strong and sympathetic partner for Parker. McGhee was part of the infamous July 29, 1946, record date for the Dial label at which Parker's physical and mental health collapsed (see the review of "Bebop" and "Lover Man" later in this anthology), McGhee was also one of the first to be called that evening when a disoriented Parker was arrested at his hotel. (Ross Russell arrived later and reported that Parker had accidentally started a fire in his room, but McGhee saw no evidence of it.) When Parker was released in early 1947, they resumed playing together but the two went their separate ways later that year.—CW

Howard McGhee: When Dizzy came out there [to California] with Bird, it really did pick up, because Bird was something . . . an institution within himself. I mean, pshew.

Ira Gitler: That got everybody going, huh?

Howard McGhee: Oh, I'm telling you, it was somethin' else, man. And Charlie Parker was *mean*. I learned a whole lot from that man, you know. Of course, I guess he learned something from me, too, but I really learned a lot from him. Because there was nothin' he couldn't play. He knew everything, and he hipped me to, like, Stravinsky and all those guys. I didn't know nothin' about Stravinsky. So Bird was the first one to tell me about it. So like, *The Rite of Spring,* he brought it over to the house and let me hear it. And I said, "Yeah, this cat, he's kind of cool, you know; he knows what he's doing." Then I went and got a couple of more things that he had wrote . . . Bird used to come over to my house all the time to listen to them. Because I mean, I liked them myself. I mean, Stravinsky was a hip dude, you know, as far as writing music was concerned. He had this thing down.

Ira Gitler: Well, of course, you had known Bird and Diz back in the East, as we talked about.

Howard McGhee: Oh, I knew them from the East, yeah.

Ira Gitler: So when they came out to California, you must have felt . . .

Howard McGhee: Yeah, well, I felt like part of the family which they had, you know. And Bird didn't know anything about California. I mean, he had no idea what California was like. And he jumped up and quit Dizzy, and he should have stayed with Dizzy and gone back to New York, because California wasn't in his groove. There was nobody out there using no dope as far [as] heroin and shit like that. And out there they charged fifteen dollars a cap for heroin, and Bird was shootin' them up like they were going out of style! Well, what can you say? If a man's got a habit, he's got a habit. He's got to feed it, or else it hangs him, you know.

Ira Gitler: And that wasn't the place for it.

Howard McGhee: That wasn't the place for it, because fifteen dollars a cap . . . And Bird used to walk around with a clarinet case *full* of heroin, man. He told me the first time I saw him . . . We were in Philadelphia when I was with Barnet, and I asked, I said, "What's all of that in that clarinet case?" So he said, "Oh, you don't want to know nothin' about that, man. That ain't no good for you." "It ain't huh? Okay. If you say so, I'll leave it like it is." And I never thought about it any more until he got to California, and then he told me that he had a problem and that he was sick, and that he had to have a certain amount of heroin a day to keep operating. And that's when I really realized that the man was strung and he was really sick. But I had to try [to] step in and try to help him the best way I could, but he was draining my loot fast as I could get it. He was taking it all, you know. And I couldn't afford that. And Bird's old lady wasn't doin' nothin'. And he had to have money for this and money for that. Then I told him, "Look, man, the best thing for you to do is go back to New York."

But he didn't last that long. We did a date, I think we started doing the date for Dial Records, and Bird cracked up . . .

Ira Gitler: Well, at that time was he working with you? Were the two of you working in a club?

Howard McGhee: Well, not when we did the date.

Ira Gitler: No.

Howard McGhee: We did go into a place called the Finale Club, and I had an eight-piece band there and four saxes and four rhythm.

Ira Gitler: Was that with Sonny Criss?

Howard McGhee: Sonny Criss, Teddy Edwards, Gene Montgomery, and Bird. So the band was beautiful, but we weren't making any money. I mean, people would enjoy it or be loaded, but people would come into the joint that was in there before we'd come in, and we couldn't chase them out and say, "You've got to come back and pay admission." So we played there and it turned out pretty nice. But we wasn't making a lot of money.

Ira Gitler: You had told me that you wanted to get someone to record that band, and nobody would record it.

Howard McGhee: Yeah, I tried to get a record date for it, with Modern Records, because that's the guy that I had been dealing with. He didn't have no eyes for Charlie Parker. He had heard Charlie was a bad guy and all that jive, you know. So he didn't want to touch him, you know.

Ira Gitler: Now, you had already started recording.

Howard McGhee: Yeah, I had already been recording with him . . .

Ira Gitler: For Modern.

Howard McGhee: Yeah, with Modern, because I had made something with Pearl Traylor, I think it was, some Blues singer, a piano player that sang the blues, too. Anyway, whatever, Jules wanted to make it, and I was on it. So I had me a connection, man. But he didn't have no eyes for Bird.

Ira Gitler: That was Jules Bihari [owner of Modern Records, along with his brothers].

Howard McGhee: Yeah, that was Jules.

Ira Gitler: There were two brothers, right?

Howard McGhee: There were three brothers.

Ira Gitler: Three brothers?

Howard McGhee: Yeah. But anyway, Jules was the man that had the say-so. He said what happened with the company. And the younger brother, he was like the businessman of the chain (?).

Like, I tried to tell them . . . I said, "Man, come out and *hear* the band." I said, "I just want you to hear it." He never would even come by the club to hear the band. He just wasn't interested in Charlie Parker.

Ira Gitler: Now, had you met Ross Russell by this time?

Howard McGhee: Yeah, I had met Ross, but Ross wasn't in no position to do anything. He only had a little store, you know.

Ira Gitler: He wasn't really into Dial yet.

Howard McGhee: No, he wasn't into Dial.

Ira Gitler: He had the Tempo Music.

Howard McGhee: Yeah, he was in Tempo Music. That was his thing. He couldn't just say, "Well, okay, I'll record the band." But when he did get his hands on enough money together to record it, he gave us this date that Bird cracked up on. So when Bird cracked up, that really blew . . . Because he thought he had lost his ass! He finally got all this money together, and now this cat can't play. So he was very much disturbed by it. And I don't blame him; I guess I would have been too. But I tried to pull it out for him, because I knew that he had to have *something* out of that to put out, so maybe he could make enough money back to continue his recording thing or something. Which he did! He recorded "Trumpet at Tempo" . . .

Ira Gitler: And "Thermodynamics."

Howard McGhee: And "Thermodynamics."

Ira Gitler: Were they done the same day?

Howard McGhee: The same day, you know—yeah. Well, Bird, his hand was shooting up in the air and he was turning around, he couldn't stay still and so forth. So . . .

Ira Gitler: Do you agree with the story that was told that Bird had a lot of bennies in him?

Howard McGhee: It wasn't benzedrine. He wished he had had some benzedrine. He needed some benzedrine, and he could have stood some. I didn't have any to give to him, because I never used them . . . I never used bennies at that stage of the game.

Ira Gitler: *But he didn't have any horse [heroin].*

Howard McGhee: No, he didn't have any horse. So he needed somethin'!

Ira Gitler: *Something. And what was he doing? Was he drinking?*

Howard McGhee: He tried drinking, but drinking don't do it. It takes you another direction.

Ira Gitler: *So that's why he was . . .*

Howard McGhee: Yeah, he was in trouble.

Ira Gitler: *He had nothing to calm him or . . .*

Howard McGhee: Nothing to relieve him.

Ira Gitler: *In any which way.*

Howard McGhee: Yeah. No way possible for him to come out of that. His horn was shooting up in the air and he couldn't stand still, he couldn't sit down, he was . . .

Ira Gitler: *He just was, what would you say, in extreme anxiety?*

Howard McGhee: Right, in extreme . . . He didn't know what to do. Nobody had nothin' to give him, and he wasn't hip enough to go to a doctor and tell the doctor what his problem was, or maybe the doctor might have helped him, you know. But he didn't have enough sense to do that. And I didn't know if he should go to a doctor! I thought if he'd go to the doctor they'd have you locked up or something for you being a drug addict. But anyway, they . . .

Ira Gitler: *Did you know his connection, Moose the Mooche?*

Howard McGhee: No, I didn't know him. I knew about him, but I didn't know him personally. I guess maybe he'd been using his connection all the time he was out there with Dizzy, because he was out there with Dizzy for eight weeks in Billy Berg's, and I guess he had been using him all the time. And he run out of money, and then took his ticket and turned that in, and got the money, and got enough dope to let him skate for a week or so. But really, when it came down to it, boy, he was uptight, man. He didn't have no one to turn to. And I wasn't making that kind of money where I could give Bird forty-five or fifty dollars a day just for his habit. I said, "No, I can't make that, Bird. You have to do something."

But anyway, they took him to Camarillo, and I used to go out there and see him every day. But they . . . First the man where Bird was staying at, at this hotel, the guy was a Japanese fellow that had the hotel . . . So he called me and told me, he said, "Man, your friend is actin' awful funny down here. He's walking around here nude." I said, "What!?" So I got dressed and got in the car and drove down to where he was staying. And when I got there and Bird . . . the cops had already taken Bird to the hospital. So I get in the car and go to the hospital to see what's happening.

When I walked in, Bird said, "Hey, Maggie!" He was fine. And I said, "Damn, what's goin' on, man?" He said, "Oh, everything's fine, everything's fine. Give me my clothes. I want to get out of here." So I went and talked with one of the cats: "What's happening? What are they doing to Bird?" So he said, "Well, the Police brought him in here, and he's on a warrant. We've got to hold him because he was sitting in the car buck naked, and he can't be doing that in *California*," you know. So I went and told him, I said, "Bird, well, I can't get you your clothes because they won't turn you loose."

Ira Gitler: *The story was that he had set fire to the hotel room.*

Howard McGhee: No-no-no, he didn't set no fire.

Ira Gitler: *It was a cigarette or something on the mattress . . .*

Howard McGhee: No. No-no. He went . . .

Ira Gitler: *How did that story get started?*

Howard McGhee: I don't know. Somebody told that lie. I don't know what . . . But it was a lie, because I *know*. I went down and talked to the man, and he said, "No, he walked out of here with [   ] and was sitting on top of a car, and the police came."

Ira Gitler: Sitting there naked.

Howard McGhee: Nude! Yeah. But somebody said he had set fire to the hotel. He didn't set no fire to no hotel. Because when I got down there, there hadn't been no fire there. So the guy told me, said, "Well, I think they took him to the mental hospital."

So like I said, when I walked in there, Bird was smilin' and laughin' and talkin'—"Maggie [McGhee], what are you doin'?" you know. I said, "Gee, I expected to see you laid out, man." He said, "No, I'm fine, man." He said, "Get me my clothes; I'm ready to go." I said, "Well, it ain't quite like that, Bird. I can't get you out like that. You have to go to court and all that shit. I don't know what the fuck they got against you, but they got something against you." And I said, "It sounds kind of bad." He said, "What is it?" I said, "I think they got you for nudity." In California they don't like for you to do *nothin'* wrong. They'll throw the book for the least little thing you do. "So you have to go to court for that."

So he went to court, and they put him in Camarillo to see if he's crazy or insane, because they really don't understand nobody here sittin' on top of a car buck naked. They don't dig that! And that's what they did to Bird. They put him in the thing there. And I used to go there all the time, and I'd take Doris out there to see him and keep track of him, to see if he was all right. And Bird . . .

Bird was all right. He ran the psychiatrists crazy. There was a cat that was supposed to be taking care of him . . . ?—and Bird was taking care of him! He was talking about things, and this cat didn't know what Bird was talking about. Bird would be talking some heavy shit! Because Bird knew what was going on. Let's face it, he had a mind that was somethin' else. He could talk to you about anything you wanted to talk about.

You could ask him about a carburetor, he'd tell you how to fix it and so forth. Because one night we was driving along, and my car started chug-chug, like it wasn't getting enough gas. So Bird said, "Pull over to the side." So he walked into . . . We pulled up to a thing with (?), went in there and screwed up something, and he said, "Now start it up, Maggie." So I started it up, and it ran just like brand-new! I said, "Yeah!" I didn't even know what the hell he did. He had adjusted the carburetor so that the air wasn't getting in there too much, the gas was flowing even. . . .

So Bird was a smart guy. A lot of people didn't know that, but Bird had a mind on him that was something else. Well, his horn tells you that! His music, man, whatever he played, it was right, correct, and you can't see that. . . . There was nothing *wrong* with it.

A funny thing, too, I was just reminded of it. . . . I asked Johnny Hodges, when Bird first come on the scene . . . I said to him, "What do you think of Charlie Parker?" He said, "Ah, he don't play nothin'. He don't play nothin'." I said, "No?" He said, "He ain't got no sound." I said, "Charlie Parker ain't got no sound?" So I said, "Okay." So I got a chance. . . . When I worked with Duke, I asked Johnny . . . It's the first thing I did. I said, "What do you think . . . ?"

Ira Gitler: How many years later was that?

Howard McGhee: This was way later. I said, "What do you think of Charlie Parker?" He said, "Oh, he was beautiful." I said, "But Johnny, you told me he didn't have no sound." He said, "Well, I didn't know what I was talking about. He's one of the baddest. . . . " But I mean, that was after they had made that Blues thing . . .

Ira Gitler: Right, for Norman Granz.

Howard McGhee: Yeah. Ha-ha, Bird let *everybody* know where he was at. But anyway, I just brought that up because I think that people should know about such things.

Ira Gitler: Yes, I do, too.

Howard McGhee: People say . . .

Ira Gitler: "Funky Blues."

Howard McGhee: Yeah. Just a funky blues, and Bird played the shit out of it! Johnny Hodges, I felt sorry for him, because if I was him, I wouldn't have played! "Let him finish making this record; I don't want to make this one." But boy, it was somethin' else.

Ira Gitler: So you went out to see him quite often . . .

Howard McGhee: Oh yeah.

Ira Gitler: And eventually got his release.

Howard McGhee: Yeah. Well, what's his name, Ross Russell had a lot to do with that. He went out there. . . . Like I told you, Bird ran this psychiatrist crazy. In fact, he committed suicide, that guy did—that psychiatrist. He had never met nobody like Bird. He didn't believe nobody could be like him. But Bird had a hell of a mind on him, man. He knew what he was doing and he knew what he was talking about.

I guess that drugs does do something to you, makes you aware of what's happening, going on in the world. Because I didn't know nothin' about all this shit he was talking about. I didn't know nothin' about it. I hadn't even heard of Stravinsky. Now, you know where I was. I was a dumb stud when it comes to knowing my own music. But Bird hipped me to a lot of things I didn't know about.

But anyway, after we got Bird out of Camarillo, we went into a place called the Hi-De-Ho Club. It was just me and Bird and Hampton Hawes, and Dingbod [Bob Kesterson], and Roy Porter.

Ira Gitler: This was '47?

Howard McGhee: Yeah, this was in the last part of . . .

Ira Gitler: No, it had to be the beginning . . .

Howard McGhee: Yeah.

Ira Gitler: The last part of '46 and the beginning of '47.

Howard McGhee: Yeah, and the beginning of '47. No, it had to be a little further down than that. I think they kept him in there until '47.

Ira Gitler: Well, he came back to New York in the Spring, but he made that record date with you . . . it must have been February or March or something like that.

Howard McGhee: Yeah, I think it was done in March.

Ira Gitler: *When you did "Carvin' the Bird" and all those things.*

Howard McGhee: Yeah, that was around March.

Ira Gitler: *Then he came back to New York after that.*

Howard McGhee: Well, no. . . . Then we went into this club and we worked together there. Then we played a gig in Chicago at the Pershing. . . . We played a couple of one-night stands there and in Gary, Indiana. And then we came to New York. I came to New York with him, but I wasn't hangin' out with him.

DIZZY GILLESPIE (WITH GENE LEES)
THE YEARS WITH YARD (1961)
Down Beat, May 25, 1961

Charlie Parker once called Dizzy Gillespie "the other half of my heartbeat," and the admiration was clearly mutual. They were close friends, and they were musical partners. In the early 1940s, when Gillespie and Parker first met, they recognized each other as kindred spirits. They were both setting high technical standards on their instruments, and they were both interested in exploring harmonic, melodic, and rhythmic sophistication in music. This article is a fond reminiscence of the two musicians' history and an appreciation of Charlie Parker's greatness, written by Dizzy Gillespie, whose own greatness is unexcelled.

Note: Although Gillespie did join Cab Calloway's band in 1939, the trumpeter probably did not meet Charlie Parker in Kansas City until 1940 (the person who introduced them said it was in 1940, and Parker was based in New York for much of 1939). —CW

It's very hard for me to believe that Charlie Parker has been gone six years. To tell the truth, it doesn't seem to me that he is gone.

And in fact, he isn't gone. It sounds like a cliché to say that his music will be here forever, but that is the truth. And there are precedents for believing this.

The same thing could be said of Charlie Christian and Lester Young. They are not gone either. These three men left a heritage; they set the rules. Therefore, they are still with us.

I haven't heard an alto player who wasn't close to Bird. Of course, the closest to him that I have heard is Sonny Stitt. When I hear a record sometimes, I won't be sure at first whether it's Sonny or Yard. Sonny gets down into all the little things of Charlie Parker's playing. The others just play his music; Sonny plays his life. If they ever make a movie about Charlie Parker, Sonny Stitt is the man to play the part.

It's hard, too, to remember when I first knew Bird. It seems to me that I always knew him, as far back as I can recall, though that isn't true, of course.

In South Carolina, we heard none of the Kansas City bands. They didn't come through that part of the country. We heard only the bands from the east coast.

But I knew little Buddy Anderson, the trumpet player. Later, he developed tuberculosis and had to quit playing, but he was a fine trumpet player.

When I joined Cab Calloway's Band, we went to Kansas City. This was in 1939. Now, Buddy Anderson was the only trumpet player I knew who had the idea of exploring the instrument through piano. I played piano, too, and sometimes we'd spend the day at the piano together, never touching a trumpet. And he kept telling me about this Charlie Parker.

One day while we were in Kansas City with Cab, Buddy brought Charlie Parker over to the Booker T. Washington hotel and introduced us. We understood each other right away.

Yard had brought his own with him. The three of us played together, in the hotel room, all that day. Just the three of us. You didn't find many musicians who could show you on the piano what they were doing. But Charlie Parker could, even then. He was only a kid. We were both only kids.

I returned to New York, and then Charlie Parker joined Jay McShann's Band and came to New York, too.

In 1941, I left Cab. I played two weeks with Ella Fitzgerald and then with Benny Carter, at Kelly's Stable. In the band was Charlie Drayton on bass, Sonny White on piano (he's with Wilbur DeParis now), Kenny

Clarke, drums, and Al Gibson on tenor. Nat Cole and Art Tatum were playing opposite us. Did we hear some piano playing!

After that, I went out with Charlie Barnet for three weeks in Toronto, then rejoined Benny, then went with Coleman Hawkins. This was getting on toward 1942 or 1943. I worked with Earl Hines and Billy Eckstine in 1943-44. Then, in late 1944, Oscar Pettiford and I formed a group, as co-leaders. And we immediately sent Charlie Parker a telegram asking him to join us.

By the time we heard from Yardbird, we'd been in there for several weeks, Don Byas had come in to work as a single, and Oscar Pettiford and I had broken up the group. In fact, I was co-leader across the street from the Onyx with Budd Johnson, and Bird *still* hadn't showed up. Budd and I were there six weeks. By then, Charlie Parker was just getting into town . . . and I no longer had a group for him to work *with*!

But Yard was in New York, and that was the main thing, and a number of us were experimenting with a different way of playing jazz. . . .

There has been a lot of talk about where and when so-called bebop started.

But a simple answer to the question is impossible. It depends on your viewpoint and on what you consider were the important contributing factors.

If you consider that Charlie Parker was the prime mover, then bebop started at Clark Monroe's Uptown House, because that was where Yard used to go to jam. If you consider that Thelonious Monk was the prime mover, then it was Minton's, where Monk was playing after hours with Joe Guy, Nick Fenton, and Kermit Scott. I was in an odd position: I was jamming at both places, and ducking the union man at both places!

Bird used to come to Minton's to play, too, but he was jamming mostly at Monroe's.

Who do I consider was the prime mover in the bebop movement? I would answer that with another question: What is the most important ingredient in spaghetti sauce?

But this much I can say: it is true that we used to play unusual substitute chords and extensions of the chords to throw some of the other musicians who came up to sit in. That did have a lot to do with it.

I can remember when nobody except us played the chord progression A-minor seventh to D seventh to D♭. That was one of the chord progressions I showed Monk. But Monk was the first to use E-minor seventh with a flatted fifth, or as some call it an E half-diminished. Monk just called it a G-minor sixth with an E in the bass.

By this time, Bird and I were very close friends.

He was a very sensitive person, in the way that many creative people are. Everything made a profound impression on him. He also was very loyal, and he had a terrific sense of humor.

I remember one incident that illustrated all these characteristics.

It was after the period of Minton's and Monroe's Uptown House. We were with the Earl Hines Band. I was sitting at the piano one night in Pine Bluff, Ark., and some white fellow came up and threw a quarter on the bandstand to me and said, "Hey, boy! Play 'Darktown Strutters' Ball.'" I paid him no mind and kept playing.

When the dance was over, I went to the men's room. As I came out, this guy hit me on the side of the head with a bottle. Blood was spurting, and I grabbed for a bottle myself. Some people grabbed me, before I could crown him with a bottle of Seltzer.

They took me off to the hospital. I remember as they were taking me out, Charlie Parker—he wasn't very big—was wagging his finger in the man's face. I'll always remember his words. He told the guy: "You cur! You took advantage of my friend!"

He was such a wonderful person, and I have seen so much written about him that is false or unimportant. I remember him as a person as much as a great musician.

I was the first one to join Earl Hines, though Yard came with the band right after.

I had been with the Lucky Millinder Band. He fired me in Philadelphia, in 1942. I worked a club there for a while and then joined Hines in '43. We all started asking Earl to hire Bird. Unfortunately, there were already two alto players in the band. That didn't stop us. Billy Eckstine said, "Let's get him anyway—he can play tenor."

So Yard joined the band right after that, on tenor.

He played superbly with that band. I remember Sarah Vaughan would sing "This Is My First Love," and Bird would play 16 bars on it. The whole band would be turned to look at him. *Nobody* was playing like that.

We stayed with Earl Hines until Billy left to form his own band. Sarah left, too. Yard and I joined Billy. Gale Brockman and Benny Harris were in the brass section with me, and Billy Frazier, Dexter Gordon, Lucky Thompson, John Jackson, Charlie Rouse, and Gene Ammons were in the sax section at one time or another with Bird. That was a radical band. It was the forerunner of all the big modern bands. But a lot of ballroom operators didn't dig it. They thought it was just weird. But it was a very fine band, very advanced.

I can't recall whether Charlie Parker and I left the band together. We must have, because from the band, we went into the Three Deuces. That was in early 1945. The group was in my name, and the members included Stan Levey, Al Haig, Curly Russell, and Bird. We were there for several months. In December, 1945, we went to Billy Berg's club on Vine St. in Hollywood. Ray Brown had replaced Curly Russell, and Milt Jackson had been added on vibes.

I wasn't always sure Bird would show up, and that's why I hired Bags [Milt Jackson]. The contract was for only five men. With Bags we were sure to have at least five men on the stand whether Bird showed up or not. Later, Billy Berg said we needed more body! And he had us hire Lucky Thompson on tenor. That gave us up to seven pieces.

We stayed there eight weeks. Ah, it would be nice to work eight weeks in one club again. The musicians out there were all over us. We had a ball, but we didn't do too well as far as the public was concerned.

But by now, bebop was well established. Fats Navarro, Howard McGhee, Wardell Gray, Freddie Webster, and, if memory serves me, Miles Davis were all on 52nd St. in New York when we returned from California in 1946.

Bird had stayed on to gig on the coast. Bebop was getting lots of publicity, there had even been articles in *Life* magazine.

Clark Monroe, who owned the Uptown House, helped me put together a big band in 1946. When we got back to New York, the Three Deuces wanted us, and Clark wanted us for his new Spotlite club—he'd moved downtown, you see. He offered us a deal. If we didn't go into the Three Deuces, we could come into the Spotlite for eight weeks with a small band and then eight weeks with a big band. He said we could build it from his club.

At one time, for a one-week date in the Bronx, I had Yardbird, Miles, and Freddie Webster in that band. That was only temporary, of course. While I had the big band, Bird had his quintet. He had such people as Miles, Max Roach, and Duke Jordan with him.

I didn't know it, but the job in Hollywood had been the last time Bird and I were ever to work together in a permanent group.

Bird's contribution to all the jazz that came after it involved every phase of it. He sure wasn't the beginning, and he wasn't the end—but that middle was *bulging!* But even he had his influences.

You see, Charlie Parker had a Buster Smith background. And, of course, there was Old Yard—an old alto man—in Kansas City. He had that same feeling. Charlie came up under the aegis of Lester Young and Buster Smith. Regardless of what anyone says, there's so much music out there in the air, all you have to do is get a little bite of it. Nobody can get more than a little bit, but some guys get more than others. Charlie Parker bit off a *big* chunk—I'll tell you! Still he had influences—Lester and those others. But he added to it.

One thing he added was accent—the way of stressing certain notes. And a different way of building melodies. When he was playing a B chord, he was playing in the *key* of B.

Another thing was rapidity with sense—not rapidity just for the sake of rapidity, but *melody* rapidity. He was so versed in chord changes and substitute chords that he was never lost for melody. Regardless of what chord was being played, he never lost melody. He could play a blues and sound just like a blues singer, just like he was talking.

I saw something remarkable one time. He didn't show up for a dance he was supposed to play in Detroit. I was in town, and they asked me to play instead. I went up there, and we started playing. Then I heard this big roar, and Charlie Parker had come in and started playing. He'd play a phrase, and people might never have heard it before. But he'd start it, and the people would finish it with him, humming. It would be so lyrical and simple that it just seemed the most natural thing to play. That's another important thing about Charlie Parker—his simplicity.

And Charlie Parker was an accompanist. He could accompany singers like they never had been accompanied. He'd fill in behind them and make little runs. He could make a run and make it end right where it should. This is very hard to do. What a mathematical mind he had.

I remember one record date for Continental especially. It was with Rubberlegs Williams, a blues singer. Somebody had this date—Clyde Hart, I believe. He got Charlie Parker, me, Oscar Pettiford, Don Byas, Trummy Young, and I don't remember the drummer's name. The music didn't work up quite right at first. Now, at that time we used to break inhalers open and put the stuff into coffee or Coca-Cola; it was a kick then. During a break at this record date, Charlie dropped some into Rubberlegs' coffee. Rubberlegs didn't drink or smoke or anything. So we went on with the record date. Rubberlegs began moaning and crying as he was singing. You should hear *those* records!

Yard used to come and play with my big band. He'd never heard the arrangements before, but you'd think he'd written them. The brass would play something and cut off and bang! Charlie Parker was there, coming in right where he was supposed to. It's a shame that when he was making those records with strings that the music wasn't up to his standards. There should have been a whole symphony behind him.

I doubt, though, whether he knew *everything* he was playing. I'll bet that 75 percent of his playing he thought of, and the other 25 percent just fell in place, fell under his fingers. But what he did was enormous. You hear his music everywhere now. And yet it's still hard for me to talk about him—not because he's dead because he's not really gone to me, but because it's hard for me to think where my life ends and his begins; they were so intertwined.

You hear so much about him that I don't like to hear—about his addiction and all sorts of irrelevant nonsense. What kind of man was Beethoven? Perhaps he wasn't a very admirable individual, but what has that to do with listening to his music?

Not that I didn't think Bird was admirable. He was. But people talk too much about the man—people who don't know—when the important thing is his music.

The Negro people should put up a statue to him, to remind their grandchildren. This man contributed joy to the world, and it will last a thousand years.

PART FIVE

Back Home Blues:

The Kerouac Connection

Many American writers of the 1950s related strongly to jazz. In his 1957 essay "Disengagement: The Art of the Beat Generation," Kenneth Rexroth compared Charlie Parker to the poet Dylan Thomas. Jack Kerouac related very strongly to jazz, and the idiom figures in many of his books. In *Mexico City Blues*, Kerouac wrote that he wanted "to be considered a jazz poet," and explained how his 242 poetic "Choruses" were like those taken by a jazz musician at a jam session. Here are Parker-related excerpts from that book of poems by Kerouac and a much later CD review that invokes Kerouac and other writers.—CW

JACK KEROUAC
THREE CHORUSES FROM *MEXICO CITY BLUES* (1959)

Charlie Parker died on Kerouac's thirty-third birthday, and Kerouac wove his feelings about "Charley" Parker into some of the last of the 242 Choruses of Mexico City Blues. *Kerouac's writing here of not "answering" Parker's gaze is evidently a reference to a passage in* The Subterraneans *in which he writes of Parker's looking directly into his eyes, "as if he knew my thoughts and ambitions."—CW*

Charley Parker Looked like Buddha
Charley Parker, who recently died
Laughing at a juggler on the TV
after weeks of strain and sickness,
was called the Perfect Musician.
And his expression on his face
Was as calm, beautiful, and profound
As the image of the Buddha
Represented in the East, the lidded eyes,
The expression that says "All is Well"
—This was what Charley Parker
Said when he played, All is Well.
You had the feeling of early-in-the-morning
Like a hermit's joy, or like
                the perfect cry
Of some wild gang at a jam session
"Wail, Wop"—Charley burst
His lungs to reach the speed
Of what the speedsters wanted
And what they wanted
Was his Eternal Slowdown.
A great musician and a great
                creator of forms
That ultimately find expression
In mores and what have you.

Musically as important as Beethoven,
Yet not regarded as such at all,
A genteel conductor of string
                orchestras
In front of which he stood,
Proud and calm, like a leader
                of music
In the Great Historic World Night,
And wailed his little saxophone,
The alto, with piercing clear
                lament
In perfect tune & shining harmony,
Toot—as listeners reacted

Without showing it, and began talking
And soon the whole joint is rocking
And everybody talking and Charley
                    Parker
Whistling them on to the brink of eternity
With his Irish St Patrick
                    patootle stick,
And like the holy piss we blop
And we plop in the waters of
                            slaughter
And white meat, and die
One after one, in time.

And how sweet a story it is
When you hear Charley Parker
                    tell it,
Either on records or at sessions,
Or at official bits in clubs,
Shots in the arm for the wallet,
Gleefully he Whistled the
                    perfect
                    horn

Anyhow, made no difference.

Charley Parker, forgive me—
Forgive me for not answering your eyes—
For not having made an indication
Of that which you can devise—
Charley Parker, pray for me—
Pray for me and everybody
In the Nirvanas of your brain
Where you hide, indulgent and huge,
No longer Charley Parker
But the secret unsayable name
That carries with it merit
Not to be measured from here
To up, down, east, or west—
—Charley Parker, lay the bane,
    off me, and every body

Francis Davis has written about music for many publications, including Musician, Down Beat, *and* The Village Voice. *His books include* Outcats: Jazz Composers, Instrumentalists and Singers *and* In the Moment: Jazz in the 1980s. *Davis uses the occasion of a music review to discuss the artistic milieu of writers like Jack Kerouac, Chandler Brossard, and John Clellon Holmes. See the Discography for a more recent CD release of* The Legendary Dial Masters.—CW

"Charlie Parker looked like Buddha," Jack Kerouac declared in a poem about the alto saxophonist who was the single most important figure in the gestation of modern jazz. Kerouac wasn't indulging in fancy: some photos of Parker, showing him with a pot belly, round face, and eyes that Kerouac described (in *The Subterraneans*) as "separate and interested and humane," do suggest a likeness to one popular image of Buddha. But Kerouac's analogy depended less on Parker's physical appearance than on his vibe—on an awed perception of his music as godlike in its complexity.

Kerouac wasn't alone in ascribing divinity to Parker. There were hipsters in California who swore that Parker once walked on water. Soon after his death in 1955, at the age of thirty-four (from the cumulative effects of heroin and hard liquor, although lobar pneumonia was the official cause), the graffito "BIRD LIVES" began to appear on New York subway walls. If interpreted to mean only that Parker's music was immortal, the message was indisputable. But who knows what else some of his more frenzied apostles had in mind?

Among fellow musicians, Parker was in the eye of the beholder: what he was like as a person depends on whom you ask. In the recently published *Miles: The Autobiography*, Miles Davis, who played with Parker as a neophyte trumpeter in the 1940s, portrays him as an id-driven monster willing to pawn a borrowed horn or pocket his sidemen's wages if that was what it took to stay high. According to Davis and others who knew him, Parker was a man of insatiable appetites and few inhibitions. In Davis's book, there's an amusing anecdote not meant to be amusing, about Parker in the back seat of a taxi, "smacking his lips all over [a piece of] fried chicken," while a white woman on bended knees on the floor of the car smacks her lips all over him (much to the embarrassment of an uncharacteristically prim Miles).

Yet what sticks in most musicians' minds about Parker was his erudition, not his self-indulgence. Even Davis marveled at him as "an intellectual [who] read novels, poetry, history, stuff like that." The alto saxophonist Frank Morgan, who was still in his teens when he chose Parker as a role model, remembers being as much impressed by Parker's elocution and vocabulary as by his mastery of his horn. John Lewis, a pianist sometimes accused of overrefinement in his role as music director for the Modern Jazz Quartet, defends himself by observing that he often used to run into Parker at classical concerts—the point being that no one would accuse Parker's jazz of being too refined. And Sheila Jordan, a talented singer who says she was "chasin' the Bird, just like everybody else," when she moved from Detroit to New York as a young woman in the 1950s, describes Parker as "a gentleman" who took her out for drinks and passed along musical knowledge but never exploited her worship of him to get her into bed.

On the subject of Parker and drugs, the only certainty is that he used them flagrantly and in prodigious amounts. Everything else is open to conjecture. In jazz, no less than in the world of arts and letters, the early 1950s were a Scoundrel Time, but for a different reason. Heroin addiction was rampant, and you still hear rumors of how this or that well-known junkie kept his own butt out of jail by agreeing to name names. Some of Parker's contemporaries continue to wonder how he avoided arrest despite public knowledge of his habit.

What of Parker's role in turning others on? For many younger musicians, he was a walking advertisement for heroin; despite lectures from him to the contrary, they decided that the junk he was shooting into his veins must be the most vital of his creative juices. "You have to realize that [he] wasn't only a great musician," says the tenor saxophonist Sonny Rollins, one of several acolytes whom Parker tried in vain to discourage from following his path. "He was also a very sick man who was dying from self-abuse and felt guilty about the example he had set for others." But as the trumpeter (and nonuser) Art Farmer remarks, "Telling people to do as I say, not as I do, is never very effective advice."

Parker, who was born and started his career in Kansas City when it was a wide-open Nighttown, is such a creature of myth and supposition that it might be difficult for us to imagine that he ever really existed if not for the hard evidence of his recordings—and even these leave gaps. Parker, Dizzy Gillespie, and a handful of others planted the seeds of bebop (the name given their music, in onomatopoetic imitation of its quick, evenly accented quarter notes) in big bands during the waning days of the swing era. But due to a two-year musicians' union ban on studio recordings beginning in 1942, our knowledge of bebop's beginnings is largely based on hearsay. And most of the concert albums you'll find in front of Parker's name card in record stores give a misleading impression of what he must have sounded like in the flesh: The majority of these are from poorly recorded tapes made on the sly by Birdlorists who followed Parker from coast to coast, inadvertently removing him from his creative context by preserving only his solos, not those of his sidemen.

Parker did the bulk of his official recording for three companies: Dial, Savoy, and what became Verve. His complete Savoys and Verves have been in general circulation, in one format or another, since his death. Not so the thirty-five numbers that he recorded for Dial beginning in February 1946, when Ross Russell, a writer and Hollywood record store owner, founded the label to take advantage of Parker's temporary residence in southern California.

Parker's Dials, including every surviving alternate take, were collected in a six-record series on a British collectors' label in the early '70s, and in a Warner Brothers limited-edition box set later in the decade. But if my experience is typical, most jazz fans now between the ages of thirty-five and fifty first discovered these classic performances in haphazard fashion on fly-by night budget labels, or on the long-defunct label bearing Parker's name and operated by his legal widow in the early sixties.

The Legendary Dial Masters, Volume One and Volume Two (Stash) mark the first coherent reissue of this material on compact disc. All thirty-five "masters" are included, along with nine alternate takes and eight abbreviated performances recorded live at an L.A. jam session that bring the total playing time to just under two and a half hours. This music has never sounded better, thanks to the superb digital remastering. Parker's rhythm sections have been brought into sharper focus, and now you can actually hear—rather than merely sense—the sparks flying in both directions between him and his most tuned-in sidemen (the pianist Dodo Marmorosa and the drummer Max Roach, in particular). And as a thoughtful added touch, of special aid to novice listeners, the CD booklets identify Parker's raw material: his "originals," like those of many bebop musicians of the 1940s, tended to be derived from the twelve-bar blues ("Relaxin' at Camarillo," for example) or on the chord changes of a few familiar standards ("Bird of Paradise" from "All the Things You Are," "Ornithology" from "How High the Moon," and "Moose the Mooche," from "I Got Rhythm," to cite just three).

Pop songs and the blues have served as launching pads for jazz impro visers almost from the beginning, but Parker and his confederates radicalized the procedure by disguising the material they appropriated almost beyond recognition, in an abstract of sleek harmonic lines and daredevil rhythms that gave the impression of blinding speed even at moderate tempos. Before beginning his affiliation with Dial, Parker had already recorded "Ko Ko," his most dazzling performance in this vein, at his first session as a leader, for Savoy in 1945. But the Dials represented his first sustained exposure on record and introduced (on the sessions recorded in New York in 1947, after Russell followed Parker back east) Parker's first truly compatible working group, with Roach, Miles Davis, the pianist Duke Jordan, the bassist Tommy Potter, and—on the last few titles—the trombonist J. J. Johnson. These were the recordings with which Parker virtually wrote the stylebook of modern jazz, originating phrases that would turn up again and again over the decades in solos by other musicians (for example: the ten-note "o-o-oh-baby, you-make-me-feel-so good" figure that Parker plays during "Moose the Mooche" served as the foundation of James Moody's "Moody's Mood for Love," itself an influential and much admired recording).

Once you hear Parker, he changes the way you hear what came before him and what came after. On "Don't Blame Me," for example (a ballad interpretation as elegant as the more celebrated "Embraceable You," which is also included here), the melodic surge of his uneven-length phrases confirms both his lineage from Lester Young and Young's importance as an oracle of bebop. And Parker's out-of-the-gate-and-running blues chorus in advance of the flatted theme on "The Hymn," though quintessential bebop, could be cited as a prototype of free-form.

In addition to a session on which Parker overcomes Erroll Garner's incongruous piano accompaniment and Earl Coleman's out-of-tune Billy Eckstine imitations, *Volume One* also includes the performance of his most likely to elicit a subjective reaction. Cut off from his drug suppliers due to a police crackdown, he was hours away from complete collapse when he recorded "Lover Man" and three other numbers on July 29, 1946. Yet the bassist and composer Charles Mingus, asked to name his favorite Parker performance, chose this version of "Lover Man," which the trumpeter Howard McGhee (who was on the date, playing over his head, as though in compensation) told the jazz critic Ira Gitler he preferred to a second, more self-assured version that Parker recorded five years later. "He didn't have the strength or the stamina to run through the horn," McGhee told the jazz critic Ira Gitler. "He was just barely getting the sound out, but I thought it was beautiful like a son-of-a-bitch." Heard now, this from-the-abyss solo sounds wild and uncertain. But it rivets you with its pain.

Some twenty years ago, the jazz critic Martin Williams complained that very little in the growing body of literature on Parker focused on his musical accomplishments. This was no longer true by the late 1970s, by when analysis of bebop in general and Parker's contributions to it in particular became the backbone of an emerging jazz pedagogy. But in the aftermath of *Bird*, Clint Eastwood's murky 1988 film biography, discourse has shifted back to Parker's legendary excess.

This extramusical line of inquiry isn't as irrelevant as some would argue, if only because it reminds us that bebop's original cult audience included the real-life models for the nomadic juicers and hopheads who hit the road in Kerouac's *Desolation Angels* and *Dharma Bums* and the blocked existentialists who wander from party to party, halfway between euphoria and despair, in Chandler Brossard's *Who Walk in Darkness* and John Clellon Holmes's *Go!*, post-World War II novels that could be retitled *Bebop and Nothingness*. In a period in which molds were being shattered, the beat poets, Abstract Expressionists, method actors, and scatological comedians who romanticized themselves as self-destructive enemies of society recognized a prototype in Parker's sex, drugs, and flatted fifths (jazz would never again be in such close promixity to the other arts). And for well-read mystics like Kerouac, Parker's genius was living proof that excess really was the path to wisdom.

PART SIX

Scrapple
from the
Apple:
Nightclub
and Concer
Reviews

Charlie Parker's night club and concert appearances were reviewed with surprising infrequency in *Down Beat* and *Metronome* magazines. Here are three lesser-known reviews from *Metronome*.—CW

BARRY ULANOV

DIZZY DAZZLES FOR AN HOUR: REST OF CONCERT DRAGS (1945)

Metronome, October 1945

As writer for Metronome *in the mid-1940s, Barry Ulanov was an early proponent of the music of Dizzy Gillespie and Charlie Parker. The concert that he reviewed in this column was under Gillespie's leadership, and, while Parker gets nothing but praise, the trumpeter gets most of the coverage. This is consistent with the progression of the two musicians' careers. Parker was addicted to drugs and his inconsistent behavior was not career-enhancing. By contrast, Gillespie was clear-headed and had a personality, style of dress, and sense of humor that was quickly accessible to casual listeners. When Parker returned from California in 1947, however, the jazz audience was more aware of his artistry, and his career took off.—CW*

The New Jazz Foundation was well-served on Wednesday evening, May 17 at New York's Town Hall, when Dizzy Gillespie made his and the organization's concert debut. Dizzy was in magnificent form; I've never heard him play so well, muff so few notes, and reach such inspired heights. Though nine-tenths of a concert is too much for a small band of the nature of Dizzy's, he and his associates acquitted themselves so well that the superfluity of chromatic runs, daring intervals, and triplets, did not get on one's nerves.

The reason Dizzy and Charles Parker (on alto), Al Haig (piano), Curley Russell (bass) and Harold West (drums), had so much to play was that most of the announced guests didn't show. Dizzy's boys played through the first half of the concert unrelieved, and the effect was stunning. "Shaw 'Nuff" (named for booker Billy Shaw), "Night in Tunisia," "Groovin' High," "Be Bop," "'Round about Midnight," and "Salt Peanuts," played in programmed order, were run off magnificently by Dizzy and Charley and rhythm in that opening half. Dizzy and Charley played their unison passages with fabulous precision, no easy achievement when your lips and fingers are so tangled up in mad running-triplet figures. Charley's solos almost never failed to get a roar from the audience because of his habit of beginning them with four-bar introductions in which the rhythm was suspended (as in a cadenza), then slamming into tempo, giving his listeners a tremendous release, an excited relief. Al Haig played pleasant piano in Dizzy's groove and Curley and Harold played well; the former with an unusual regard for pitch and a feeling for Dizzy's style, all the more impressive when you realize that he is not his regular drummer.

The second half almost went to pieces. Guests didn't show and Symphony Sid, who was announcing the concert, became flustered and communicated his nervousness to Dizzy and the band. They did well with "Cherokee" and "Blue 'n' Boogie" and "Dizzy Atmosphere" and "Confirmation," but not well enough to offset the obvious bewilderment on everybody's face and the long stage waits. And nothing could balance, for me, at least, the frantic jive of Symphony Sid, who is a creditable announcer on record shows, but much too anxious to knock you out with a hip vocabulary. So sharp he was bleeding, he laid too much New Jazz Foundation hype on that audience. Somehow he didn't dig that we had our boots tightly laced; as a matter of fact, that audience seemed to me about the most hip I've ever seen *or* heard.

In spite of the limitations cited, this was an enjoyable concert, one which presented the right kind of music and musicians, one which justified the Foundation's claim that it is "not so much interested in the origin and historical background of jazz as . . . in its present status and its chance for growth in the future." Now, if Monte Kay and Mal Braveman, who are the NJF, will stop calling the art by that horrible name "jazz music," and will program their evenings with greater variety and more polish, we may local forward to the emergence of a society of real benefactors of jazz.

BARRY ULANOV

CHARLIE PARKER (1950)

Metronome, August, 1950

Not long before this review, Charlie Parker's first recordings with strings had been released (see the Metronome *review of those selections, page 245). Ulanov was critical of those recordings and appreciated hearing some of the same selections at Café Society with only a rhythm section accompaniment. Ulanov also mentions hearing and enjoying Parker with his string ensemble in person at Birdland. His relatively positive opinion of that engagement was not shared by an anonymous* Down Beat *reviewer (August 25, 1950) who said that Parker's tone had become "a flat, monotonous, squawking thing" and that Parker had "allowed his playing to degenerate into a tasteless and raucous hullabaloo."—CW*

Charlie Parker played a dance date at Café Society in June and early July and added another shining gem to his already glittering diadem. In the show, which Bird emceed with great charm, he restricted himself to a couple of tunes from his recent album, "Just Friends" and "April in Paris," which to these ears at least sounded far more effective with rhythm section backing than with the tritely scored strings. Between shows, the bright Parker quartet (Al Haig on piano, Tommy Potter on bass, Roy Haynes on drums) polished off dance sets, with Bird's horn settling comfortably on show tunes and jazz standards, shuffling off rumbas and generally keeping a lovely sound and a bumptious beat going which were, to coin a phrase, the swinging end. In all, this engagement was a delightful reminder of what used to be an accepted fact, that a distinguished jazz band inevitably plays the best sort of dance music.

In later July, Bird took five strings, a harp, an oboe, and his rhythm section into Birdland and proved that the combination of his brilliant horn and the more subdued backing could be a lot more effective than his album indicated. Better rehearsed, better performed, the same scores were much more listenable. Bird himself was in fine form, even as at the Cafe.

GEORGE T. SIMON
PARKER AT BIRDLAND (1953)
Metronome, July 1953

Artistically speaking, 1953 was a good year for Charlie Parker. Although Parker made some good studio recordings for Norman Granz in 1953, the best documents of Parker's music of the period are found in live recordings. Parker was nonprofessionally recorded in good form in Montreal, Boston, Toronto, and New York City. In an off-the-air recording of a radio broadcast from one night (May 9, 1953) of this Parker Birdland engagement, the announcer comments on the same plastic saxophone that Simon writes about. Parker played the horn six days later in the famous concert at Toronto's Massey Hall that featured Dizzy Gillespie, Bud Powell, Charles Mingus, and Max Roach.

Note: The part of this article that reviewed trombonist Kai Winding's group has been omitted.—CW

Charlie Parker appeared at Birdland on the same bill with [Kai] Winding's group. He was blowing as wonderfully as ever, seemingly in thorough command of everything, blowing absolutely fabulous runs on his new alto, one of those plastic English jobs which has a very mellow tone but which doesn't permit the brilliance that comes out of the brass instruments.

Bird was backed by a rhythm trio of John Lewis on piano, Curley Russell on bass, and Kenny Clarke on drums. John played some very nice things with his right hand, sort of an arranger's piano, but Curley and Kenny as a team were a big disappointment for the former always seemed to be pulling ahead of the latter—or was the latter pulling back from the former? In any case, it was not a good, unified beat that they laid down, and I'm surprised that Bird was able to blow as well as he did. But then there's only one Bird, who, when he's as right as he was on this particular night, doesn't need anybody to show him the way!

PART SEVEN

Making Wax

Parker on Disc

Surveys of Parker's Recording Career

Charlie Parker's complete discography is quite lengthy and some-times confusing. It includes many studio recordings under Parker's name and others' leadership, along with a still-expanding list of nonprofessional recordings of Parker that are usually issued on a bootleg basis (without the permission of Parker's estate).

Between 1940 and 1943, the young Charlie Parker's performances were professionally recorded only a few times, so it has been difficult to trace the development of his style. Luckily, many noncommercial recordings of the period have surfaced in recent years, and this sec-tion leads off with a survey of these early documents. Beginning in 1945, Parker primarily recorded as a leader, for three companies: Savoy, Dial, and the Verve group (Clef, Norgran, and Verve). Here are two authors' discussions of Charlie Parker's studio recordings as a leader with a few nonprofessional live recordings mentioned where relevant.—CW

CARL WOIDECK
CHARLIE PARKER'S APPRENTICESHIP RECORDINGS, 1940-43 (1997)
ADAPTED FROM *CHARLIE PARKER: HIS MUSIC AND LIFE*,
UNIVERSITY OF MICHIGAN PRESS, 1996

This is an edited version of a chapter from my study of Charlie Parker and his music. The musical analysis has been simplified, the transcribed musical examples have been omitted, and the extensive footnotes have been either integrated into the text or eliminated. Those who are interested in a fuller study of Parker's music, more precise documentation, and/or transcribed Parker solos are encouraged to seek out the entire book, Charlie Parker: His Music and Life.—CW

CARL WOIDECK
CHARLIE PARKER'S APPRENTICESHIP RECORDINGS, 1940-1943

In general, Charlie Parker's "apprenticeship" years are those during which he formed working relationships with older, more experienced musicians to better learn his craft. These years could be said to have begun in the mid-1930s when he quit school and tried to make a living as a musician, seeking tips from other musicians and freelancing with various groups for short periods of time. In a more traditional sense, though, his more structured jazz apprenticeship began around 1937 with his being taken under the wing of saxophonist Buster Smith, who both advised him and employed him. His apprenticeship reached a new level in early 1940 when he rejoined the band of pianist Jay McShann, who was then beginning to tour over a wider area with an expanded band. Smith and McShann were "master" craftsmen in that they were slightly older and possessed knowledge and experience that Parker valued.

Terms like "apprentice" and "master" are borrowed from the trades and crafts, but do not always have precise meaning when applied to the arts. During the mid-1930s, Parker (born in 1920) was more of a teenage hopeful than an accepted member of his Kansas City jazz community. After having a major musical breakthrough in the summer of 1937, Parker's status gradually changed to his being regarded as a talented up-and-comer. By the time of his departure for New York in early 1939, he was ready to build upon his knowledge in a regularly working and touring band, an experience that would have to wait until his formally joining McShann at the beginning of 1940.

1940 is the earliest we can study Parker's apprenticeship period simply because that is the first year from which we have recordings of Parker. By then, he had already advanced beyond many of his McShann bandmates and was moving into a higher level of training. The term apprentice applies less to the times when he and Dizzy Gillespie became their own and one another's teachers. Still, Parker would continue to hone his skills in big bands led by older, more established musicians (most notably Earl Hines) through most of 1943. That was simply the most common way to break into the national jazz arena.

Reinforcing the use of the term "apprentice" is the fact that Charlie Parker was one of the greatest students of jazz that the idiom has known. Study of his 1940-1943 recordings (especially the informally made ones) reveal just how broad Parker's sphere of listening was. A rich indicator of his early listening habits is his use of quotations—the interpolation of one melody into another piece. The musical quotations found in his pre-1944 recordings reveal that Parker the student drew from a wide range of sources, learned them well, and used the source materials creatively rather than simply reproducing them. During the period, he was clearly listening to many players of the previous generation and did not limit his research to his own instrument, a habit that today's students would do well to emulate. Parker was blessed with a phenomenal mind for sounds; he could readily hear another jazz artist's idea (or indeed any musical idea), absorb it, retain it, and reproduce it in whatever key he later happened to be playing in (the same was true for pop song melodies).

For many years after his death in 1955, Charlie Parker's available apprenticeship recordings (those made prior to 1944 on which he is clearly audible) amounted to six titles. These six official recordings with Jay McShann for the Decca company from 1941 and 1942 include four improvised Parker solos, one embellished theme statement, and one chorus of quiet "fills" behind a vocal solo. Parker's officially recorded solo legacy from this period (those made for established recording companies, in Parker's case, Decca) totals about seventy-two measures and the whole of his solo efforts (leaving aside the spare vocal accompaniment) takes just over two minutes to listen to.

Based on such a small sample, it's clear why Parker's pre-1944 musical development was not well understood. Too few and too short were the available examples of Parker improvising. Fortunately, beginning in the 1970s and continuing up to the present, a remarkable number of informally recorded items featuring Parker from this period have come to light and have been made available to the public. Just one of these recently discovered discs alone ("Honey & Body") features Parker in the foreground for more than three minutes, by itself exceeding the total pre-1944 Parker previously available.

As of this writing, approximately thirty of these developmental or apprenticeship recordings featuring Parker solos have been released (Parker's solo participation on a few items is debated, making the number uncertain). These recordings add a tremendous amount to our knowledge of Parker. First of all, they fill in chronological gaps in his discography. Previously, we had examples of Parker's early improvisational work from only 1941 and 1942. The new releases expand documentation of his early development to the years 1940 though 1943, inclusive. Secondly, the developmental recordings now display Parker in the widest possible of musical settings, from solo saxophone without accompaniment to a full jazz big band for support. Finally, the newly available recordings feature Parker soloing over a much more varied repertoire of songs and tempos than would otherwise be available.

But even if these new discoveries did nothing to fill in gaps of chronology, setting or repertoire, they would be of great interest to the listener for the amount of time on each disc that Parker is in the foreground, either improvising or stating a given melody. In his mature work (1944 and later), Parker was not known for long solos, either in "live" settings or in the recording studio. At least six of the newly released performances feature Parker in the foreground for more than three minutes each. The pre-1944 period, once characterized by particularly short recorded Parker solos, now contains documentation of some of Parker's longest uninterrupted work, regardless of period. At last we are in a position to examine thoroughly Charlie Parker's apprenticeship or developmental work, noting influences and describing stylistic evolution.

Parker's 1940-1943 music already suggests most of the stylistic qualities associated with his mature work. These qualities are generally in a developmental state, but are consistent with the better-known later Parker. In comparison with his bandmates of the period, Parker more than holds his own with respect to command of instrument. At up-tempos, he is regularly the most comfortable of all the soloists, and at ballad tempos, he is already highly complex both rhythmically and melodically. From the earliest Parker recording, he displays a great inner sense of swing that is quite compelling. His early improvisations also reveal much of the quickness and playfulness associated with his later music. His developmental recordings already contain an essential feeling for the blues, if not at the profound depth of his later work.

There is also a striking sense of freshness to these early recordings. Parker was certainly in the midst of an exciting period of artistic discovery, but more than that, his approach to improvisation seemed to emphasize the spontaneous creation of melody in the manner of tenor saxophonist Lester Young. Of course, he employed a certain amount of prepared melodic material ("licks"), but his art had not yet become codified into a lick-based language as it did in the 1950s.

In contrast with his later career as a band leader, Parker during this early period did not choose his own repertoire because he was usually working under the leadership of others (McShann or Hines, for example). Even when recording on his own (on the nonprofessional recordings), his repertoire fell within the common practice of the day—that is to say it was based on the 32-measure popular song form and the 12-measure blues form. Although Parker is sometimes credited as co-composer of "Hootie Blues" and arranger of "The Jumpin' Blues," compositions clearly and solely by Parker are not documented on the early recordings. (Parker did write at least one original song, "What Price Love?" while he was with McShann, but it was not recorded until 1946 when it was retitled "Yardbird Suite.")

Parker performed this repertoire at tempos well within the common practice, ranging from approximately quarter note = 84 to quarter note = 280, and did not quite approach the extremely rapid tempos of his later work. He often seems more at ease than his fellow players on the faster material, though he did not yet have the up-tempo virtuosity of an Art Tatum.

Similarly, Parker's early range of note values is broad, but not as broad as his later work. Parker from his first recording displays an interest in double-timing on slow pieces, but was evidently technically unable to sustain it on faster material. By 1943 he was beginning to incorporate short bursts of double-timing on medium-swing material. Parker had already developed the tendency to accent the high points of his melodic lines. Those accents often fall on the beat, because he had not developed full flexibility to accent freely within a subdivided beat. Syncopation, whether produced by accentuation or cross-rhythm, is less varied than in his mature work.

Parker's early work employs vibrato more often and at a slightly faster rate than found in his later work and in fact occasionally seems nervous. He does, when "sweet" material calls for it, employ a more-nearly constant vibrato in the popular tradition, a practice he would soon abandon. Parker's alto sax tone evolved subtly between 1940 and 1943. Aural evidence suggests his tone gradually became less edgy, but because of the low fidelity of the amateur recordings, conclusions are difficult to make.

Especially in the earlier developmental solos, Parker often stops to begin a new thought at or near the dividing points of a song's form. The later solos within this period show more freedom to build phrases that truly cut across such structural divisions. Many melodic figures may be noted that continued to be employed in his mature work, although his early repertoire of building blocks was more limited. Parker's practice of "quoting" one piece in the performance of another was already prevalent. As in his mature work, he was more likely to use quotations outside the formal recording studio, although some shift in the sources of the material borrowed seems to have occurred between his apprenticeship and his masterful work. Especially in his early work, Parker's use of quotations provides strong clues as to his formative influences and early listening habits.

The apprentice Parker was already interested in an enriched harmonic palette and arrived at the desired chromaticism within a framework of functional harmony through a variety of means that were simply less developed than in his mature period. Already present in his work are altered dominant chords, chord substitutions, side slipping, and melodic sequencing.

Small-Group Recordings on Alto Sax

Before 1944, Charlie Parker was recorded on four occasions (as far as is known) playing alto sax in intimate settings ranging from solo to octet. In each case, these were informally recorded sessions that were never intended for release. Because these recordings all find Parker playing alto sax during the same period in non–big band settings, because many feature him in the foreground at greater-than-usual length, and because several songs appear in more than one session, it makes sense to discuss them together. (Parker's concurrent alto sax work with the full McShann big band and his tenor sax recordings of 1943 will follow later in this chapter.)

Honey & Body

An ideal starting-point for the appreciation of Charlie Parker's apprenticeship period is what is often thought to be his first recording, "Honey & Body." Consisting of both a medium-swing section and a ballad section, it exemplifies many of the musical qualities associated with early Parker.

Sometime around 1940, Kansas City trumpeter Clarence Davis

recorded on an amateur disc-cutter alto saxophonist Charlie Parker improvising a medley of two songs. Although the performance has been referred to under a variety of names (such as "Variations on 'Honeysuckle Rose' & 'Body and Soul'"), Davis labeled his disc simply "Honey & Body," and that is how it will be referred to here. "Honey & Body" is unique in the discography of Parker in that it is the only known recording of him playing unaccompanied saxophone (in this case, the alto) continuously for any length beyond a few seconds. The date of recording of this disc has been debated among Parker scholars. One claim (by the disc's last-known owner, Carroll Jenkins) states that it was recorded in 1937 when Charlie Parker was sixteen or seventeen. It is known that Clarence Davis played with Parker in 1937, making this date possible. But careful listening and analysis provide important clues that make certain a later date of recording for the disc. One clue is that Parker melodically quotes Roy Eldridge's version of "Body and Soul" (at 2:58 on the CD) that was recorded on October 10, 1938. The other clue is another quote—Parker seems to refer to the melody of the Jimmy Van Heusen popular song "I Thought about You" (3:01), which was copyrighted in 1939 and first recorded by jazz musicians in October of that year. Charlie Parker returned to Kansas City from the East Coast at the end of 1939 or the beginning of 1940, and all signs point to very late 1939 or the first half of 1940 for this Kansas City recording of Parker.

Unfortunately, the version of this performance that has been most commonly available in the United States (see the Discography entry for *The Complete Birth of the Bebop*) fades out at the point when the needle stuck in the groove when transferring to the original disc to tape. Significantly, another version now available as a French import (see the Discography entry for *Young Bird, Volumes 1 and 2*) continues beyond that point without sticking and offers a significantly more complete performance.

"Honey & Body" is in two parts, one an improvisation upon the chord progression and form of the composition "Honeysuckle Rose," and the other a performance of "Body and Soul." Both parts relate to Parker's disastrous experience sitting in with Jimmy Keith's band in the mid-1930s. In a taped interview, Parker told the story to jazz scholars Marshall Stearns and John Maher:

> I knew how to play—I'd figured—I'd learned the scale and (could)—I'd learned to play two tunes in, in a certain key, in key of D for your [alto] saxophone, F concert? . . . I'd learned how to play the first eight bars of

["Up a] Lazy River," and I knew the complete tune to "Honeysuckle Rose." I didn't never stop to think about there was other keys or nothin' like that . . . so I took my horn out to this joint where the guys—a bunch of guys I had seen around were—and the first thing they started playin' was "Body and Soul," long beat [implied double-time] you know, like this . . . so I go to playin' my "Honeysuckle Rose" and [unintelligible], I mean, ain't no form of conglomeration [unintelligible]. They laughed me right off the bandstand. They laughed so hard [unintelligible].

Upon first listening to "Honey & Body," it becomes apparent that even at this young age, Charlie Parker had a highly developed sense of swing. Even without a rhythm section, the performance has a pleasing forward motion and "drive." From a harmonic standpoint, the absence of chordal accompaniment means that the responsibility to outline tonal areas, cadences and chord progressions falls solely on Charlie. He cannot rely upon his accompanists to contextualize his melodic improvisation; the improvisation harmonically sinks or swims on his ability to imply tonality, cadences, and progressions. By the same token, he is not harmonically limited by his accompanists; any ingenuity or flights of fancy need not be justified by preset harmonies provided by another instrument. Thus, the state of Charlie's harmonic knowledge and imagination is made quite clear.

The Wichita Transcriptions

The so-called Wichita Transcriptions (see the Discography entries for *Young Bird* and *Early Bird*) were recorded at Wichita radio station KFBI on November 30th, 1940 by members of the Jay McShann Orchestra including alto saxophonist Charlie Parker. They are called "transcriptions" because they were once thought to have been recorded ("transcribed") for later radio broadcast, but in fact jazz fans Pete Armstrong, Fred Higginson, and musician Bud Gould recorded the band simply out of their own enthusiasm. The radio station simply offered good recording facilities and easy access through Gould's job in the house band at KFBI. Parker historians knew that the session had taken place, but most assumed that the discs were long lost. Miraculously, the discs were found in surprisingly good condition by jazz historian Frank Driggs in 1959, and were first legitimately released in 1974.

On the date, a septet (two trumpets, trombone, alto sax, tenor sax, piano, bass, and drums) recorded two pieces, "I've Found A New Baby" and "Body and Soul." On the same date (not at a later date as originally believed), a similar septet recorded five pieces, "Moten Swing," "Coquette," "Oh, Lady Be Good!," an untitled blues (later released as "Wichita Blues"), and "Honeysuckle Rose." Even though the group is not quite the full McShann band (four McShann players reportedly did not attend the session), the Wichita Transcriptions add to our understanding of the group with respect to the band's repertoire and Parker's role in it better than the "official" McShann studio recordings on the Decca label (see page 199). Parker is featured on all but one of the band pieces, although 32 measures is the most space he receives on a given performance.

While still somewhat thin and edgy, Parker's tone throughout the Wichita recordings is subjectively less shrill than on "Honey & Body." Much of the difference may be ascribed to the more-professional recording techniques. Parker's vibrato seems more under control and less nervous, although it remains more in evidence than in his post-1943 recordings. Of the pieces on which he is featured, the slowest is "Body and Soul" and the fastest is "Honeysuckle Rose." These tempos are within the common practice in jazz of 1940, but it should be noted that, at twenty years of age, Parker is already the most comfortable of the players at the latter tempo. Given a rhythm section, his sense of swing is even more solid than on "Honey & Body." He lets the band propel him, and swings on top of their beat. Parker does not attempt passages that imply double time except in the slow "Body and Soul." He simply did not yet have the instrumental virtuosity to bring off this difficult technique except at ballad tempos.

Although Parker had a wide range of listening habits and musical influences, a dominant influence was certainly Lester Young, who was based in Kansas City through late 1936. Parker may have heard him play in-person and definitely studied Young's recordings. When Young first recorded in 1936, he offered an alternative to Coleman Hawkins with regard to tenor sax timbre, vibrato, approach to swing, and melodic line. One attraction for Parker was Young's sparing use of vibrato (usually employed only on sustained tones). In a magazine interview, Parker said: "I never cared for vibrato . . . because they used to get a chin vibrato in Kansas City . . . and I didn't like it. I don't think I'll ever use vibrato." Interestingly, Parker tried to minimize Young's influence upon him: "I was crazy about Lester. . . . But I wasn't influenced by Lester. Our ideas ran on differently." The early Parker recordings, however, reveal a considerable

Young influence, and in fact Parker's pre-1944 recordings contain more references to Young than to any other musician. This is quite appropriate because Parker was one of the greatest students of jazz in his researching, emulating, absorbing, and finally transcending of his early models.

One of the Count Basie/Lester Young records that Charlie Parker took with him to study during his pivotal stay in the Ozark mountains in 1937 was a performance of George Gershwin's pop song "Oh, Lady Be Good!" (often called simply "Lady Be Good") with a 64-measure solo by Young (for contractual reasons, the record was released under the name of "Jones-Smith Incorporated"). "Oh, Lady Be Good!" is in a 32-bar AABA song form, and is performed by both Jones-Smith and McShann in the key of G concert. Its simple harmonies do not present the more difficult modulations of a "Body and Soul," and lend themselves to a diatonic, "horizontal" approach as favored by Young. Several authors have suggested comparing the 33⅓ RPM Jones-Smith and McShann versions of "Oh, Lady Be Good!" by manipulating turntable speed, either by slowing down Parker's alto sax solo to 16 RPM or by speeding up Young's tenor sax solo to 45 RPM. The latter scheme (which raises the speed by thirty-five percent) works best because it transposes the B♭ tenor almost exactly a perfect fourth higher, into the same range as the E♭ alto. The results are striking; at normal speed, Parker's timbre, melodic contours, and sense of swing are remarkably similar to a sped-up Young.

The Jerry Newman Disc

"Cherokee" (see the Discography entries for *Young Bird* and *Early Bird*) is another nonofficial recording that was not available to most critics and listeners before 1974. It was found in the estate of Jerry Newman who, while he was a Columbia University student, brought a portable disc recorder to several Harlem after-hours night clubs for the purpose of capturing jazz in an informal "live" setting. He was fascinated by the established Swing Era players, and recorded them prolifically. He also managed to single-handedly document the legendary after-hours musical explorations of such forward-looking players as Charlie Christian, Thelonious Monk, Kenny Clarke, and Dizzy Gillespie. Were it not for these recordings, we would be missing much more of the transitional period between the Swing Era and modern jazz. How sympathetic Newman was to these explorations is not known; he most likely recorded Monk and Clarke because they were accompanying established players in their role as the "house" rhythm section at Minton's Playhouse. Charlie Parker was evidently not a strong interest of Newman's; "Cherokee" is the only item including Parker that has surfaced from Newman's estate (likewise, he recorded Dizzy Gillespie only a few times).

"Cherokee" is nearly as fast as the fastest Parker recording of this period, the Wichita Transcription of "Honeysuckle Rose," but still far short of the fastest tempos of his mature period. As usual, Parker is at ease and swings hard at up-tempo. The basic rhythmic unit of the solo is the eighth note, with sixteenth notes used only for embellishments and pick-ups. Double-timing is not employed, nor would it usually be at this tempo even in his mature-period recordings. Accents, as expected, fall on the high points of a melodic line and usually on the beat. Because of the limited fidelity and surface noise of this disc, Parker's alto saxophone tone on "Cherokee" is difficult to discuss in comparison with the other recordings. His tone has the streamlined, "cutting" sound we associate with him, but it is not reproduced well enough to draw any conclusions as to its evolution in aesthetic or technical terms.

From a harmonic standpoint, the A sections of "Cherokee" are not particularly sophisticated for a 1930s popular song, nor do they present the improvisor with particularly difficult problems. The B section, however, *is* unusual harmonically for the period and had a reputation of being difficult to improvise upon. (For an example of its daunting effect on improvisors of the time, one need only listen to Count Basie's 1939 extended [two sides of a 78 record] version of the song; no soloist improvises on the B section, and indeed, after the first two complete AABA choruses, the A section is repeated *fourteen* times, with the B never being heard again! Significantly, Parker's model Lester Young only solos on the A section.) The reason for this avoidance was the bridge's chord progression, especially the first eight measures. Because of Charlie Barnet's 1939 hit version of the song, big bands were expected to play "Cherokee." Parker sought out rather than avoided the song as a vehicle for improvisation. Indeed, in 1939, he had a pivotal musical breakthrough in New York while playing "Cherokee" and Parker understandably viewed the song's B section as a special challenge. Gene Ramey, who played "Cherokee" many times with Parker in the McShann band, said in an interview:

> I am sure that at that time nobody else in the band could play, for example, even the channel [B section] to "Cherokee." So Bird used to play a series of "Tea for Two" phrases against the channel, and, since this was a melody that could be easily remembered, it gave the guys something to play during those bars.

The B sections on the Jerry Newman disc contrast with the other sections in that Parker uses much more repeated and prepared melodic material. As inventive an improvisor Parker already was, he clearly found the need to memorize material to get him through the difficult "bridge" of "Cherokee."

The Charles White Discs

These discs were recorded in Kansas City when during one of Charlie Parker's visits to his hometown (see the Discography entries for *Young Bird* and *The Complete Birth of the Bebop*). Parker is accompanied only by Efferge Ware on guitar and Edward "Little Phil" (or "L'il Phil") Phillips playing some sort of quiet percussion. Until the early 1990s, the discs were in the possession of Charles White, an acquaintance of Parker. White originally stated that the four selections thus-far released (two others were reportedly recorded but have not been found) were recorded in September 1942, but one of the compositions, "My Heart Tells Me," was not copyrighted until September 2, 1943. The song was featured in the motion picture "Sweet Rosie O'Grady," which was released October 20, 1943. Its earliest recording, by Glen Gray and the Casa Loma Orchestra, first entered the Billboard magazine charts November 27, 1943. Clearly, Parker could not have heard this song and recorded it until the fall of 1943, after he had left the Earl Hines band. Most likely, this session took place in late 1943 or early 1944 when it is known that Parker had returned to Kansas City and was working at a local club.

Three of the four songs ("Body and Soul," "I've Found A New Baby," and "Cherokee") had already been recorded in earlier versions by Parker. "Cherokee" in particular continued to fascinate him. This version, although slower, is very similar to the earlier Jerry Newman disc. Despite a somewhat stiff accompaniment, Parker's internal sense of propulsion provides enough swing for the whole group.

"My Heart Tells Me" and "Body and Soul" are the last two examples of the state of Parker's ballad playing until the November 1945 session for Savoy that produced "Meandering." As expected, he double-times with ease, but partly because of the rigid four-beat accompaniment, Parker's improvisations do not approach the suppleness and flexibility of just a few years later. Like the Wichita version, this version of "Body and Soul" begins at ballad tempo, then doubles in speed and finally concludes as a ballad à la Chu Berry and Roy Eldridge. In this case, however, Parker is the only horn player and thus is able to solo at both tempos. Parker again quotes Roy Eldridge as he modulates into the B section of "Body and Soul."

Parker had recorded "Found a New Baby" in 1940 among the Wichita Transcriptions, and it's interesting to compare the two versions. Although the Wichita version of "Found a New Baby" is more similar to Lester Young's in key and tempo, this later version contains more explicit references to Young and is perhaps Parker's last major recorded homage to a formative musical influence. During "Found a New Baby," Parker quotes both Lester Young's composition "Tickle Toe" (at 0:16 on the CD) and Young's improvised solo (Young's second B section) from the 1936 Jones-Smith recording of "Shoe Shine Boy" (1:56). Although Parker later minimized Young's influence, it should be evident in this chapter that Young's influence on Parker's sense of swing, the spinning of melody, timbre, and vibrato, was dominant and went far beyond mere quotations.

The Jay McShann Big Band Sides

Charlie Parker joined Jay McShann's mid-sized band in Kansas City around January, 1940. Between then and July, 1942, most of Parker's recordings were made in the setting of the McShann big band (by the time Parker left, the band had grown to fourteen pieces). Because these recordings all find Parker playing alto sax during the same period in big band settings, because these performances feature generally shorter solos than the previous group, and because several songs appear in more than one session, it makes sense to examine the McShann-Parker big band recordings in one sweep.

The Decca Sides

Until 1974, these 1941 and 1942 recordings for the Decca company by the full Jay McShann Orchestra were the sole artifacts of Charlie Parker's first style period available to most listeners. Ironically, at about seventy-one measures of solo or foreground material, these recordings now represent the *smallest* portion of his 1940–1943 work available today. The Decca recordings (see the Discography entries for *Blues from Kansas City* and *Young Bird*) are not truly representative of the McShann band because the group was not allowed to record its usual blend of pop songs, blues, "jump" tunes, ballads, and original compositions, nor were they able to adequately feature their strongest soloist, alto saxophonist Charlie Parker.

The band was typecast by Decca as a blues band and, indeed, three of Parker's four Decca solos are on blues (two twelve-bar blues and one sixteen-bar modified blues). In addition, the band had to shorten many of its pieces to fit the limits of the 78 RPM record, either by cutting out parts of arrangements and/or by shortening solos.

In Dallas, Texas, on April 30th, 1941, two pieces featuring Parker solos were recorded, "Swingmatism" and "Hootie Blues." Parker's timbre on the Dallas sessions has a new richness and depth, whether because of different equipment (mouthpiece, reed, or saxophone), better recording techniques, or a change in his concept of saxophone timbre. His use of vibrato is sparing and under control, and most in evidence in the slowest piece, "Hootie Blues." His sense of swing continues to develop, as heard in not only rhythmic authority in the fastest pieces, but also in the sureness he brings to the slowest blues.

Parker's solo on "The Jumpin' Blues" is most famous for its opening phrase (at 1:03 on the CD) that trumpeter Benny Harris adapted (in a new key) for his "Ornithology," which became a bebop anthem. Lester Young had played a very similar passage in his 1936 "Shoe Shine Boy" solo and may have been the actual source of the phrase. That Parker was familiar with the Young solo has been reported by saxophonist Lee Konitz:

I was on tour with Charlie once and I was warming up in the dressing room—I happened to be playing one of Lester's choruses—and Bird came noodling into the room and said, "Hey, you ever heard this one?" and he played "Shoe Shine Boy" about twice as fast as the record.

The Savoy Broadcast

Between the Chicago and New York Decca recordings discussed above, the Jay McShann big band was recorded nonprofessionally off the air during a February 13, 1942, NBC Blue Network broadcast from New York's Savoy Ballroom. This material (see the Discography entries for *Young Bird* and *Early Bird*) was first issued in 1991, and fills in our picture of Parker's role in the McShann band.

Even more than the Wichita Transcriptions, these recordings present the most accurate example of the Parker-era McShann big band in repertoire, solo space for Parker, and overall length of the pieces. Of the five full selections presented (not counting the brief closing theme), only two are blues. The other three pieces are an "I Got Rhythm"–derived swinger, an Ellington ballad, and a dated pop song set in swing. Parker definitely solos on four of the five pieces; his solo participation on a fifth piece is unclear (the 8-bar melody statement on "I Got It Bad" could be either alto saxophonist John Jackson or Parker).

Not only is Parker the beneficiary of more solo opportunities, he also doubles his solo length on the two pieces that had previously been recorded for Decca, "Hootie Blues" (previously 12 bars) and "Swingmatism" (previously 16 bars). Even with those extensions, his longest unbroken appearance is less than a minute long (five of the small-group recordings discussed above have Parker in the foreground for at least three minutes). Nevertheless, discovering any new Parker is valuable, especially material from his less-documented apprenticeship period. By definition, this was a time of assimilation and gradual transformation of his musical influences. An illustration of Parker's continuing reliance on the phraseology of his prime influence, Lester Young, is Parker's solo on "St. Louis Mood," during which every phrase is consistent with Young's musical vocabulary.

The Redcross Discs

Although these performances (see the Discography entries for *Young Bird* and *The Complete Birth of the Bebop*) were recorded soon before the Charles White discs (discussed with the small-group alto sax recordings above), Parker's use of *tenor*, not alto, saxophone on these small-ensemble recordings suggests that they be examined separately. Like the Wichita Transcriptions, the Redcross discs were known to have been recorded, but for many years, no one thought to determine if they still existed. In the early 1980s, through a misunderstanding, they were thought to be lost forever; it was not until 1985 that they were discovered by collectors and 1986 that they were released to the public. These discs were made on a nonprofessional disc recorder in an informal setting; the amateur recording engineer was Bob Redcross, friend of singer Billy Eckstine, who in early 1943 held mini–jam sessions in room 305 of Chicago's Savoy Hotel. Earl Hines's band (which included Eckstine, Charlie Parker, and Dizzy Gillespie) was in town, and Redcross committed some of the music they played to disc.

From the standpoint of Parker's music, these recordings are important for several reasons. From July 1942 (the New York Deccas) to September 1944 (the Tiny Grimes session for Savoy that marks the beginning of Parker's mature-period recordings), Parker did not record commercially, and it was thought that there were no documents tracing the evolution of his art during this period. Parker was with the well-known Earl Hines band for approximately the first ten months of 1943, but an American Federation of Musicians ban on recording by union members prevented this unit from leaving an official record (many radio transcriptions of big bands survive from this period, but so far, none have turned up of this Hines big band). The Hines big band was an early gathering place for many forward-looking musicians who were in transition between the Swing Era style and that of modern jazz (or "bebop"), notably Charlie Parker, Dizzy Gillespie, Bennie Green, Wardell Gray, and Sarah Vaughan. Documents of Parker during this period fill in important blanks in his musical development, a time when he was for the first time allied with a group of like-thinking young players. Another reason for the importance of these recordings is that they feature Parker on tenor sax instead of his usual alto. When tenor saxophonist Budd Johnson quit the band in December 1942, Earl Hines needed a replacement on that instrument, so a tenor sax was bought for Parker. Although Parker continued to prefer (and possibly practice on) the alto, he necessarily had to make adjustments to the larger and lower-pitched horn, merging some new stylistic qualities with ones already discussed. Later in his career, Parker was commercially recorded playing tenor sax on only two occasions, so these informal discs contribute significantly to our understanding of his approach to the tenor.

The first item of musical discussion must be Parker's timbre (or tone quality) on the tenor sax. Parker's timbral concept on alto sax was outside the mainstream and was controversial for some listeners. Critics of his alto sax tone quality considered it shrill and edgy, while adherents found it fittingly stripped down and unsentimental, and probably none found it sensual in the manner of a Johnny Hodges or a Benny Carter. Parker's tenor sax timbre by contrast, is full, smooth and sensual.

Revealing the influence of Lester Young, Parker's tenor sax timbre is not generally treated with a constant vibrato, rasp, or growl. There is one exception: held notes in the upper register are sometimes treated with a pronounced vibrato of uncharacteristic speed and depth, a practice associated with the Coleman Hawkins school of tenor playing. As expected, Parker once again exhibits a strong internal sense of swing whether he is rhythmically accompanied by bass or guitar or just by a pair of drummer's wire brushes.

"Sweet Georgia Brown" is performed at a "medium swing," approximately quarter note = 256, although the tempo varies. Parker's two lengthy solos are bursting with ideas and represent some of his best work of the period. His long eighth-note lines swing with compelling power, tremendously aided by the young but already accomplished bassist, Oscar Pettiford. Parker also seems inspired by the presence of trumpeter Dizzy Gillespie, who not only solos inventively, but also audibly urges Parker on. With only two instruments, Parker and Pettiford admirably hold together the improvisations, although in one section, they seem "turned around" in the form.

The Redcross disc of "Body and Soul" contained the only substantial ballad-tempo playing from Parker on these sides. Unfortunately, the beginning and end of the disc were too damaged to play through, so the CD version picks up during the guitar interlude and later omits the return to the ballad tempo. In general, the performance follows the Chu Berry and Roy Eldridge's slow-fast-slow scheme, although Parker and the guitarist imply double-time before actually doubling the speed. From Parker's first ballad recording ("Body"), he had demonstrated the ability to imply double-time; on the Redcross version of "Body and Soul," he has several passages in implied *quadruple*-time (thirty-second notes). Despite playing a horn that he once called "too big," Parker showed that, at twenty-two years of age, he possessed technique and rhythmic sureness that surpassed nearly every jazz musician of the time (Art Tatum would be a likely exception).

* * *

If jazz historians had to assess the stylistic contributions of Charlie Parker strictly on the basis of his commercial and amateur recordings made by the end of 1943, they would today finally find a sufficient body of work to do so. He might be seen as an advanced but nevertheless transitional figure between the swing era style and modern jazz, (as some view Charlie Christian and Jimmy Blanton, both of whom died before modern jazz's full flowering), who stopped recording before the maturation of the new style. His debts to Lester Young, Buster Smith, Coleman Hawkins, Art Tatum, and others would be traceable, and his own burgeoning contributions to a new musical direction would likely be recognized. Of course, Parker continued recording; we know how his style evolved, the nature of his post-1943 innovations and the extent of his influence on other players. But appreciation of his mature work should not take away from the inventiveness and uniqueness of his apprenticeship recordings.

During that apprenticeship period, Parker combined and then developed ideas from the most advanced of his swing era predecessors. His influences and original ideas were in flux as they would be at no other point in his career. Partly because of this artistic flux, Parker's 1940–1943 recordings are particularly vital examples of Parker because they present him at his most spontaneous; he had not yet codified his musical vocabulary, and he took an impromptu approach to the spinning forth of melody, much like his prime influence, Lester Young. In addition, Parker's work of the period is marked by a stunning pace of growth, strong sense of discovery and a rare appetite for new ideas. Each recording exhibits new facets of Parker's evolving art. The spontaneity and discovery found in these recordings reward the listener in unique and satisfying ways; for all these reasons, Parker's apprenticeship recordings stand on their own within Parkeriana.

MAX HARRISON
A RARE BIRD (1997)

Max Harrison is a well-known jazz author whose writings on jazz range from Bunk Johnson to Ornette Coleman. I read Max's chapter "Charlie Parker's Savoy Recordings" in his book A Jazz Retrospect *and asked him for permission to reprint that section in this Parker anthology. I was planning to find some other way to cover Charlie Parker's concurrent Dial recordings, but I wasn't sure how. Max surprised me with the suggestion that he supply a new essay that would survey Parker's Savoy and Dial recordings plus a few live recordings. Because Parker's work for the two companies overlaps considerably in time period and personnel, and because I regard the Savoy and Dial recordings as essential, I am pleased to accept his offer.—CW*

I

The received image of Parker implies more than one paradox. His progress between the earliest recordings with McShann and the first of those for Savoy and Dial is such as nearly to seem alarming, like the rapids before a waterfall, and appears to argue for the iconoclastic status always accorded him by friend and foe alike. The profoundly traditional nature of his music, with its strong orientation to the blues, rejects, however, all the tarnished glamour of the revolutionary label, and this despite the rivers of ink set flowing by bop. Yet, as if explicitly to subvert his work's deep roots in the past, he broke new ground in all essential aspects of jazz.

By a further contradiction, we have in more recent years been asked to see him as a rather artlessly spontaneous swinger, only requiring from the bands in which he played a simple, easily devised backdrop for his own efforts.

A conservative who innovates as drastically as did Parker might be termed a rare bird, and he is likely to spread incomprehension.[1] But all paradoxes are resolved in the music itself, where accepted and innovative procedures are related so that one enhances the other. A convenient example is the theme of "Billie's Bounce" [Savoy], a continuous 12-bar melody in which strikingly fresh uses are made of phrases which are traditional to the blues by fusing them with elements new to that idiom, the whole coalescing into a single unified statement.

Though he may not have been, or wished to appear, verbally articulate on such matters, it is a pity that Parker was seldom interviewed competently. Like other men of genius, he combined boiling ambition with considerable naïvety, but it would have been interesting to know whether he saw the forging of a surpassingly brilliant style of solo improvisation as an end in itself. Or were his personal horizons wider? Did he understand that he had achieved a renewal of the musical language of jazz comparable only to that of Louis Armstrong before him (and Ornette Coleman since)?

There are no easy answers where Parker's music is concerned, and so many factors thrust themselves forward. We do well to remember Balzac's dictum that the main events in a writer's life are his books, in a musician's life his notes, and though biographical matters can seem important, we should distinguish between the miseries of Parker's existence and the remarkable insights into the human condition that his work embodies. We never would confuse a stone block with the statue a sculptor draws from it, and we ought to be able to separate the shapeless raw material of life from the disciplined form and content of Parker's music. If he seems ambiguous as an instance of the relationship between an artist's work and his day-to-day existence it is because in his life he appeared to be a prisoner of his own liberty, the opposite of what we find in his music, where freedom arises out of order.

He preserved the hair-trigger emotional responses of adolescence, lived exposed to the storms of the inner self, and so his improvisations can be

---

1. This was sometimes to comic effect, as when Frank Kofsky on page 21 of his inexhaustibly entertaining *Black Nationalism and the Revolution in Music* (New York: Pathfinder Press, 1970) declared that Parker achieved only "a single innovation." See also the footnote supposedly relating to Parker on pages 278–79 of Kofsky's tome.

unnerving in their nakedness of expression. Deep in his temperament ran a vein of rage that was not always concealed by an affable public mask. As we shall see, there were quite other sides to his art, but it is tempting to echo Igor Markevitch's description of Schoenberg as "a great self-destructive personality." Parker may have been one of those rare people who kill themselves so as not to kill their own legend, yet we must still regret, not merely in commentators but in musicians themselves, that *nostalgie de la boue* which has led to the destruction of some of the best talents in jazz. This feeds, too, the stereotypical misconception of Parker as a "chaotic" genius, which in turn reinforces notions of his "instinctive" spontaneity. However seductive this romantic view of him may be—and his mastery as an executant strengthens it further—we must be sure that the message we discover in his music, amidst all the emotional variety and technical interest, is *his*, not our own or somebody else's.

Our best guide will be the music he recorded when he had the fullest control of the situation, and that means his sessions for the Dial and Savoy labels. Some musicians, like Ornette Coleman,[2] have always felt that Parker sounded better under studio conditions than on recordings of his public appearances. The fact remains that what with the 22-LP Limited Edition set of 1940-54 "live" and private recordings, to which have now been added the often mesmerising fragments of the Mosaic 10-LP/7-CD set of Dean Benedetti's Parker recordings, the accumulation of non-studio examples of his music, which can have few parallels among other jazzmen, towers over the studio output so far as quantity is concerned. And it sometimes offers a different sort of quality, in particular a greater surface intensity. But intensity is not everything, and it is by the studio performances, if he thought about such matters, that he would have expected to be remembered.

Certainly Parker responded extremely well to the studio situation, the consistency of his inspiration on most of the Savoy and Dial sessions being among the wonders of recorded jazz. We therefore are fortunate that both the Dial and Savoy companies have provided a large number of alternative takes of these items. In fact the issue of such material, which started in the late 1950s, has given us a liberal education in appreciating groups of closely similar yet significantly different jazz performances. Incomplete pieces and even false starts have also emerged, and these heighten our sense of the music's growth and development as each session unfolds.

---

2. Quoted in Whitney Balliett, *Jelly Roll, Jabbo and Fats* (New York: Oxford University Press, 1983), p. 192.

These recordings find him shaping nearly all performances towards specific and consistent ends. Jazz being the kind of music it is, not all the initiatives are Parker's, of course, and there is creative work here by at least a dozen others. Yet nearly everything played reflects, seldom passively, what is heard from the alto saxophone. This is to suggest that inherent in his music was not just a method for improvising solos but also one for ordering ensembles, and that is a measure of how thoroughgoing his renewal of the jazz language was. In this he went further than Armstrong (though not further than Coleman), his great predecessor, who was proverbially indifferent to the poor quality of the bands in front of which he performed. But we shall have to be specific about what Parker actually did before detailing the effect on those who played with him and then looking at the results in his recordings.

II

His art and what it has to tell us are too subtle to be polarised between, say, the brilliance of "Ko Ko" and the blueness of "Now's the Time" [both Savoy]. In fact his solos embody a complex manipulation, more volatile than any hitherto in this music, of pitch, rhythm, harmony, and expressive instrumental tone, the constantly shifting relationships between them ordered by the demands of melody. This is to say that each element operates in conjunction with all the others. Separating them analytically, however, can provide insights which heighten our appreciation of his work, and our first question must ask what holds together the several aspects of this complexity, controlling and even directing them? Quite central is a two-way, and even contradictory, process whereby he rooted his music in the constraints of commonplace 12- and 32-bar chord sequences and in the rhythm section's regular pulse, and then did everything to challenge, even subvert, these.

Remembering that in Parker's time, and for a considerable while before and after, jazz was taken to be an inherently progressive music, it is surprising that attention was only drawn much later to the restricted number, and the simplicity, of the harmonic frameworks that he used. These were the 12-bar blues plus "I Got Rhythm" and a quite small selection of rather old 32-bar AABA format popular songs. Lennie Tristano and his school likewise confined themselves, and there is a parallel with Bix Beiderbecke employing ODJB pieces as anchors for his innovations. Such restrictions can be another way of challenging the imagination, and in pursuing his creative fantasy Parker subjected this plain material to considerable sophistication, introducing, for a start, notes outside the harmonies stated by the rhythm section. It is normally said that these result from his using the upper intervals of the chords, ninths, elevenths, thirteenths. Other features are notes, some of them chromatically altered, which imply passing chords not stated in the accompaniment, and anticipations and prolongations of notes from chords that may or may not be heard from the rhythm section. But it goes further than that. Sometimes his solos imply harmonies which are not simply extensions of, or interposed between, those stated in the accompaniment but are substantially different. In effect polyharmony is arrived at when one chord sequence is imposed on another.[3] And in some ways more extreme instance of this is referred to in Miles Davis's familiar account, quoted in many texts and hence not given here,[4] of what he called "turning the rhythm section around." What this misleading term meant was that Parker might begin playing in, say, the eleventh bar of a 12-bar blues, improvising on the first bar of the chord sequence and continuing thus. With the rhythm section holding to its original place, he would therefore be two bars out of phase with his accompaniment, a large-scale effect of polyharmony being thereby produced. Bearing in mind these various devices, it will be obvious that Parker's harmonic rhythm was often different from that of the rhythm section.

Given the unity of his mature style, which reached its first complete expression at the November 1945 Savoy session, it is no surprise that Parker's employment of rhythm itself was as flexible and inventive as that of harmony. His rhythmic approach derived from Lester Young and hence ultimately from Armstrong. But whereas in Young's case alternations of tension and relaxation were produced by his placing notes on and between the beats, Parker more consistently played just behind the beat while at the same time introducing a wide range of accentual displacements and crossrhythms. As a result, his lines have an almost infinitely varied internal rhythmic life that goes beyond a rapid ebb and flow between tension and release and is in a sense organic. A good miniature illustration is his famous break on "A Night in Tunisia" [Dial]—yet although this example is always cited, he surpassed it later, as on the 1947 Carnegie Hall concert performance and on that notable occasion in 1953 at Massey Hall, Toronto. Debates as to who was the "greatest" jazz improviser reduce

---

3. See Scott Sandvik, "Polyharmony, Polymeter and Motivic Development in Parker's *Klactoveeseds-tene*" in *Jazzforschung* 24 (1992).
4. The original can be found in *Esquire*, March 1959.

music to the level of athletic contests, yet a case could be made for Parker as this music's rhythmically most imaginative player.

His irregular placing of accents, sometimes acting with his use of silence, which is to say pauses between phrases such as we find in take 2 of "Scrapple from the Apple" or take 4 of "Relaxin' at Camarillo" [both Dial], quite often result in groupings of notes, normally eighth notes, that imply bar lengths, and hence of course time-signatures, different from the rhythm section's 4/4 [see footnote 3]. This polyrhythmic aspect is heightened by the irregular punctuations of piano and drums, the latter, in the finest performances, complementing with particular closeness the soloist's invention and the whole emphasising the need for the bassist in a bop rhythm section to state the underlying pulse more strongly than in earlier styles.

Asymmetry on the harmonic and rhythmic planes is naturally confirmed in the melodic usage of Parker's solos, but it is also necessary to recognise that he can read a conventional melody with so exact a grasp of its essential meaning that, in Timothy Evans's phrase, "it yields up its Platonic ghost."[5] In his improvisations on such material, as in the Dial ballads, it is as if the music's (harmonic) corporeality is metamorphosised into spiritual grace, and pieces like "Embraceable You" [Dial] contain numerous feathery, form-making feints like the brushwork of a great painter, shaped with the gentleness of supreme strength. But concerning such achievements we ought long since to have learned from Bach that, in Donald Tovey's words, "a great artist's feeling is often more profound where his expression is most ornate."[6]

From such elaboration emerges discontinuity as well as asymmetry: observe both the airing-out of solos like that on take 1 of "Klact-oveeseds-tene" and the other examples referred to above, plus the way in take 1 of "Dexterity" [both Dial], for instance, that phrases are placed across the main eight-bar divisions of the chorus. A more negative way of appreciating Parker's shifting balance of asymmetries is to compare his phrases with the superficially very similar yet far more four-square ones of Sonny Stitt. Parker's asymmetry and discontinuity are emphasised in solos like that on take 2 of "Moose the Mooche" [Dial], where he reconciles a group of seemingly quite disparate ideas. In such cases phrases can seem inconclusive, even contradictory, yet they usually add up to a balanced whole; the

5. See Timothy Evans, "Jazz from the Forties on Onyx" in *Journal of Jazz Studies*, June 1975, pp. 96–103.
6. Donald Tovey, *Essays in Musical Analysis*, vol. 7 (London: Oxford University Press, 1944), p. 132.

mind is searching restlessly but is always in control. Illustrating what appears to be an almost opposite tendency, we find the same ideas, or parts of them, employed years apart. Sometimes these are used to considerably different effect because the dialogues with and within the rhythm section are different; but there is an element of self quotation here, and it points in two directions.

Parker's quotations come from both inside and outside his own music, the latter from inside and outside jazz, and they range, in all cases, from the wryly unobtrusive to the clownishly emphatic. Even these last can sometimes be ambiguous: while there is no doubt of the humourous message carried by the "Kerry Dance's" heavily underlined appearance in the Royal Roost performance of "Out of Nowhere" dated December 18th 1948, the same fragment, abruptly terminated, has a rather different resonance in the studio "Ah-Leu-Cha" [Savoy]. Snatches of the traditional "High Society" clarinet solo appear equally outlandish in both "Ko Ko" and take 1 of "Merry-Go-Round" [both Savoy], and though Parker referred (Queen [I] 002) to "Diggin' Diz" as "a satire on 'Lover,'" the aim of some of his quotations seems to lie beyond either humour or irony. Good examples are the allusions to "Cocktails for Two" near the end of "Warming Up a Riff" [Savoy], and to "Charmaine" in the Royal Roost "Oop Bop Sh'bam" of January 22nd 1949. These, something like the unaltered fragments of ragtime and *bal musette* tunes which Satie had, a generation earlier, embedded in his ballet *Parade,* are divorced from their normal associations and are infused with meanings all the more disconcerting for our being unable to define them.

Aspects of Parker's solo on take 4 of the Savoy "Billie's Bounce" recur in his four choruses on this theme recorded in Los Angeles the following year (Spotlite [E] SPJ123). As do elements of his take 4 solo on the Savoy "Now's the Time" in his 1953 Boston public performance of this piece [Phoenix (A) LP10]. Such self-quotations, especially when spanning several years, raise further questions. Are they the same thing as his development of ideas on a single recording date, as when his solo on take 3 of "Moose the Mooche" [Dial] reshapes elements from takes 1 and 2? On take 1 of "Dark Shadows" [Dial] he glances back to his 1941 "Hootie Blues" solo recorded with McShann, and some of his basic ideas do appear to have survived a rather long time. The resemblance between the opening phrase of his solo on McShann's "The Jumpin' Blues" and the first idea of "Ornithology" has often been noted, and the same thought is clearly behind the main phrase of the "Perhaps" theme; hear also the bridge of "Thriving on a Riff" [both Savoy].

Conditioned by myths about the "spontaneity" of jazz, we may be surprised by this kind of recycling, although what may be called formulaic improvisation occurs frequently in all jazz styles. The term is here unfortunate, suggesting procedures which are prefabricated, even mechanical, yet Parker's imagination is seldom more evident than in the deployment of his music's basic motives. Around a hundred of these have been isolated[7] and they are normally recognisable by intervallic content rather than by actual melodic distinction. In his solos they are joined together, fragmented, extended, condensed, played with all manner of different combinations of note values and rhythmic accentuations, in different positions within a phrase, starting on every beat and between beats, over different chord changes, even upside down and/or backwards while usually remaining identifiable under analysis.

Improvisation has normally been something like this, and to take for perspective an example well removed from jazz, Weber reported that Hummel, whose virtuosic piano improvisations were received with almost unanimous approval in the 1820s and early '30s, "used, with masterly control, figures of all kinds in a supremely logical way in innumerable positions."[8] Certainly Parker employed a well defined vocabulary in an astonishing variety of ways and with a facility that in no sense lessened the expressive force of the results, leaving no doubt that he was the most adept formulaic improviser that jazz is likely to see. True, his basic motives would occasionally be too near the music's surface, and, as Michael James has written, "The very plenitude of his ideas could lead to an agglomeration of breathtaking fragments rather than a cohesive statement."[9] This is quite different, of course, from the carefully measured linear discontinuity of his most daring flights, and, as André Hodeir pointed out, the contents of Parker's motivic vocabulary "are never stereotypes, because they form an integral part of what he happens to be saying."[10]

Given his fundamentally traditional stance, it is not surprising that while the great majority of Parker's melodic cells are evidently original with him, some few are traceable to Lester Young, and there are instruc-

---

7. See Thomas Owens, "Charlie Parker: Techniques of Improvisation," unpublished dissertation, University of California at Los Angeles, 1974.

8. Quoted in Derek Bailey, *Improvisation, Its Nature and Practice in Music* (Ashbourne: Moorland Publishers, 1980), p. 48.

9. Max Harrison, Michael James, Alun Morgan, Jack Cooke, and Ronald Atkins, *Modern Jazz—the Essential Records, 1945–70* (London: Aquarius Books, 1975), p. 16.

10. André Hodeir, *Jazz—Its Evolution and Essence* (London: Secker and Warburg, 1956), p. 107.

tive cases like that of "Cool Blues" [Dial]. A simple riff tune, this, like "Buzzy" or "Constellation" [both Savoy], is not really characteristic of Parker, yet he alludes to its basic idea in take 4 of "Yardbird Suite" [Dial], take 2 of "Cheryl" [Savoy], and more fleetingly in bar 7 of take 1 of "Embraceable You" [Dial]. It was also used by John Kirby's band, and this may be whence Parker got it, because he knew Russell Procope, a member of that ensemble. Yet it goes farther back, at least to a unison saxophone section figure in Duke Ellington's "Blue Ramble" of 1932, and is a good example of Parker's use of the *lingua franca* of jazz. He sometimes appears especially original in pieces like "Bird's Nest" [Dial] and "Bird Gets the Worm" [Savoy], which are untamed in manner yet full of subtle feeling. The point of such performances is not that they are so fast but that they contain so many ideas. Are his solos in fact tightly packed, rather than closely argued from within? Are they less organic than their purely rhythmic dimension, as noted above, leads us to suppose?

Certainly the underlying motivic network of Parker's improvisations results in a constant challenge to the four- and eight-bar phrase-lengths which dominated jazz up to his time and beyond, this being evident in the melodic asymmetry already referred to. While tightly packed, the best of his solos are not in the least overcrowded, and the formulaic approach should be seen, in his case at least, not as a limitation but as a means of control. It provides a background consistency, with the large number of original motives, which are used at all tempos, balancing the small number of simple harmonic frameworks.

Aside from the ballads recorded for Dial, most of the themes heard on his sessions were composed by Parker on those same few chord sequences, and they are shaped, just like his improvisations, by all the factors mentioned thus far. These themes appeared cryptic when new, but their expressive implications are rich and diverse, arising out of their various sorts of interlocking complexity. Occasionally he would begin a solo with the theme's last phrase, as in his sequences of three blues choruses on both "Cheryl" and "Bird Feathers"; and note the wonderful reshaping of the main phrase in the last eight bars of his improvisation on take 1 of "Yardbird Suite" [all three Dial]. But, like other bop musicians, he based his solos—or variations on his motivic repertoire—chiefly on the chords. Despite this, we do to some extent get different Parkers when he improvises on different themes, the Dial session of March 1946 well demonstrating this.

His themes have received little separate attention, but did he value them more than we assume? This is implied by cases like "Relaxin' at

Camarillo" [Dial], an outstanding blues theme that is not easy to play (hear McGhee on take 1). Parker's two choruses on take 3 form probably his best solo of that date, yet take 5 was chosen for the initial 78-RPM issue, apparently because it has the most cleanly executed account of the theme.[11]

The intricacy of many Parker, and some other, bop themes was fully matched by Tristano, although rather than composers both men were theme makers in precisely the sense that Hodeir coined that term. Parker's approach was as varied in this aspect of his music, however, as in others. Some of his themes are melodically most attractive, like "Marmaduke" [Savoy], and others, such as "Confirmation," are distinctly ingenious, even if the latter is not, as sometimes claimed, a "continuous linear invention . . . with no repeats"[12]: the second and fourth eight-bar phrases are subtle and different variants of the first. Occasionally a theme is revealed only at the end, as in take 3 of "Thriving on a Riff" [Savoy] and the version of "Dewey Square" [Dial] (take 1) issued as "Prezology." Even when a non-Parker title is given, as with "Embraceable You" [Dial], the original melody is quoted only tangentially, and in cases such as "Bird Gets the Worm" and "Klaunstance" [both Savoy] no theme is stated at all. At the opposite extreme are the strange canonic themes, "Ah-leu-cha" and "Chasing the Bird" [both Savoy]. What was he after here? Both have the "I Got Rhythm" sequence in the background yet the effect is one of poly-harmony as both lines imply the chord changes and because the trumpet starts a bar after the alto one instrument is out of phase with the other. Both themes work quite well as counterpoint, however, and we must regret that Parker did not undertake other such ventures, although they bore a kind of fruit in George Russell's "Odjenar" and "Ezz-thetic," which were recorded by Davis and Lee Konitz in 1951.

With his most original themes and in his finest improvisations Parker achieved a re-ordering of new and traditional materials, this amounted in the latter case to a defamiliarisation of common musical elements and pro-

---

11. The problems that these themes presented lesser musicians inevitably led to bowdler-ization, even caricature. Suitably "adjusted" by Andy Gibson, "Now's the Time" became a big hit in 1949 as "The Hucklebuck." Far more reprehensible was the coarsening of this music by real jazz musicians, and dire assaults on "The Hymn" by Clark Terry's Jolly Giants [Pye Vanguard (E) VSD79365] and by Archie Shepp on "Confirmation" [Improvised Music (A) SR114] can stand for many similar cases of reverse alchemy, of gold being turned into lead.
12. Martin Williams, *The Jazz Tradition* (New York: Oxford University Press, 1983), p. 147.

cedures. A powerful agent in this is the sound in which his thoughts are clothed. One of his most considerable innovations may be seen in the difference between, say, the idealising romanticism of Johnny Hodges's tone and the mortifying realism of his own, even if the latter is illuminated from within by a soft lyrical underglaze. His sound, like all other dimensions of his work, had several aspects, and whatever the refinements of his playing in terms of the theory of music, the sheer intensity of life he got into his phrases is as central when he performs quietly at slow tempos as when loudly at fast. And tone interlocks with all other facets of his music—rhythm, for instance, being not just a matter of his placement of accents but of sometimes executing adjacent notes with substantially different degrees of force, from fiercely emphatic to barely stated (ghosted). This feeling of unified contrast is obviously central to his music, and the three takes of "Out of Nowhere" [Dial], all of them studies in double-time at slow tempo, provide revealing comparisons. Note especially how he shifts between different levels of intensity during each solo, exploiting contrasts of volume, force of execution, and accentuation, adding further point to his ideas by shading his tone with much subtle variation.

The haunted lyricism of Parker's further improvisations on "My Old Flame" and "Don't Blame Me" from the same date, and on "How Deep Is the Ocean" from the next one, draws attention, if they are set beside the blazing assertion of the rather aptly named "Crazeology" [all four Dial], to the music's diversity of feeling. Different again is the finished elegance of his solo on take 1 of "Scrapple from the Apple" [Dial], and it is worth repeating that, despite regular assertions to the contrary, his music is far from being unrelievedly harsh and dark. Much bop is indeed aggressive, but Parker's world is large enough to encompass furious anger and blithe unconcern, often on the same recording session and occasionally in a single improvisation. The climate can change with disquieting abruptness, and it was this depth and variety of emotional content that made the richness of technical means so necessary.

An equally indispensable vehicle was instrumental mastery, and if Parker was among the most creative virtuosos of his century it is because the end of his playing was never mere display but always emotional exploration fused with technical innovation. Even in the furious double-timing of "Another Hair-do" [Savoy] or the whiplash phrases of the Swedish "How High the Moon?" [Spotlite (E) SPJD124/5] every note is essential. Although the foregoing outline of Parker's method and style perhaps makes it seem complex, even overloaded, he at best achieved a perfect matching of ends with means that showed every detail to be natural and necessary.

Like other great jazz soloists, he could make a dazzling impression despite thoroughly poor support, but as suggested earlier it is important to recognise where he is heard to fullest advantage, and why. "No man is an island," some less than others, and far from being content with a simple backdrop to his own playing, Parker, because of all the changes he had wrought in the soloist's language, needed answering changes in the ensemble. This is most apparent at the rhythmic level in the close correspondence between alto and drum contributions, the latter showing, indeed, that Parker's requirements were quite precise. He was not a natural band-leader like Ellington or Davis, and had little skill or interest in the day-to-day running of a regular working combo. But he knew what he wanted musically and how to get it, and the results naturally benefited from the personnel being stable.

We cannot say whether he grasped how far ahead of the other players he was, but he understood that contrast has as dramatic a potential in the organising of ensemble music as in the construction of a solo. Hence the choice not of a virtuoso trumpeter such as Fats Navarro to duplicate his own brilliance but of the lyrically introverted Davis. Not that this matter is altogether simple: the latter trumpeter's emerging talent for asymmetry and displacement echoed some aspects of Parker's music rather faithfully. But only on one studio session did he employ Powell, a pianist very close to him in style, preferring such men as Jordan, Haig, Lewis, and Marmarosa. On pieces like "Klaunstance" and "Bird Gets the Worm" [both Savoy], Jordan's sparse yet melodious solos are a perfect foil to his voluble leader, and the refined lyricism of all four pianists accords interestingly with what Davis was contributing to the band as well as helping balance the polyrhythmic activity of Parker and Roach.

Contrast and integration did not depend simply on a choice of suitable players but were worked out in the sequence of events on each track. A good instance is "The Hymn" [Dial] (alias "Superman"), where four impassioned alto blues choruses yield at last to the sedate, tidily harmonised theme, risking yet entirely avoiding anticlimax.[13] An entire session like the Savoy date of November 1945, might be arranged so as to offer as many different but related avenues of expression as possible. Here are two pieces based on familiar AABA chord sequences—the simple "I Got Rhythm," called "Thriving on a Riff," and the more complex "Cherokee," titled "Ko Ko";

---

13. This theme is also used in an accompanimental role in "Blues" (properly "Wichita Blues") recorded with McShann in 1940, and reappeared in Davis's 1956 "Trane's Blues."

two 12-bar blues in F—one traditional, "Now's the Time" one more complicated, "Billie's Bounce"; and one slow ballad, "Meandering," on the chords of "Embraceable You." So much for this music being off-hand in organisation! It is unlikely that Parker would so consistently have achieved such well balanced and acutely expressive results within the formality of studio conditions and 78-RPM time limits if he had been an unthinking wailer. At least when his health permitted, he was *very* clear-headed musically.

This is already evident from some of the music recorded with Tiny Grimes in 1944, when the durable work, as on the session of February 19th 1947, was hurriedly squeezed in at the end of the date. This combo offered 52nd Street swing, one of the sources out of which bop was in the process of being born, and Grimes's neatly patterned triteness obviously had nothing to say to Parker. His 4/4 strumming merely obscures the astute Clyde Hart's discontinuous and more relevant support. "Tiny's Tempo" is a blues by Grimes and Hart which includes three fine alto choruses, while "Red Cross" [both Savoy] is a 32-bar theme from Parker on the "I Got Rhythm" chords with quite interesting harmonic moves implied on the bridge. Although his tone does not have its full expressive power, he is splendidly fluent, well on course for next year's recordings with Gillespie.

By the time he reached the November 1945 session Parker was absolutely ready, but his instrument was not and he was plagued by reed squeaks and other troubles. These recurred on later occasions too. Luckily he was not put off, and his three choruses on take 4 of "Now's the Time," like his solo on take 5 of "Billie's Bounce" [both Savoy], are, to coin a phrase, really the blues. The earlier versions of both tunes have interesting yet not always original ideas, standard blues phraseology looming too large. The final takes show (like take 4 of "Barbados" [Savoy]) an almost disconcerting improvement in their concentration and have a classic simplicity, no note or nuance being superfluous. This emphasises that Parker did need all these takes to produce his best work in the recording studio— public performances giving rise to other considerations. He makes a marked improvement between takes 1 and 3 of "Thriving on a Riff" (take 2 being a false start), and should have been given one more take to bring it up to the level of "Now's the Time," "Billie's Bounce," and "Ko Ko" [Savoy]. "Billie's Bounce" is the first of a series of blues themes, including "Relaxin' at Camarillo" [Dial] and "Barbados," which illustrate the density and originality of thought he achieved in this idiom.[14]

---

14. However, minor-keyed blues do not seem to have interested him much. Despite a few pieces such as Ellington's "Ko-Ko" of 1940 we had to wait for themes like Horace Silver's "Señor Blues" of 1956 before much use was made of blues in the minor. Even in the major mode, choice of key does not appear to have been of great importance to Parker.

Following the preliminary study of "Warming Up a Riff," which begins during Parker's first chorus and fades after his third, "Ko Ko" [both Savoy], with its 64-bar chorus, is an exception to what might be called his 12- and 32-bar rule. Framed by a tonally indefinite introduction and coda which state no harmony, the alto solo stands with several others done for Savoy and Dial among the greatest in recorded jazz, the flow of ideas and the emotion behind them irresistible. It is wild, melancholy, elevating.

To follow this with Thornton's dreadful "Thriving on a Riff" [Savoy] playing is like being pitched over a precipice. Otherwise, the limitations of Davis's trumpet work and Gillespie's at the piano are in a largely positive balance with their leader's virtuosity. Davis, only 19, then had a big, rather dead, vibratoless open sound that was much improved by the mute, as shown in "Thriving on a Riff" (alias "Anthropology"). He is quite self-possessed here but sounds much like Gillespie. His best solo of the date is on take 3 of "Billie's Bounce," though according to Benny Bailey this is a reproduction of a solo of Freddie Webster's.[15] Several thoughts are prompted by Parker's intention of using either Bud Powell or possibly Thelonious Monk on this session. Either would have had a rather considerable effect on the results, particularly Monk. But in the event neither was available on the day and this let in Thornton.

A further uncommon 64-bar AABA theme, George Handy's "Diggin' Diz" [Dial], uses the "Lover" harmonic sequence and is the sole survivor of a Dial session of February 1946 that was chaotic for non-musical reasons. Gillespie comes off best among the soloists, with his phrases unemphatic yet finely chiselled, although there are two lucid 16-bar keyboard passages from Handy.

At this point it is relevant to refer again to the session recorded "live" at the Finale Club, Los Angeles, probably in the following month [Spotlite (E) SPJ123]. Besides Parker and Davis, this has Joe Albany at the keyboard, Addison Farmer (bass), Chuck Thompson (drums), and is of as much interest for the piano as for the alto work. One is irresistibly reminded of Armstrong and Hines's creative dueling 18 years earlier, for example on "Billie's Bounce," where Parker's four choruses are matched—fully matched—by five from Albany; and on "Ornithology," which is obviously a trial run for the famous version recorded later in the month. In fact Albany's contribution should be compared with Marmarosa's, especially on take 4 of the studio performance. Albany provides an aggres-

---

15. Quoted in Jack Chambers, *Milestones*, vol. 1 (Toronto: University of Toronto Press, 1983), p. 38.

sively participating accompaniment of Parker here, then holds back behind Davis prior to the superb piano solo with which he follows him. "All the Things You Are" can be heard both as an advance on the reading with Gillespie of February 1945 and as another preliminary study, this time for the "Bird of Paradise" version of October 1947 [Dial]. Parker's solo on this piece at the Finale Club that night was unusually inventive, even for him. Especially when muted, Davis is more confident than in the November 1945 occasion, for instance on "Blue 'n' Boogie." The main point here, though, is another magnificent sequence of choruses from Albany—a potentially great jazz pianist who got lost.

There are of course no alternative takes to these "live" recordings, but on the studio date later in March 1946 we hear Parker, spurred on by Marmarosa and taking full advantage of the taut resilience of the McMillan-Porter beat, sometimes developing an improvisation from take to take, as in "Moose the Mooche," at others making a new departure each time, as with "Yardbird Suite" [both Dial].[16] In both sets of cases the differences of emotional tone from one solo to another are considerable. There are other fruitful divergences, as between the restraint of "Ornithology" and the verve of "A Night in Tunisia" [both Dial], yet it is often the lyrical, intimate side of Parker that emerges here. His execution is better than in the previous November, and there is great work on, for example, take 4 of "Ornithology," take 5 of "A Night in Tunisia." Aside from on take 1 of "Moose the Mooche," Davis is muted throughout, and Thompson is much better than on "Diggin' Diz" [Dial].

V

That was almost as much a landmark occasion as the November 1945 session, but, in the saddest of contrasts, the following July's date produced Parker's worst recordings, and his resentment over their being issued is perfectly understandable. He was on the verge of a complete breakdown in his health and was defeated by fast tempos, not completely by slow. His attention to detail was blurred, and only a halting paraphrase of "Lover Man" is offered, while "The Gypsy" [both Dial] is simpler still, even if something of his tone and timing survive. The literature on Parker contains plenty of rhapsodising over the stricken "Lover Man," but a more

16. "Yardbird Suite," on the chords of Hines's "Rosetta," was at first titled "What Price Love?" and was a vocal number from the McShann days. The thought of Parker as a song-writer is an odd one.

sensitive response is that of Charles Fox, who rightly says that such a performance "turns the listener into an involuntary *voyeur*."[17] There is good work from McGhee and especially Bunn here, carried out in difficult circumstances.

The recordings of February 1st 1947, made quite informally, are our first glimpse of Parker after his emergence from Camarillo State Hospital, where he had been confined for six months as a result of various sorts of non-conformist behaviour. The three items titled "Home Cookin'" [all three Dial] are based on different chord sequences. "Home Cookin' I" is on "'S Wonderful" but with the "Honeysuckle Rose" bridge, "II" is on "Cherokee," "III" on "I Got Rhythm." "Home Cookin' I" is another piece we enter in midstream (like "Warming Up a Riff"), and, far from being impaired by the lay-off, Parker's playing is more forthright than ever, more directly melodic, and certainly more optimistic. This is so not only for the "Home Cookin'" pieces but also for "Lullaby in Rhythm" and the very badly recorded "Yardbird Suite" [both Dial].

Taken down later the same month, "Cool Blues" [Dial], at any rate take 4 of it, may be Parker's most familiar record. His own title for this theme was "Blues Up and Down" (not to be confused with the Stitt–Gene Ammons "Blues Up 'n' Down"). Garner found the pace of takes 1 and 2 (later issued as "Hot Blues" and "Blowtop Blues") too fast while Parker considered 3 too slow, even though Garner has his best solo on this theme here. The famous take 4 is an effective compromise. "Bird's Nest" is an improvisation on the "I Got Rhythm" sequence, although the bridge is close to that of "Dark Shadows" [both Dial]. Garner does well on take 3. The sole justification for Earl Coleman's imitations of Billy Eckstine are that they allow us to hear Parker in an accompanimental role—which he performs most sensitively—and that they give rise to his solos on "Dark Shadows." Part of his improvisation on take 3 of this found its way into Woody Herman's "I've Got News for You," and he used some of the same ideas in condensed form on take 4.[18]

Largely because of Garner's presence, this date is off Parker's main path, and the direction he had signalled with the "Home Cookin'" pieces was taken up at a session later in the month. This was originally issued as

17. See Max Harrison, Charles Fox, and Eric Thacker, *The Essential Jazz Records—Ragtime to Swing,* vol. 1 (London: Mansell, 1984), p. 457.
18. After Garner's death the preposterous claim was made on his behalf that he had *composed* "Bird's Nest" and "Cool Blues." The former has no theme, of course, and the background of the latter is given in the main text. One might as well boast of having contributed a cup of water to the Victoria Falls as of supplying Parker with an idea.

by Charlie Parker's New Stars—a reference to Gray, Marmarosa, Kessel, Lamond, and Callender, who had worked and recorded together in various combinations. The glowing vitality of this music, its rhythmic density—in terms of the amount of activity on that level—and relaxed swing made the occasion exceptional. It reminds us, too, that the richness of Parker's music is such that it almost inevitably contains initiatives that were never followed up. The four-man rhythm team here puts forward an alternative to the polyrhythmic approach he normally favoured. It is a sort of modernisation of the Basie rhythm section, retaining the fluid pulse while allowing the piano and guitar—rather than the drums—greater freedom. This complements the horns' invention in an original and telling way, leading everyone to reach their highest level at some points. Again, Parker sounds notably optimistic, take 1 of "Cheers" being an outstanding instance. This theme and those of "Stupendous" and "Carvin' the Bird" [both Dial] are supposed to be McGhee's, although the former is by the trumpeter Melvyn Broiles and the latter has been credited to Kessel, who recorded it as "Swedish Pastry" (as did Benny Goodman with Stan Hasselgard). "Relaxin' at Camarillo" [Dial], as already stated, is Parker's, his title for it being "Past Due." It was renamed in imitation of Muggsy Spanier's "Relaxin' at the Touro," and it gives rise to a memorable introduction and coda from Marmarosa.

Back in New York Parker resumed the practice started with "Now's the Time" and "Billie's Bounce" [both Savoy] and not quite continued by "Carvin' the Bird" and "Relaxin' at Camarillo" [both Dial], of including two contrasting blues themes, one simple, one complex, on most dates. Among the May 1947 items, they are "Buzzy" and "Cheryl," while other pairings are "Blue Bird" and "Another Hairdo," and "Parker's Mood" and "Barbados" [all six Savoy]. Not that "simple" themes are such easy assignments as we might suppose. Riff tune though it is, "Buzzy" needed five takes; and observe the unusual grace notes in the "Bluebird" [Savoy] main phrase. This session, like its predecessor, again raises the point that the "master" takes chosen for 78-rpm issue do not necessarily carry the best improvising. On the last Los Angeles date, Marmarosa's finest solo of the day was on take 1 of "Stupendous" [Dial], whereas take 2 was first chosen for issue. Similarly, Davis's reputation suffered for some years because his best solos were on early takes and it was usually later ones that were released. If satisfying solos by him with this band did appear, they were on pieces such as "Cheryl" where there were few takes. This helps explain Davis's subsequent practice as a leader of recording only in single takes.

Even if he was too close to Parker stylistically to be the ideal pianist here, there is excellent Powell on "Cheryl" and "Buzzy" [both Savoy], and it is a pity in both cases that he has to give way to dull bass solos. As for Parker, his improvisation on take 1 of "Buzzy" stands very high in terms of newly-minted ideas if not in execution; admittedly takes 3 and 5 unfold more smoothly. The sequence of "Donna Lee" [Savoy] takes also develops unevenly, with all hands sounding tentative at first and 4 being best for Davis, 5 for Powell and the leader.[19]

Despite Parker's presence, the Savoy session of August 14 1947 is part of the trumpeter's story rather than his own. Issued as "by the Miles Davis All-Stars," it was the trumpeter's debut as a leader and an early step on the road to *The Birth of the Cool* and far beyond. From the viewpoint of jazz history the significance of these performances is their demonstration of Davis's having ideas of his own that were already at a remove from bop, though naturally still influenced by it. "Milestones"—not the piece the trumpeter recorded in 1958—was perhaps composed by Lewis, and Boyd may have had a hand in "Half Nelson." But Davis certainly wrote the others, arranged them all, and chose the personnel. The themes have more of a *legato* flow, although this is productively in tension with the dense harmonies, for example in "Sippin' at Bells," which has 18 chords to its 12-bar sequence, largely defusing any blues feeling. The tempos are more sober and the ensemble texture is cooler, not least because Parker is on tenor saxophone, an instrument with which he would record again under Davis's leadership for Prestige in 1953. Its effect is to bank his fires down, allowing the trumpeter to emerge more decisively. Not that Parker was overshadowed here or in 1953, his solos on both takes of "Half Nelson" showing that he had lost none of his early mastery of the tenor. Takes 2 and 3 of "Little Willie Leaps" (based on "All God's Children Got Rhythm") are rather different, 2 being slowish with a good open solo from Davis while 3 is faster, less relaxed, yet still with excellent solos from all. Take 2 of "Milestones" is splendidly played and although the trum-

---

19. This piece, on the "Indiana" chords, was long credited to Parker, but following remarks by Gil Evans it was reassigned to Davis. If Davis's, then "Donna Lee" was the first theme he contributed to a Parker date. However, there are three Benedetti recordings on "Indiana" made in March 1947, when Parker was still in California and had McGhee, not Davis, on trumpet, during which Parker skirts closely enough around the "Donna Lee" theme to put the matter into question again. Davis always claimed this theme was his (e.g., *Down Beat*, February 16, 1961), but for more extensive comment see Douglass Parker's "Donna Lee" and the Ironies of Bebop," which appears in Dave Oliphant, ed., *The Bebop Revolution in Words and Music* (University of Texas at Austin: Harry Ransom Humanities Research Center, 1994), pp. 161-201.

peter is less well focussed on 3 the careful preparation and rehearsal paid off particularly well on this date.

Only now, in October of what supposedly was Parker's most productive year, do we get a session with the Davis-Jordan-Potter-Roach line-up that is thought, with almost sufficient reason, to have been the finest he ever led. Indeed, of the 16 dates examined here only four have this personnel—plus one that adds J. J. Johnson. Aside from "The Hymn" [Dial], an essentially traditional fragment, all the themes are Parker's, and it is a further indication of his prowess as a bandleader that a different ensemble sound, especially from the horns, is achieved on each piece. This is to varying extents true of other sessions, of course, but it is particularly noticeable here.

Parker's solos on both takes of "Embraceable You" [Dial] are peaks of recorded jazz improvisation, especially the first. While not, as often supposed, growing entirely out of its initial phrase, take 1 is more closely argued from within than most of his solos, being less dependent on—though by no means free of—his vocabulary of basic motives. Jordan provides worthy preludes on both takes and on the first Davis offers the most affecting solo he contributed to these sessions, no small feat in view of what Parker had just played. The pair of alto solos on this piece are a reminder that our grasp of the richness of Parker's invention can be heightened by hearing one take while following a transcription of another on the same theme. These two accounts of "Embraceable You" should also be compared with "Meandering" and "Quasimado" [both Savoy], which use the same chords and are vivid illustrations of the different results he could get from the same sequence (even if there is a hint of take 1 of "Embraceable You" in take 1 of the brisker "Quasimado").

VI

There are further beautiful solos in "Bird of Paradise" [Dial], which is not the Jimmie Lunceford piece of that name but is based, as already noted, on "All the Things You Are." Again the atmosphere is exquisitely maintained by Davis and Jordan and when the trumpeter is heard for a second time he is gently counterpointed by Parker on take 2, more assertively on 3. Regarding the latter's "spontaneity," while all three Dial takes of this piece show obvious differences, comparison with the Finale Club performance proves that he had his ideas pretty well sorted out in advance. All of these, plus the 1945 reading with Gillespie, use the same introduction and coda, which first was recorded, rather incongruously, as part of Eckstine's "Good Jelly Blues."

An attraction of take 1 of "Dewey Square" [Dial], is that it has 64 bars of the leader as against 32 on 2 and 3. He is rather cool on 1, less so on the others, and had a way of sometimes hotting up as work on a theme proceeded. "Scrapple from the Apple" [Dial] is another example. "Bongo Bop," not to be confused with "Bongo Beep" [both Dial], is a blues with some Latin-American rhythms, this being an occasionally recurring vein of Parker's. A pity they decided to waste time by playing the theme twice. As for "Dexterity" [Dial], Stitt pretended it was his and renamed it "Sonny Side."

More time is thrown away on a bass solo—almost this band's sole recurring weakness—in "Bird Feathers" [Dial] (alias "Schnourphology"), but Parker is near his optimistic best. This theme has a certain relationship with "Moose the Mooche"; and the "Klact-oveeseds-tene" [Dial] idea, based with alterations on the "Perdido" chords, had been recorded the previous June by Wardell Gray and Dexter Gordon as "The Chase." Take 1 of "Out of Nowhere" [Dial] includes a Jordan solo later unfortunately eliminated, but a main point about the three performances of this piece is their illustration of the way Parker would sometimes come up with entirely new thoughts on the last take, abandoning others that had been tried and apparently found wanting. An instance is the sliding thirty-second note triplet figure heard on takes 1 and 2 but missing from 3.

Davis and Johnson are muted in all ensemble passages on the first of the two December 1947 dates [Dial] and the three horns blend excellently. The trombonist in no way impedes the band, even on the very fast "Crazeology"; his only open solos are in the two accounts of "How Deep Is the Ocean" "Crazeology" employs an interestingly altered version of the "I Got Rhythm" sequence and was recorded by other artists as "Bud's Bubble," "Little Benny," and "Ideology." "Drifting on a Reed" (not the Hawkins-Monk piece of 1944) is a blues that has Parker improvising with great intensity on all three takes. Some of these were issued as "Giant Swing," "Air Conditioning," and Curtis Counce recorded it as "Big Foot" in 1956; Parker himself often announced it with this title. "Charlie's Wig" is an ABCD 32-bar theme based on "When I Grow Too Old to Dream" that once more has everyone improvising very well, even if Johnson manages a bit less variety than Parker or Davis. Confusingly, various takes of this were issued as "Bongo Bop," "Bongo Beep," and "Move." The real "Bongo Beep," is a Latin-American-tinged blues—as is "Bongo Bop." Still more confusingly, some versions of "Bongo Beep" appeared as "Bird Feathers" and "Dexterity." Dial's mistitling of Parker alternative takes deserves a chapter to itself. But Davis, now far indeed from the November 1945 session, is quite virtuosic on the second take of "Bongo Beep" and the third "Crazeology." Parker's musical perception was such that he never really inhibited the trumpeter from following his own direction.

In contrast, the second December 1947 [Savoy] date appears to have been rather casual. "Bird Gets the Worm" and "Klaunstance "(for which Parker's strange original title was "Klausen's Vansen's") are rapid theme-less improvisations on "Lover, Come Back to Me" and "The Way You Look Tonight" respectively. They have been mentioned on earlier pages. "Bluebird" (not the George Wallington theme of that name) is a blues, and "Another Hair-do," also a blues, seems like a simple riff except that the first two takes soon break down. The theme chorus, in fact, has three bars of riffing, six bars of improvising by Davis and the leader, then another three bars of the riff. This is obviously an unorthodox way of splitting a 12-bar chorus, and it is regrettable that Parker did not try such things more often.

The final two sessions were for Savoy and took place the greater part of a year later. Hence there are personnel changes, most significantly Lewis is at the piano. "Barbados," another blues with a Latin-American accent, is among the most engaging of Parker's themes, just as "Constellation," a mere scale-pattern riff, is the dullest. For all their elaboration, the quite unpredictable surges of sixteenth notes, thirty-second notes, quintuplets and sextuplets in take 5 of "Parker's Mood" distil a sombre poetry which makes this one of the greatest instrumental statements in the blues idiom. It draws particular attention to his deviations from theoretical norms of equal-temperament tuning, to variations of speed and width of vibrato, these being largely unmapped territories in the study of Parker's music.[20] They are always factors, of course, but are more noticeable here because of the specific character of this performance.

A comparison between "Ah-Leu-Cha" and the earlier canonic piece "Chasin' the Bird" emphasises the superiority of this later band, and not only because the contrapuntal passages are more cleanly executed. Significantly or otherwise, "Ah-Leu-Cha" was the only Parker theme Davis recorded after they went their separate ways. He did so twice, once respectably a few months after the great man's death in 1955, and then, carelessly and much too fast, at the Newport Festival of 1958. Parker had persistent reed trouble on both of these September 1948 sessions, and 6 takes were necessary for both "Perhaps" and "Marmaduke." There is a highly personal statement from Davis on "Steeplechase," and it may be

20. However, see Thomas Owens, "Applying the Melograph to *Parker's Mood*," in *Selected Reports in Ethnomusicology*, vol. 2, no. 1 (1974).

unnecessary to note that "Merry-Go-Round" is not the Ellington piece of 1935. As these are the last items of all, however, it is entirely apt that both takes contain tremendous Parker.

In all this music there is a masterly fusion of European and non-European elements, though whether the latter can honestly be called "African" is another matter entirely. Some were original with Parker, and the rest might be thought of more sensibly as American. Such was the richness of his work that it had the potential for still further variation if coupled with real formal extensions. It is not surprising that he was reported in later years to be improvising longer and longer solos; but that would only have been a beginning. The words Hodeir ascribed to him, "There's too much in my head for this horn,"[21] are entirely appropriate, and provided we believe jazz to have any kind of meaningful unity, the complexities imply not just an answering ensemble style but larger overall structures. Hence Parker's brushes, however inconclusive, with Edgard Varèse and Stefan Wolpe.

The further and faster he recedes from us in time the greater does his stature appear. But the light by which he searched was also the fire that consumed him. For a while, as they say in *The Winter's Tale*, "all men's ears grew to his tunes," but familiarity can spread like poison through our perceptions, and Parker's music, ever ready to scorch our ears with the lasting and unmistakable sound of truth, will always need listening to with care and humility.

PHIL SCHAAP

THE VERVE SESSIONS (1988)
ADAPTED FROM "THE SESSIONS," IN *THE COMPLETE CHARLIE PARKER ON VERVE*, VERVE RECORDS, 1988

Phil Schaap is one of the most devoted and thorough jazz afi-cionados. Although many jazz fans may not know his name, Phil's resourceful work is responsible for many archival jazz discoveries in recent years. His behind-the-scenes production work and atten-tion to detail have been responsible for making many jazz reissues definitive rather than merely well chosen. For his efforts, Phil has received Grammy awards for production, engineering, and liner

21. André Hodeir, *The Worlds of Jazz* (New York: Grove Press, 1972), p. 72.

note writing. In addition, he is an expert on the music and life of Charlie Parker. Phil's Bird Flight *radio program has aired on New York's WKCR since 1970. Phil also teaches the course* Jazz in American Society *at Princeton University.*

This piece is adapted from a much longer (and highly recommended) essay in the ten-CD set, The Complete Charlie Parker on Verve. *Charlie Parker recorded too much material for Norman Granz's Clef and Norgran (and later Verve) labels to be surveyed in full here. Instead, I've chosen and edited Phil's descriptions of ten Parker-Granz sessions, one for each of Parker's nine years of affiliation with Granz, with an extra session included for the year 1953.—CW*

MONDAY JANUARY 28, 1946—JAZZ AT THE PHILHARMONIC— Philharmonic Auditorium, Los Angeles

BIRD, alto saxophone; Al Killian, trumpet; Willie Smith, alto saxophone; Lester Young, tenor saxophone; Billy Hadnott, bass; Lee Young, drums. Plus Dizzy Gillespie, trumpet; Mel Powell, piano; on "Sweet Georgia Brown"; Howard McGhee, trumpet; Arnold Ross, piano; on all other items.

Norman Granz's first concert of 1946 was an expanded presentation. Granz was producing the Down Beat Award Winners Concert. In reality, this meant the standard Jazz at the Philharmonic jam session plus a few added superstar attractions and an awards ceremony at intermission (when the 1945 Down Beat trophies would be distributed). This was the first time Charlie Parker ever played for Norman Granz.

"Lady Be Good" left the most lasting impression on the jazz world. Charlie Parker plays two stunning choruses. Bird had done his early woodshedding by mimicking Prez' early recordings, and even in Parker's last years, he would toss off all sixty-four bars of Lester's first classic "Lady Be Good" improvisation—and at triple tempo—as a dressing room warm-up. But here, in front of the master creator, Charlie Parker eschews any lick, riff, or quote from Young's famous version and creates his own masterpiece. It remains the most popular of Parker's JATP improvisations. (Two generations of musicians have copied Bird's solo and vocalist Eddie Jefferson set lyrics to it, recording it as "Disappointed" with James Moody.) Most amazing here, is that the participating players know the worth of Parker's solo instantaneously: after Bird finishes, nobody dares follow him. Pianist Ross had already soloed and a drum solo at this juncture would be quite odd, so for the first time, Jazz at the Philharmonic has a bass solo (by Billy Hadnott), and a long one at that.

All this is, of course, entirely unplanned; but off-stage Howard McGhee, Al Killian, and Willie Smith are plotting. Since they feel that only Lester Young among them can answer Bird's "Lady Be Good" they shove Prez on stage. Again we hear applause for a musician's surprise entry from the wings. As Prez approaches the bandstand we can hear his good nature, if not his actual words, in acknowledging this situation. Imagine the magic of Bird and Prez standing together on stage in front of thousands.

DECEMBER 1947—THE JAZZ SCENE
(Carnegie Hall, New York City)

CHARLIE PARKER QUARTET: BIRD, alto saxophone; Hank Jones, piano; Ray Brown, bass; Shelly Manne, drums.
CHARLIE PARKER with NEAL HEFTI ORCHESTRA

Neal Hefti: Going back to the original Jazz Scene conception. Norman Granz came to seven or eight people and told them to write anything they wanted for this upcoming limited edition *album*—before LPs, an album combined 78 RPM discs; in this instance *12 inch*. Anyone could do anything they wanted to with an orchestra of any size, within reason. They only had to do one tune. He was going to sell it for maybe fifty dollars which in those days was a hell of a lot of money, and he was only going to do ten thousand albums and he was going to number each one. It was really [a] limited edition—sort of a snob appeal album. Everyone throughout the year did their one side wherever they were. Ralph Burns, Duke did his, George Handy did his, Flip Phillips did his, Machito did his, and whoever he engaged to do this one side. I was in New York in the month of December 1947 and there was to be a record strike as of January 1, 1948—which there was—the AFM went on strike against recording. So Norman Granz booked a date for the one side, just the one side! That is in the album under the name of "Rhumbacito." He asked me about two days before if I could come up with two other sides for a 10 inch single; as long as the orchestra was there "as long as you got this group there." We recorded it at Carnegie Hall because every other studio in town was totally booked, because of the upcoming record strike. In fact, I think we even started close to eleven o'clock or at midnight so that we could hire some musicians, because they were all booked up. . . .
The first tune I did was the Bill Harris single side. They were going to go

back-to-back "Repetition" and Bill Harris'. I called it "Chiarina" which was Frances' [Hefti's wife] Italian name. So we did that first as sort of an easy warm-up and then I did the "Rhumbacito" which was sort of like a suite. We had about 15 minutes left to do the other side of the proposed single and that was "Repetition" which was just the way it is without the Charlie Parker solo. We went through and sort of reprised the first chorus a little bit and then I had a sort of ending, etcetera. We ran it down a couple of times and Norman came over and said 'Charlie Parker is here. Can you use him?' I said I really hadn't planned it for any kind of soloist but if he wants to just jam over the last chorus when we reprise the melody, there's no problem. I didn't even have a title for it and called it, as a working title, "Repetition" because we went back and repeated the first chorus.

Manny Albam: We started working on "Repetition." And Bird kind of walked in in his overcoat and he had his horn case and he walked into the house rather than on stage. He kind of just looked around and he looked at the band . . . I was looking down at the music and suddenly I heard Bird playing it. I thought he was just coming in to listen to the date.

Another thought is, why would Bird walk in Carnegie Hall—and with his horn—after twelve midnight? Well, Norman Granz needed one side of Charlie Parker for his *Jazz Scene* and it too had to be recorded before the strike. In hiring Carnegie Hall Recording Services, Granz had set up two sessions: Charlie Parker in a quartet upstairs in the recital hall and the large Neal Hefti Orchestra on the actual Carnegie Hall stage. The drummer for both bands was Shelly Manne.

Norman Granz got a usable take of the "The Bird" (based on Eddie Durham's "Topsy") before Manne went downstairs. When Norman gave up trying to record Bird in a drumless trio, he came down to supervise the end of Hefti's session. Bird was with him and you know what happened. With no part for Bird, Hefti might well have turned over the score to Parker. Violinist and concertmaster Gene Orloff remembers vividly:

It was the most phenomenal thing I ever saw. The lead sheet for him or whatever he had to blow changes on was spread out, a sheet of about ten pages and he had it strewn out over the piano. He was like bending down then lifting his head up as the music passed by, reading it once or twice until he memorized those changes and then proceeded to become godly.

MONDAY DECEMBER 20, 1948—CHARLIE PARKER, SOLOIST, And MACHITO AND HIS ORCHESTRA—*Recording Studio, New York City*

The important merger of Jazz and Latin music reached a pinnacle when Charlie Parker was featured with Machito and His Orchestra. On two separate occasions (8/73 and shortly before his death on 4/15/84) Machito said that working with Charlie Parker was his greatest thrill and the highlight of his career.

Most of the arranging and some of the composing for Machito was done by Mario Bauza, his brother-in-law and musical director. Bauza's vision had been the blending of African and Cuban music, a triumph he furthered by fusing it to jazz. Mario remembers that Norman Granz had become a fan of the Machito Orchestra and introduced the idea of recording it with Parker, among other jazz stars.

> I had no material, no special material for these people. When number one for recording, they just came in there: "Let's make a head arrangement recording." And I said, no-no-no-no No. I cannot do that. So Charlie said to me, "Well Mario bring me something home, that stuff that you all play, regular Cuban music." I remember I say, "But all I have is vocalists." He said, "Never mind let me hear it." So, I played him, I gave him "Mangue." He said "I goin' play that. The only thing, when the vocal chorus come just give me the cue and I'll play through there myself."

WEDNESDAY NOVEMBER 30, 1949—CHARLIE PARKER WITH STRINGS

BIRD, alto saxophone; Mitch Miller, oboe, possibly English horn; Bronislaw Gimpel, Max Hollander, Milt Lomask, violins; Frank Brieff, viola; Frank Miller, cello; Myor Rosen, harp; Stan Freeman, piano; Ray Brown, bass; Buddy Rich, drums; Jimmy Carroll arrangement, conductor.

Charlie Parker: When I recorded with strings, some of my friends said "Oh, Bird is getting commercial." That wasn't it at all. I was looking for new ways of saying things musically. New sound combinations.

This date's first selection, "Just Friends," was Parker's biggest single. The collection of all six titles on three 78s in a binder became a hit album. But some purists felt Bird had sold out, and they have influenced a generation of record buyers to such an extent that these wonderful recordings have been passed over for too many years.

Charlie Parker was fascinated with classical music and totally in awe of symphony musicians. His exposure to Stravinsky and Bartók as well as Beethoven, Brahms, and Bach, however limited, motivated him to bridge two worlds. His need to prove his own worth as a player pushed him towards a meeting where he would play with classical music's great craftsmen and technicians. This insecurity of Parker's led to this famous showdown in the fall of 1949. It is an important story. It was a musical triumph for Charlie Parker.

Norman Granz chose to honor Bird's request for strings. He called Mitch Miller (yes that Mitch Miller) and assigned the A&R work to him. Miller had a childhood buddy, Jimmy Carroll, whom Miller felt would make the right arrangements for standards, strings, and soloist. Miller's selections for the strings included Max Hollander (Lorin's father), cellist Frank Miller (Toscanini's first chair, who taught Leonard Rose who taught Yo-Yo Ma), and violist Frank Brieff who became a successful conductor. The rhythm section would have to swing, so Granz regulars Ray Brown and Buddy Rich were recruited, but Mitch Miller chose a studio man, Stan Freeman, to play piano. Freeman also played jazz and, in fact was the only other soloist. Rehearsals were foregone and the arrangements were simply run down at the sessions.

Violist Frank Brieff describes the final session:

He somehow just astounded all of us by his great method of improvisation. And of course we had arrangements. He just played around with it all the time. Sometimes we would repeat it a few times and he changed every time with his improvisations until he liked what he heard. He was a shy individual. He had a marvelous tone. Playing with the strings as he did at that time was something new. He had always been involved with brass, trumpets and trombones. The thing that touched me, he was really so proud to have us there because apparently he was told about us and what we had done in the music world. He felt that we were greater musicians than he was and that wasn't true at all. He had a great regard for us, it was very sweet. He was, himself, an extraordinary man in the sense that he did things and he didn't know how and why he did them. He had such innate quality that was really marvelous. It reminded me very much of the time I asked Maestro Toscanini one day, I said, "Maestro, do you teach conducting?" and he looked at me and said, "No, conductors are born, they are not made." Up to a certain point that is true of any kind of art. You can develop a wonderful technique but there is something that is born with you that is there or it isn't there. And he had this marvelous quality, this Charlie Parker.

TUESDAY JUNE 6, 1950—CHARLIE PARKER AND HIS ORCHESTRA—
Recording Studio, New York City

BIRD, alto saxophone; Dizzy Gillespie, trumpet; Thelonious Monk, piano; Curly Russell, bass; Buddy Rich, drums.

Bebop reached its pinnacle when Dizzy Gillespie and Charlie Parker performed in a quintet, specifically the quintet which played 52nd Street and made historic recordings during 1945. This session is an update on these two giants in the same type of group.

It is also a reunion—sixty percent of that 52nd Street band is present. But now a unique co-conspirator in the bebop revolution is at the piano. We shall always be thankful that Charlie Parker hired Thelonious Monk for this session. These are the only recordings Monk made from July 1948 to July 1951. Happily, it is also a brief period in Dizzy's career when he is not bound by contract to another label. These are the last studio recordings of Bird and Diz together.

Enthusiasts are always interested in the meaning of the song titles. Here, most can be explained. At the time jazz DJs were being celebrated in song by jazz artists. (Lester Young cut "Jumpin' with Symphony Sid," for example.) "Bloomdido" is for a broadcaster named Bloom. Charlie later tried to convince his manager, violinist Ted Blume, that "Bloomdido" was written and named for him. Ted had learned to spot a put-on by Bird and questioned the spelling. Parker replied that these kinds of errors were common in the record business. When Parker with Strings was on tour, Blume met Bloom, and once again challenged Parker's false contention that Bird had penned it for Ted. But Charlie sweet talked him so, Blume couldn't be sure. Eventually, Ted Blume learned that "Bloomdido" had been waxed before he'd even met Charlie Parker. "An Oscar for Treadwell" was also named for a jazz radio personality, Oscar Treadwell, who broadcast at the time from Philadelphia. Trumpeter George Treadwell, who led the band at Clark Monroe's Uptown House, has been cited as the inspiration for this tune, but that information is spurious.

When Dizzy Gillespie's Quintet featuring Charlie Parker opened at the Three Deuces on 52nd Street, the bassist was Ted Sturgis. (Curly Russell came in after a week or two.) If this is surprising, it should be known that

Mr. Sturgis was the bassist in Earl Hines' Orchestra when Bird & Diz were members. Ted has always been the bassist of choice for Roy Eldridge who is Dizzy's mentor and an early idol of Yard's. Sturgis' half-century old nickname is "Mohawk," and the third title here is his namesake.

"My Melancholy Baby" is the perennial drunkard's request, and one night in '45 at The Three Deuces, Bird and Diz silenced one by actually playing the old warhorse. They never got over their impromptu performance that night, so it was reprised at this session.

On "Leap Frog," the musicians play a musical game, jumping over each other's blowing—hence the title.

The only mystery is "Relaxin' with Lee." Is it for Cur*ly*, Monk's wife, Nel*lie*, or altoist *Lee* Konitz, whom Bird dug? I have asked all three of these people, but got no 'confirmation.' Recently, I tried the question on Dizzy Gillespie. He replied, "'Bloomdido' is still my favorite."

WEDNESDAY JANUARY 17, 1951—CHARLIE PARKER AND HIS ORCHESTRA

BIRD, alto saxophone; Miles Davis, trumpet; Walter Bishop, Jr., piano; Teddy Kotick, bass; Max Roach, drums.

There are some essential elements to this session. First is the reunion of Miles Davis and Max Roach with Charlie Parker. It is a one-shot deal, just a record date, but its musical significance is increased by the fact that it's a bebop quintet, the way these giants had performed in 1947–48. There is little to suggest any design was at work in reacquainting these players. Miles Davis had spent much of late 1950 in California, during which time he had been arrested and acquitted on a drug charge. Miles returned to New York and took steps to pick-up his career. Parker got Miles this gig, perhaps in an effort to help. Miles Davis soon would have many other record dates as he signed with Prestige, and on the very day of this session(!) began his long series of studio sides for that label. The Clef files seem to suggest that Max Roach was a sub or hired at the last minute.

Miles and Max represent Parker's old guard, his original unit. Walter Bishop, Jr. and the late Teddy Kotick (6/4/28–4/17/86) were new elements in Parker's band and they would stay until the end. Walter Bishop, Jr. agrees with Max's description of how the day went except for "Star Eyes":

The intro, Bird suggested that. That was Bird's intro. I never heard the tune before, I didn't know the tune. So he played it right there, a couple of times.

"Au Privave," the rest of those, he had music paper for Miles and it looked like chicken scratches . . . Bird showed me the melody of "She Rote" then he laid it out for me, how it came out of "Beyond the Blue Horizon."

This date also marks a change back to straight ahead jazz in terms of Norman Granz's presentation of Charlie Parker on disc. But the key element, of course, is the surviving music. "Au Privave," in its initial issue, was gobbled up by young musicians, including Ornette Coleman. Today it is a staple in jazz repertoire. To the public, however, "Au Privave" was the B side and "Star Eyes" the hit. "Star Eyes" must have been important to Charlie Parker as well. He recorded it twice and paid particular attention to the motif which opens and concludes both versions. It's different music here than on the 1950 quartet version, but the idea is the same.

FIRST HALF OF JUNE 1952—NORMAN GRANZ JAM SESSION—*Radio Recorders, 7000 Santa Monica Boulevard, Hollywood, California*

BIRD, alto saxophone; Charlie Shavers, trumpet; Benny Carter, Johnny Hodges, alto saxophone; Flip Phillips, Ben Webster, tenor saxophone; Oscar Peterson, piano; Barney Kessel, guitar; Ray Brown, bass; J. C. Heard, drums.

In 1946, Charlie Parker had appeared on an Armed Forces Radio broadcast show called *Jubilee* with Benny Carter and Willie Smith. But this second Alto Summit finds Johnny Hodges on hand with Bird and Benny "King" Carter.

Although there can be no doubt that Buster Smith is the primary alto saxophonist among Yardbird's various influences, Charlie Parker studied Carter and Hodges intently. He kept up with these definitive swing alto masters throughout his professional career.

Charlie "Bird" Parker loved Johnny "Rabbit" Hodges. Here's Bird's reaction to Rabbit when Duke Ellington's "Passion Flower" was played for him by Leonard Feather in a blindfold test.

(Charlie's face lit up in a beautiful grin as he recognized the altoist.) That was Duke—featuring Johnny Lily Pons Hodges! I always took off my hat to Johnny Hodges 'cause he can *sing* with the horn; oh, he's a beautiful person.

Dizzy Gillespie states that the young Bird was at times grooming himself in the Carter mold. Bird's K.C. chums and Big Apple jamming buddies remember that same period as a real trial for Parker while he tried to out-grow most of his Carterisms so as to forge his own style. Benny Carter has acknowledged jazz's debt to Parkerisms. Before Benny performed Bird's "K.C. Blues" at the 1982 Chicago Jazz Festival, he addressed the audience, stating that Parker was the most important instrumentalist in jazz history.

Norman Granz was responsible for this definitive "Alto Summit." He has been responsible for a lot of amazing musical happenings, but his greatest idea is to place before the public the music that musicians play for their own amazement. That is the concept behind Jazz at the Philharmonic. On these sessions Granz took his famous jams into the 'Land of Hi-Fi.' This was the first of his Norman Granz Studio Jams and the series extended to nine volumes. None, however, gained the currency of this one with its Alto Kings.

MONDAY MAY 25, 1953—CHARLIE PARKER AND HIS ORCHESTRA— DISC 9 TRACKS 7–22—Fulton Recording, New York City

BIRD, alto saxophone; Junior Collins, French horn; Hal McKusick, clarinet; Tommy Mace, oboe; Manny Thaler, bassoon; Tony Aless, piano; Charles Mingus, bass; Max Roach, drums; Dave Lambert Singers, mixed chorus (Dave Lambert, one other male voice, tenors; Jerry Parker, baritone; Butch Birdsall, bass; Annie Ross, at least one other female voice); Dave Lambert, choral arrangement; Gil Evans, instrumental arrangement, conductor.

Gil Evans had a little apartment behind a Chinese laundry on 55th Street in midtown Manhattan. Gil used to let his new friend and new idol crash and stash there. It was the spring of 1947. Bird, back from Camarillo and California, was partying and sitting in on nearby 52nd Street. When Parker was at Gil's, and awake, the two would have important musical discussions. A mutual admiration developed and also a dream.

Gil was in his second stint arranging for the lush, and at times divine, Claude Thornhill Orchestra. The Thornhill sound was built on unconventional instrumentation and the use of a chorus. One of Evans' greatest triumphs was grafting Parker's innovations onto the Thornhill sound without spoiling either. This fusion is the birth of the "Birth of the Cool," Miles Davis' nonet, which borrowed freely from the Thornhill presentation.

Later on Gil Evans would often ponder what would have happened if

Parker had played or recorded with either unit. He shared these thoughts with Charlie Parker. Their dream was to do such a recording. It was on Bird's mind when he was interviewed by Nat Hentoff in the 1/28/53 issue of *Down Beat*.

> I'd like to do a session with five or six woodwinds, a harp, a choral group, and full rhythm section. Something on the line of Hindemith's *Kleine Kammermusik*. Not a copy or anything like that. I don't ever want to copy. But that sort of thing.

Bird was still musing on how he might merge jazz with twentieth century classical music. It was a hope he often expressed. But the kind of "Eureka" which turned his run of "Cherokee" changes into a new music, bebop, eluded him in this search. Whatever was on his mind or in his ear as the synthesis of jazz and classical music, we never got to hear it.

Meanwhile, Gil Evans was already hard at work, Using the instrumentation described by Parker, Evans was not so much striving for some Bird's eye preview of Third Stream as he was toiling at the difficult task of mating Parker to the Thornhill-Davis conception.

Thornhill's band had used a mixed chorus, the Snowflakes, one of whose charter members was the late Buddy Stewart, a friend of Bird's. Evans contacted Dave Lambert, Stewart's musical partner and also a friend of the Yard's, to handle the vocal arrangements. Dave Lambert was a devotee of Willard Robison, while Charlie Parker had been particularly keen on Robison's "Old Folks" since the song was young. This explains its selection. The Dave Lambert Singers were his working unit, kept afloat economically by doing jazz-tinged jingles. Lambert wrote for their voices.

The session has been described as a disaster. Granz was so discouraged that he stopped the session before the fourth title, "Yesterdays," could be taped. They may have been heading towards overtime. Granz had reference lacquers (hand-cut 78s) sent to Evans to select two titles for a single release. ("In the Still of the Night" and "Old Folks" were released on Clef 11100—the latter actually became popular with younger players, who put it in their hard bop repertoire.)

Evans decided to get together with Lambert for a listen. It was a hot day in the early summer of 1953. To keep cool, they put the speaker in the window and went outside to listen on the stoop. Gradually their spirits brightened as their appraisal of the session's worth grew. It wasn't the music or the performance that was flawed—the engineer's balance was wrong. The voices drowned out the ensemble, the jazz rhythm section was lost. (In deference to one of Gil's last wishes, and to the extent this could be compensated for, I tried to remedy this in the remastering.)

Gil Evans and Dave Lambert went to Charlie Parker with this insight. Then, the three of them went to Granz. All three were willing to do the date over again *for free* if Granz would put them back in the studio; an action that also would have rescued the fourth title. Granz refused.

THURSDAY JULY 30, 1953—CHARLIE PARKER QUARTET—DISC 10
—Fulton Recording, New York City

BIRD, alto saxophone; Al Haig, piano; Percy Heath, bass; Max Roach, drums.

Max Roach on "Chi Chi":

> Bird came by my place one morning and I was laboring over this. This is when I was recording, when Mingus and I formed the Debut Company and I did the date with Cou-Manchi-Cou and all that stuff in it. And Bird came by and I said, "Damn!" It was like 3 o'clock in the morning. I lived on 30th Street between 3rd and 2nd Avenues and I had a basement apartment. He'd come by anytime and, of course, I let him in, whatever. He saw me laboring over this goddam music. He said "What 'cha doin?" I said "I got a session I'm producing; my first, myself, tomorrow." So he says, "OK here's a gift." And this is the truth Phil, he sat down at a little kitchen table and a cheap piano—and I wish I had saved that goddam 'script; I never throw anything away—he wrote off the tune like a letter and I did it the next day [4/10/53] with Hank Mobley. We recorded it, then Bird recorded it. That's "Chi Chi."

Bird almost didn't record nothin'! This Charlie Parker Quartet recording session was scheduled from 12:00 Noon to 3:00 P.M. It was a little bit before 1:00 P.M. when Bird's first call came to the studio saying he'd be there in fifteen minutes. Norman Granz came into the studio and told the rhythm trio to take their places. But everybody was cooling it when the second call came from Bird as it neared 1:30 P.M. Again the message was he'd be there in fifteen minutes. Another round of that game was played near 2:00 P.M. and Percy Heath was getting very nervous. Max Roach came over and told Percy Heath what the deal was: that Norman Granz was a right guy, and Bird or no Bird, he'd get his money.

It was pushing 2:15 P.M. when Charlie Parker arrived. Heath was stunned how quickly things got going. The foursome was into the first take of "Chi Chi" before 2:20 P.M. Knowing the circumstances now, you may be wondering why so much of the remaining time was spent on "Chi Chi." Max's version was getting some play so Norman had decided "Chi Chi" would be the plug side from this date. They made an effort to get a timed and flawless take for a single, then moved on at about 2:40 P.M.

Another snag was hit when Charlie Parker called "I Remember You" for the standard. Percy Heath wasn't familiar with it. Al Haig wrote out the changes and fast. Somehow, the quartet nailed it in one take.

With a quarter hour of studio time left, Bird went to the mainstem: his most famous blues, "Now's the Time." Bam! Another tune in a single take. Sticking to staples, Parker called "Confirmation." There were a couple of false steps, but the third time was the charm and "Confirmation" was in the can when the clock struck three.

FRIDAY DECEMBER 10, 1954—CHARLIE PARKER QUINTET— *Fine Recording, 711 Fifth Avenue, New York City*

BIRD, alto saxophone; Walter Bishop, Jr., piano; Billy Bauer, guitar; Teddy Kotick, bass; Arthur Taylor, drums.

Parker assembled the ensemble. He called for "Love for Sale." If you listen to the early takes, it sounds as if possibly Bird was unfamiliar with the tune. But Billy Bauer explains that he was at fault for at least some of the tentative playing:

> I knew the tune and it seemed like the others did too, but I had played it perhaps two or three times professionally. Now I'm recording it with Charlie Parker. I think Parker was using the early takes as a rehearsal, a musical explanation of what he wanted, and at those unsteady moments he's leading us and teaching us. After he was satisfied with "Love for Sale," he explained "I Love Paris" to us because he had something in mind as to how he wanted it presented.

Arthur Taylor also talks about being a little unnerved by the honor of making a record date with Charlie Parker. He was young, and relatively new to recording. He recalls being hired for the session by Walter Bishop, Jr., but otherwise can't offer much insight into why he and not one of the regulars such as Roy Haynes (probably with Sarah Vaughan) or Max Roach (certainly with Clifford Brown) made the date. Taylor—while a member of the Bud Powell Trio—had had quite a few gigs with Bird, but recording with him was a big step. With his own high standards and the precision of his playing, Arthur Taylor was unsettled by the fact that nothing had been discussed or rehearsed beforehand. Knowing Bird, however, he expected things to be that way. So A. T. found his way to Fine Sound, and on the very first tune Bird gave him a long solo!

> I should be going around New York with a sign hanging on me saying "I PLAYED THE LONGEST DRUM SOLO ON ANY CHARLIE PARKER STUDIO RECORDING!!"

A. T.'s long bit notwithstanding, it was an unfortunately short day for Charlie Parker in the studio. The deal with Granz limited it to two tunes, and the vaults only hold dubs for seven surviving takes.

Bird never recorded again.

Reviews: Parker under Others' Leadership

Charlie Parker was reviewed much more often on record than in person. In the 1940s, Metronome *magazine led the way in sympathy toward and understanding of the music of Parker, Gillespie, et al. These reviews from* Metronome *are generally quite insightful and provide a minihistory of Charlie Parker's evolution and the critical reception of it. The magazine's system of rating records from "A" to "D" (with pluses and minuses possible) allowed for quite a few gradations of evaluation. Because most of these records were 78s, each side was usually rated individually, providing even more specificity.—CW*

BARRY ULANOV AND LEONARD FEATHER
DIZZY GILLESPIE (1945)

Metronome, October 1945

These Dizzy Gillespie sides are from a May 11, 1945, session that was the second time that Gillespie had hired Parker for a recording date. Notice that the reviewers, Barry Ulanov and Leonard Feather, write that Parker shows "a striking resemblance to Dizzy . . ." as if Parker was following Gillespie's lead.—CW

"Salt Peanuts"A–
"Hot House"A–
"Shaw 'Nuff"A
"Lover Man"B+

Here at last is a session that brings to records an accurate idea of Dizzy's music. The quintet heard here is the same one Diz had at the Three Deuces this summer, except that Sid Catlett is brought in on drums for the records. The alto man, Charlie Parker, and the pianist, young Al Haig, show a striking resemblance to Dizzy in their improvisations.

"Shaw 'Nuff" is the most amazing and characteristic performance. The ensemble passages are fast, tricky trumpet-and-alto unison, with unexpected dissonances, harmonic and rhythmic subtleties that are typical of the progressive musical thinking for which Dizzy's crowd stands. "Hot House" is an ingenious variation, by Tad [Tadd] Dameron, based on the chords of "What Is This Thing Called Love?" "Salt Peanuts" is simpler than most Dizzy tunes, but with the same phenomenal solo work by Parker and Dizzy, so frantic that it not only takes your breath away, but their own breath too, with the result that some phrases are left clear in mid-air.

"Lover Man" is a vocal side featuring Dizzy's and our favorite new singer, Sarah Vaughan, but she is hampered by the band, which can't possibly give her the full, rich background needed by her full, rich voice. Dizzy's short solo on this side proves that this kind of tempo and tune is not for him. However, it's a good record, at least worth comparing with the Billie Holiday version. Recording good. (Guild 1093, 1002)

BARRY ULANOV AND LEONARD FEATHER
TINY GRIMES–CHARLIE PARKER (1945)

Metronome, October 1945

The Tiny Grimes–Charlie Parker sides were both recorded under Grimes's name on September 15, 1944, but "Red Cross" (Parker's first sole composition to be recorded) was often issued under Parker's name.—CW

"I'll Always Love You Just the Same"C+
"Red Cross"B+

The first side is under Tiny's name, featuring him as ballad vocalist on his own tune. The exciting coupling features Charlie Parker with the same quintet, doing a good riff tune named after a 52nd Street character and not the institution of the same name. Charlie Parker being the greatest new alto sax man of the year, we can't get too much of him; we also like Tiny's guitar and the work of the unnamed rhythm section here. (Savoy 567)

Reviews: Parker's Early Sessions as a Leader

BARRY ULANOV, GEORGE T. SIMON, AND LEONARD FEATHER
CHARLIE PARKER'S REE BOPPERS (1946)
Metronome, March 1946

This November 26, 1945, session for the Savoy label was Parker's first as a leader. Parker's solos on these sides have for years been considered classics of modern jazz, but these reviewers didn't see such potential. Parker's reed does squeak a bit (the saxophonist's trouble with his horn has been described by Savoy producer Teddy Reig), but Parker's two blues solos have stood the test of time and have been transcribed and studied by generations of saxophonists up to today. The "Dizzy disciple" trumpeter referred to was Miles Davis. Although he was still in the process of putting his style together, Davis's solos here already show an individual approach which does not really resemble an imitation of Dizzy Gillespie's "faults."—CW

"Now's the Time" C+
"Billie's Bounce" C+

Parker's Ree Boppers, as they are so aptly named, were in a bad slump when they made this pair. Charlie plays some inspired alto, but messes it up with a squeaky reed and slipping fingers. The rhythm section is poorly recorded. Worst of all, the trumpeter is a young Dizzy disciple who succeeds only in imitating all the faults of his mentor and none of the virtues. The result is a sound that's nothing short of miserable. Drummer Max Roach was off on this date, too. (Savoy 573)

BARRY ULANOV, GEORGE T. SIMON, AND LEONARD FEATHER
CHARLIE PARKER'S RI BOP BOYS (1946)

Metronome, May 1946

This famous recording was also made at the same November 26, 1945 session that produced "Now's the Time" and "Billie's Bounce." This side was coupled with a Don Byas track (also reviewed, but omitted here). The reviewers are correct to point out that Dizzy Gillespie plays both trumpet and piano, and they have a point that it's hard to hear the piano's chords. But surely this record is more than just a "phenomenal illustration of how Parker can run unusual chord changes at a fantastic tempo." Yes, Parker's solo is stunning; but it is also highly inventive and deeply moving. Max Roach is taken to task for his allegedly "horrible, utterly beatless drum solo," but his solo does in fact have order and logic, being a half-chorus in length (thirty-two bars; according to Parker scholar Thomas Owens, Roach omits one beat in his solo). These normally insightful reviewers seem to have paid more attention to presentation and less to content.—CW

"Ko Ko" B

Another weird product from the date that produced "Now's the Time" and "Billie's Bounce," reviewed in March. We omitted to mention that the pseudonymous "Hen Gates" who played piano on those sides was really Dizzy Gillespie. On "Ko Ko," label info to the contrary, there is no Miles Davis trumpet; it is Dizzy who plays both the trumpet and piano parts. The tune is not the old Ellington opus of the same name. It's a series of mad improvisations by Parker's alto on the chords of "Cherokee," though the recording covers up the rhythm section's chords so completely that you'd hardly know it. With better discipline on the part of the men, and without that horrible, utterly beatless drum solo by Max Roach, this could have been a great side. Even as it is, it has some phenomenal illustrations of how Parker can run unusual chord changes at a fantastic tempo. (Savoy 597)

GEORGE T. SIMON AND LEONARD FEATHER
CHARLIE PARKER (1946)

Metronome, November 1946

Metronome *briefly abandoned its usual rating system and adopted a simplified star system (two stars: "highly recommended"; one star: "recommended"; and no stars for all other records). These Parker recordings received no stars. They were recorded at the tragic July 29, 1946, Los Angeles session that Howard McGhee described in his recollections of Parker earlier in this anthology. In a short article in* Down Beat *("My Best on Wax," June 29, 1951), Parker said, "If you want to know my worst on wax, though, that's easy. I'd take 'Lover Man,' a horrible thing that should never have been released—it was made the day before I had a nervous breakdown. No, I think I'd choose 'Be-Bop,' made at the same session, or 'The Gypsy.' They were all awful."—CW*

"Be-Bop"[no stars]
"Lover Man"[no stars]

This is by no means the best bebop available. The first is fast and surfacey, pop-corny in effect, but with little to hold it together. The slower reverse is very confusing, with Parker missing entrances, etc. Apparently it was recorded shortly before the great altoist suffered his nervous breakdown. Jimmy Bunn's piano is the only saving grace of examples that don't do the new jazz form one bit of good. (Dial 1006)

Reviews: The Classic Quintet

In 1947, when Charlie Parker returned to New York City from his California hospitalization, he assembled his first long-term working group. Later dubbed his "classic quintet," this group always included Miles Davis (trumpet) and Max Roach (drums), and usu-

ally had Duke Jordan (piano) and Tommy Potter (bass). The classic quintet recorded for both the Savoy and Dial labels; here are four of the Dial sides (one with an added player).—CW

BARRY ULANOV, BARBARA HODGKINS, AND PETER DEAN
CHARLIE PARKER (1949)

Metronome, February 1949

In this review, "Bongo Bop" is praised, but regarding "Embraceable You," it's unfortunate that the reviewers focus on Parker's occasional minor reed squeaks (which suggests that this is take B; both A and B takes at various times appeared on Dial 1024) and not his rich improvisation. In later years, the first take has become the more famous version because of Parker's use of thematic improvisation.—CW

"Bongo Bop"B–
"Embraceable You"C+

Mystifyingly cloaked under its title, "Bongo Bop" offers no bongo and more straight blues than bop. Charlie himself in fine form, Miles Davis effective, pianist Duke Jordan much less than that. Reverse shows Bird reeding badly, achieves its only distinction in Miles' departure from the cloying melody (says Deuce Ulanov—Deuce Simon is not moved, Deuce Hodgkins is only a little pleased). (Dial 1024)

BARRY ULANOV, BARBARA HODGKINS, AND GEORGE T. SIMON
CHARLIE PARKER (1950)

Metronome, May 1950

Ross Russell, the owner of the Dial label, later discovered Parker's handwritten title for the composition reviewed here. Its correct title is "Klact-oveeseds-tene." The reviewers characterize

Parker's solo on that song as "fragmentary," but since this review was printed, jazz writers have praised Parker's creative use of sound and silence and the way that his initially discontinuous phrases lead to longer lines and greater continuity. Once again, Roach is criticized, this time for drowning out the piano. In his Parker book Bird Lives!, Ross Russell explained, "Special care was taken to install a tiny high-frequency microphone to catch the hiss of Max Roach's cymbal." It's interesting that the previously maligned Miles Davis (see the reviews of "Now's the Time" and "Billie's Bounce" earlier in this anthology) and J. J. Johnson (who makes "Charlie's Wig" a sextet) garner more praise than Parker.—CW

"Klactoveedsedstene" [sic] B–
"Charlie's Wig" B–

There's probably some deeply esoteric meaning to the first title, but we had neither time nor inclination to puzzle it out. Charlie's somewhat fragmentary alto, Miles Davis's neatly articulated long lines, Duke Jordan's tentative piano are all but obliterated by Max Roach's drums. The "Wig" is blown rather sloppily, with Parker again disappointing, Davis again pleasing, J. J. Johnson likewise. (Dial 1040)

Reviews: Norman Granz Recordings

By late 1948, Charlie Parker had ended his affiliation with the Dial and Savoy labels, and he recorded almost exclusively for producer Norman Granz from 1949 through 1954. Granz first worked for mainstream label Mercury, then founded his own labels, originally Clef and Norgran; these recordings were later reissued on Granz's Verve label. Granz was a strong supporter of Parker and at one point in the 1950s even paid the saxophonist a regular stipend. Granz seldom recorded Parker with his regular working groups and instead preferred to present Parker in a wide variety of musical settings, some quite inspiring and some less so. In a November 1979 Down Beat article, Granz explained that philosophy: "I think these shifting combinations bring out fresh dimensions in an established artist."—CW

BARRY ULANOV, BARBARA HODGKINS, AND GEORGE T. SIMON
CHARLIE PARKER AND STRINGS (1950)

Metronome, August 1950

This November 30, 1949 session for Granz was the saxophonist's first with a string section. Earlier in the year, Parker had performed at the International Festival of Jazz in Paris; the French treated Parker as an artist more than an entertainer and perhaps that encouraged him to ask Granz for an ensemble combining a jazz rhythm section and strings, harp, and oboe. Parker was enthusiastic about this repertoire and setting, and defended himself against charges of commercialism in Nat Hentoff's article, "Counterpoint" (see page 79). These selections were issued on an early long-playing album (LP). Apparently, Granz was unhappy with the way his artists were reviewed in Metronome, *as the writers point out here, so they had to purchase the LP themselves to review it.—CW*

"April in Paris"
"Summertime"
"If I Should Lose You"
"I Didn't Know What Time It Was"
"Everything Happens to Me"
"Just Friends"
    album rating B–

Since there is a Granz edict that bans *Metronome* from receiving any review copies of Mercury records that Norman had a hand in, we waited until this best-selling album came out on LP before acquiring it over the counter . . . Better late than never, we're here to state that with the exception of the last side "Just Friends" we're *not* for it. Bird with strings may have seemed like a good idea, and "Just Friends" proves that it could have been. But the club labeled "Play the melody" that was evidently brandished over Charlie's head is all too obvious, and we can't take the emasculated alto sounds that are all too like Rudy Weidoft on a bad day. Jimmy Carroll's writing for strings is skeletal though well-played; Stan Freeman's piano contributions on "April" and "Friends" are pleasant; Ray Brown and Buddy Rich, the only other jazz names, are inaudible; Mitch Miller's oboe which he usually blows good is here an ill wind. "Just Friends," however, is Charlie's bid for freedom of interpretation. Save for a tasteless interpolation of "My Man," it's the usual deft Parker performance of skill and inventiveness, for which it's almost worth acquiring the other five sides. (Mercury MG 35010)

BARRY ULANOV
CHARLIE PARKER (1953)

Metronome, September 1953

This May 25th 1953, session was inspired by Parker's hearing composer Paul Hindemith's Kleine Kammermusik (op. 24, no. 2), as described in Nat Hentoff's "Counterpoint" (see page 79). Instead of Parker's desire to record newly composed music inspired in part by twentieth-century classical music, the saxophonist evidently compromised with Norman Granz and recorded an American popular song repertoire. In Robert Reisner's Bird: The Legend of Charlie Parker, *Max Roach is quoted as saying: "He [Parker] mapped out things for woodwinds and voices, and Norman Granz would holler, 'What's this? You can't make money with this crazy combination. You can't sell this stuff!'" Phil Schaap describes in detail how this session was recorded in his notes to "The Verve Sessions" (see page 225).—CW*

*"In the Still of the Night"*B–
*"Old Folks"*B–

Charlie accounts for himself very well in his fragmentary alto bursts here and there amid voices (Dave Lambert's) and arrangements (Gil Evans') which clutter his way all the way through both sides. (Mercury 11100)

CHARLIE PARKER (1955)

Metronome, April 1955

This late December 1952 or early January 1953 recording was not Parker's last for Granz, but it was the last to be assigned for review by Metronome *before Parker's death. It appeared in the April 1955 issue, which went to press before Parker died on March 12th. Parker's playing is quite strong and he is evidently inspired to be recorded in a small combo setting with lots of room to improvise. Finally Max Roach is praised for his percussion work!—CW*

"Cosmic Rays"A–
"Kim"B

If you want, give "Kim" one-half a plus because it's meaty, furiously uptempo Bird with good Hank Jones and fabulous Max Roach (Teddy Kotick's bass is a fine complement to Max, too). But it doesn't hang together, or get the feeling that "Rays" does.

Few people can create at "Kim's" tempo but fewer can touch the wailing Bird on the first side, a pronouncement, a preaching if you want, on those rays, with all the sharp edges bitingly present. And then, just after Max's extraordinary, *melodic* solo, Bird ends the sermon on a pensive note. (Clef 89129)

PART EIGHT

Ornitholog

STANLEY CROUCH
BIRD LAND (1989)

Charlie Parker, Clint Eastwood, and America.

The New Republic, February 27, 1989

This piece, which originally appeared in The New Republic, *is much more than a review. The occasion was the release of director Clint Eastwood's film* Bird. *In some respects the movie was accurate to Parker's biography, and in some ways it took defendable liberties with his story for the sake of cinematic drama, but in significant ways the film either altered important facts or emphasized aspects of Parker's life that had the effect of giving a narrow view of the saxophonist. Here, Crouch uses* Bird *as a starting point to discuss Parker in a larger context, touching on racism, artistry, addiction, and other topics.*

(Note: the "unpublished" Chan Parker memoir, referred to here as My Life in E-flat, *has been issued by the Parisian publisher Plon in a French translation entitled* Ma Vie en mi bémol.*)—CW*

In the red and purple bric-a-brac that often passes for jazz criticism or jazz scholarship, Charlie Parker looms large. He is the rebel angel speared by the marksmen of the marketplace, and by the grand conspiracy of robed and unidentified klansmen. Parker was truly one of the most mysterious figures in American art. Six years ago I began the bedeviling job of writing Parker's biography. It quickly became clear that much of what was taken for granted about the alto saxophonist was a mix of near-truth, fabrication, and butt-naked lies.

Over the last few years, culminating in Clint Eastwood's very bad film *Bird*, there has been more attention than usual shown to Parker. Almost everything he ever recorded is now available, some of it reworked for sound vastly superior to the original releases. There is a coffee table book, a video documentary, and a stack of glowing reviews of *Bird* that reveal the extent to which many who would be sympathetic to Negroes are prone to an unintentional, liberal racism. That racism reduces the complexities of the Afro-American world to a dark, rainy pit in which Negroes sweat, suffer, dance a little, mock each other, make music, and drop dead, releasing at last a burden of torment held at bay only by drugs.

It must be that melodramatic notion of suffering that makes Eastwood's film so appealing. Many film critics appear to have the same problem with the depiction of Negro life that many literary critics do. Too quick to prove that they really understand the plight of the caged coon, who would be a man if only the white world would let him, they often fall for condescending, ignorant, bestial images of Afro-Americans, feeling for them as visitors to Dr. Moreau's Island did, where the noble beasts of the jungle were mutilated into bad imitations of human beings in the mad surgeon's "house of pain." In *Bird*, Negro life is such an incredible house of pain that the dying Charlie Parker summons up, with one exception, only a montage of negative experience.

The exception is his friend Dizzy Gillespie, who proudly asks an audience just served up some sensational saxophone what they think about it. Otherwise Parker on his deathbed summons up a black doctor predicting that he will die from drugs, a black saxophonist laughing at him, a black musician throwing a cymbal at him in disgust during his early, ineffectual efforts at improvisation. All that remains for him, in Eastwood's account, are images of his smiling, vibrant, white lover Chan, and of his white trumpeter buddy Red Rodney. This is a Charlie Parker in no way connected to, in no way the product of, the Afro-American culture filled with the bittersweet intricacies that were given aesthetic substance so superbly in his music.

The movie makes a perfect companion to Chan Parker's *To Bird With Love*, a huge picture book now out of print that was done with the French archivist and producer Francis Paudras. Artfully organized and intimate (it includes bills, love notes, and poignant telegrams), one would never guess from the book that its author was the last of Parker's four wives, the first two black, the last two white. A famous photograph of Parker with his first wife, Rebecca, whom he married when he was 15, their son Leon, and her subsequent husband Ross Davis is cropped so that Rebecca doesn't exist. Those are the kinds of croppings that abound in Eastwood's film, which reportedly leans heavily on Chan's unpublished memoir, "Life in E-Flat." All of the things that Chan knew little about, or preferred to ignore, remain outside the film.

Though Parker was well taken care of as a child, for example, and was quite attached to his mother, whom he called every weekend, she is only referred to once in *Bird*, when the soothsaying doctor tells that boy he better watch out for that dope. Chan is given a monologue about her own childhood and her own father and asks Parker about his early life, but he tells her in reply only about the day he discovered that he was addicted. So much for the complexity, or the vitality, of *his* past. His second wife, Geraldine, didn't play a large role in his life, and was only married to him a year; but Doris, the third, went to California in 1946 when Parker had a nervous breakdown there, visited him in Camarillo as often as she could, and returned with him in 1947 to New York, where they lived together until 1950. (Though Eastwood's stacking of the deck in Chan's favor elicits a remarkable performance from Diane Venora, there is something distasteful about the film's general slighting of black women, not least in light of Parker's friendships and working relationships with women such as Mary Lou Williams, Sarah Vaughan, and Ella Fitzgerald; only one on-screen speaking part is given to a black female, in a fictitious situation in which Bird recalls being told, when he was working his style out, "Nigger, don't be playing that shit behind me while I'm trying to *sang*.")

This film depicts not Negroes, but Negro props. No wonder, perhaps, in the light of Eastwood's comment to *Newsweek* that because he listened to a lot of rhythm and blues on the radio as a young man, "I think I was really a black guy in a white body." We get the young Parker playing a song flute as he rides on the back of a horse, a teenaged Parker with a saxophone on the porch of an unpainted house, a couple of young Negroes smoking cigarettes near him. Had Parker grown up in New Orleans instead of Kansas City, he would almost certainly have been shown on a cotton bale.

Then the movie flashes forward to Parker in 1945, roaring through the chords of "Lester Leaps In." Forest Whitaker, who plays Parker, has been directed to hump and jerk and thrust his horn outward, exactly as Parker did not. "The thing about Bird," says Art Taylor, a drummer who played with him, "is that he didn't move. He just stood there almost still as a statue, and when he finished, there was a pool of water at his feet" (Whitaker obviously has the talent to get far closer to Bird than he did; but he was not asked to do much more than another version of the Negro manchild.)

Next Parker comes home, high, in 1954, and explains to Chan that he has just been fired from Birdland, the club named for him. As he gives the details, she talks to him as though he is a child who went off without his lock and got his bike stolen. Bird refers to himself as "an overgrown adolescent," angrily taunting her for trying to "work that psychology on him." He swallows iodine, falls to the floor, and Chan stands over him, saying. "That was stupid. Now I'll have to call an ambulance." From that point in the story until its bitter end, despite an outburst here and a joke there, this Charlie Parker is forever under somebody—his wife, his doctors, his agent, the white South, the narcotics police, the court system, the music business. He is always a victim of the white folks, of the iron-hearted colored people, of himself. At best he is an idiot savant, in possession of natural rhythm, with little more than boyish charm and a sense of bewilderment. There is no sign of the sophistication, the curiosity, the aggressiveness, the regality, the guile, the charisma of which all who knew Parker still speak. Eastwood's Parker works only at getting high or not getting high.

Even the world of music is presented as something Bird isn't very involved in, other than as a way of making a living. He shows no real love for the saxophone or for jazz. There is no competitive feeling, no sense of threat, no arrogance, no appreciation of any of his predecessors. (As the pianist Walter Davis, Jr. told me, "You can't have a movie about Bird and not have him run over *somebody*. This was a very aggressive man. He took over and made things go *his* way. If you weren't strong, Charlie Parker would mow you down like grass.") He's just a colored man with a saxophone, a white girlfriend, and a drug problem. When he dies, you are almost relieved.

The critics have made much of Eastwood's love of Parker's art, and even more of the technology that he and his music director Lennie Niehaus used to extract Parker's improvisations from their original recordings so that contemporary musicians could overdub them for today's sound. That accomplishment, however, was a catastrophic mistake. The splendid remasterings that Jack Towers and Phil Schapp have done with Parker's own work on Savoy and Verve are vastly superior to this gimmicky, updated sound track. On the CD versions of *Savoy Original Master Takes* and *Bird: The Complete Charlie Parker on Verve*, there are aesthetic details never heard before. Moreover, as Doris Parker said to Eastwood after a screening of *Bird* at the New York Film Festival. "Charlie didn't play by himself. When you take him away from his real musicians, you destroy what inspired him to play what he did." What the musicians play on Eastwood's sound track is often incompatible, in fact, with what Parker's alto is doing; the music is mixed so high that the saxophone almost never rises above the background, and the drummer, John Guerin, does *not* swing.

The life of Charlie Parker was a perfect metaphor for the turmoil that exists in this democratic nation. It traversed an extremely varied world, including everything from meeting and talking with Einstein to attending parties with Lord Buckley where Communists tried to turn him. Parker was at once the aristocracy and the rabble, the self-made creator of a vital and breathtakingly structured jazz vernacular and an anarchic man of dooming appetites. He was always trying to stay in the good graces of those stunned by his disorder. His artistic power was almost forever at war with his gift for self-destruction. He was dead in 1955, at 34, his remarkable musical gifts laid low by his inability to stop fatally polluting and tampering with the flesh and blood source of his energy, with his own body.

Those musical gifts made it possible for Parker to evolve from an inept alto saxophonist, a laughingstock in his middle teens, to a virtuoso of all-encompassing talent who by the age of 25 exhibited an unprecedented command of his instrument. His prodigious facility was used not only for exhibition or revenge, moreover, but primarily for the expression of melodic, harmonic, and rhythmic inventions, at velocities that extended the intimidating relationship of thought and action that forms the mastery of improvisation in jazz. In the process, Parker defined his generation: he provided the mortar for the bricks of fresh harmony that Thelonious Monk and Dizzy Gillespie were making, he supplied linear substance and an eighth note triplet approach to phrasing that was perfectly right for the looser style of drumming that Kenny Clarke had invented.

The anomalies are endless. He performed on concert stages as part of Norman Granz's Jazz at the Philharmonic, traveling in style and benefitting from Granz's demand that all his musicians receive the same accommodations, regardless of race; but when he was at the helm of his own groups, Parker was usually performing in the homemade chamber music rooms of nightclubs. "One night I'm at Carnegie Hall," he once told the saxophonist Big Nick Nicholas, "and the next night I'm somewhere in New Jersey at Sloppy Joe's." These shifts of venue paralleled the contrasts in his personality. The singer Earl Coleman, who first met Parker in Kansas City in the early '40s, said of him:

> You could look at Bird's life and see just how much his music was connected to the way he lived. . . . You just stood there with your mouth open and listened to him discuss books with somebody or philosophy on religion or science, things like that. Thorough. A little while later, you might see him over in a corner somewhere drinking wine out of a paper sack with some juicehead. Now that's what you hear when you listen to him play: he can reach the most intellectual and difficult levels of music, then he can turn around—now watch this—and play the most low down, funky blues you ever want to hear. That's a long road for somebody else, from that high intelligence all the way over to those blues, but for Charlie Parker it wasn't half a block; it was right next door. . . .

It was not Parker's scope, however, but his wild living, and his disdain for the rituals of the entertainment business, that made him something of a saint to those who felt at odds with America in the years after World War II, who sought a symbol of their own dissatisfaction with the wages of sentimentality and segregation. Parker was a hero for those who welcomed what they thought was a bold departure from the long minstrel tradition to which Negroes were shackled. He was, for them, at war with the complicated fact that the Negro was inside and outside at the same time, central to American sensibility and culture but subjected to separate laws and depicted on stage and screen, and in the advertising emblems of the society, as a creature more teeth and popped eyes than man, more high-pitched laugh and wobbling flesh than woman.

Parker appeared at a point in American history when that bizarre image of the Negro had been part of many show business successes: minstrelsy itself, the first nationally popular stage entertainment; *Birth of a Nation*, the first epic film and "blockbuster"; "Amos 'n' Andy," the most popular radio program since its premiere in 1928; *The Jazz Singer*, where Jolson's Jacob Rabinowitz stepped from cantorial melancholy into American optimism by changing his name to Jack Robbins, changing the color of his face, and introducing the recorded voice to film; *Gone With the Wind*, Atlanta's plantation paradise lost; not to mention the endless bit parts in all the performing arts that gave comic relief of a usually insulting sort, or that "realistically" showed Negro women advising lovelorn white girls in their boudoirs. Parker offered an affront to that tradition of humiliation.

In fact, the jazzmen who preceded Parker had also addressed the insults of popular culture, and countered those stereotypes with the elegant deportment and the musical sophistication of the big bands. Parker turned his back on those bands, though; and not only because he preferred five-piece units. Manhandling the saxophone and Tin Pan Alley ditties, writing tunes that were swift and filled with serpentine phrases of brittle bravado, arriving late or not at all, occasionally in borrowed or stolen clothes so ill-fitting that the sleeves came midway down his forearms and the pants part way up his calves, speaking with authority on a wide variety of subjects in a booming mid-Atlantic accent, Parker nicely fit the bohemian ideal of an artist too dedicated to his art to be bought and too worldly to be condescended to. (Except, of course, when he chose himself to mock his own identity, as when he stood in front of Birdland dressed in overalls and announced to his fellow players that he was sure they must be jazz musicians because they were so well dressed.)

Historically, Parker was the third type of Afro-American artist to arrive in the idiom of jazz. Louis Armstrong had fused the earthy and the majestic, and had set the standards for improvisational virtuosity and swing, but he was also given to twisting on the jester's mask. Duke Ellington manipulated moods, melodies, harmonies, timbres, and rhythms with the grace of relaxed superiority, suavely expanding and refining the art in a manner that has no equal. Armstrong's combination of pathos, joy, and farce achieved the sort of eloquence that Chaplin sought, and Ellington commanded the implications of the Negro-derived pedal percussion that gave Astaire many of his greatest moments. But Parker was more the gangster hero, the charming anarchist that Cagney introduced in *Public Enemy*. The tommy gun velocity of Parker's imagination mowed down the clichés he inherited, and enlarged the language of jazz, but like Cagney's Tom Powers, he met an early death, felled by the dangers of fast living.

In many ways, Parker reflected the world in which he was reared, the wild west town of Kansas City, where everything was wide open and the rules were set on their heads. The mayor and the police were in cahoots with the local mob, liquor flowed during Prohibition and gambling and prostitution were virtually legal. When the musicians went to bed, everybody else was getting up to go to work. Parker's mother was the mistress of a deacon considered an upstanding representative of the life led by those who lived by the Bible. These were, perhaps, the origins of Parker's conviction that finally there was no law, and the double standards of the racial terrain understandably added to that view.

Parker's father was an alcoholic drawn to the night life: his mother left him when the future saxophonist was about nine. Convinced that she could keep young Charlie away from the things her husband loved by giving the boy everything he wanted, she reared him as a well-dressed prince who could do no wrong. That treatment is far from unusual in the lives of Negro innovators. It gives them the feeling that they can do things differently from everyone else. But there was also a crippling side to it. As the bassist Gene Ramey, who knew the saxophonist from about 1934, remarks in the excellent oral history *Goin' To Kansas City*, "He couldn't fit into society, 'cause evidently his mother babied him so much, that he . . . was expecting that from everybody else in the world."

But when Parker, who was known for his laziness, became interested in music in the '30s, he quickly discovered that the gladiatorial arena of the jam session made no allowances for handsome brats in tailor-made J. B. Simpson suits at the height of the Depression. He was thrown off many a stage. It was then that he decided to become the best. As Parker told fellow alto player Paul Desmond in 1953, "I put quite a bit of study into the horn, that's true. In fact, the neighbors threatened to ask my mother to move once when I was living out West. They said I was driving them crazy with the horn. I used to put in at least 11 to 15 hours a day. I did that for over a period of three or four years."

He practiced incessantly, and was in the streets, listening to the great local players. He was drawn especially to Buster Smith and Lester Young, though he told the younger saxophonist Junior Williams that it was when he heard Chu Berry jamming in Kansas City in 1936 that he actually became serious about the saxophone. (So serious, in fact, that he gave his first son Berry's name, Leon.) Berry was swift, articulate, and a great chord player; Smith had deep blues soul; Young preferred a light sound that disavowed the conventional vibrato and invented melodic phrases of spectacular variety and rhythmic daring. Parker was also taken by the trumpeter Roy Eldrige, whom he quotes in an early homemade recording, and studied the harmonic detail of Coleman Hawkins; and he was surely inspired by the unprecedented velocity of the pianist Art Tatum.

Velocity was essential to Parker's life. Everything happened fast. On the night that Joe Louis lost to Max Schmeling in 1936, 15-year-old

Charlie Parker proposed to Rebecca Ruffin and married her a week later. He was a morphine addict by the summer of 1937, which suggests that he may have mixed in an upper-class circle, since there was no heavy drug trade in Kansas City at the time. By January 1938, Parker was a father. He was also anxious to see more of the world and "rode the rails" with hobos later that year, stopping in Chicago, then continuing on to New York, where he arrived with a nickel and a nail in his pocket. It was there that Parker found the beginnings of his own style. In 1940 he returned to Kansas City for his father's funeral and joined Jay McShann's big band, becoming the boss of the reed section and the principal soloist. In a few years he headed the movement that added new possibilities to jazz improvisation and was termed, much to Parker's chagrin, "bebop."

It was during Parker's three years with McShann that the intellectually ambitious personality began to take shape. Parker was interested in politics, mechanics, history, mathematics, philosophy, religion, languages, and race relations. He loved to mimic actors like Charles Laughton, was a prankster and a comic. His problems with dissipation became obvious, too; he told his wife Doris that he had never been able to stop, and recalled that his mother would have to come and get him from a hotel where he was using Benzedrine, staying up nights and going over music. These appetites made him unreliable, and McShann had to send him home for rest often, working with his mother to try and help him handle his addiction.

Parker was also, in fine modernist fashion, a man of masks. Gene Ramey, a member of the McShann band, recalled:

> He shouldn't have been nicknamed Yardbird or Bird Parker; he should have been called Chameleon Parker. Man, could that guy change directions and presentations on you! But he also had a gift for fitting in—if he wanted to. That applied to his music most of all. Bird would sit in anywhere we went—Bob Wills, Lawrence Welk, wherever the local jam session was, anybody that was playing. . . . We used to practice together often, just saxophone and bass. We would take "Cherokee," and he would ask me to tell him when he repeated something so he could meet the challenge of staying fresh and fluent. Bird liked to take one tune and play it for a couple of hours. Then he would know every nook and cranny of the melody and the chords. He was very scientific about those things. Now he might not talk about it, but don't let that fool you into believing he wasn't thinking about it.

But beneath the masks, beneath the obsession with music, the mimicry, and the involvement in the sweep of life, there was a need. McShann says that Parker had a crying soul that always came out in his playing; and his first wife, Rebecca, observed it when he was in his early teens:

> It seemed to me like he needed. . . . He wasn't loved, he was just given. Addie Parker wasn't that type of woman. She always let him have his way, but she didn't show what I call affection. It was strange. She was proud of him and everything. Worked herself for him and all, but, somehow I never saw her heart touch him. It was odd. It seemed like to me he needed. He just had this need. It really touched me to my soul.

The refinement of Parker's rhythm and the devil-may-care complexity of his phrases came to early distinction during those barnstorming years with McShann, in his next job with Earl Hines, and in the laboratory for the new vernacular that was Billy Eckstine's big band. On "Swingmatism" and "Hootie Blues," recorded with McShann in 1941, Parker had already put together the things that separated him from the alto order of the day. His sound is lighter; he uses almost no vibrato; the songful quality of his lines have a fresh harmonic pungence; and his rhythms, however unpredictable, link up with an inevitability that seems somehow to back its way forward through the beat.

When McShann brought his band to New York in early 1942, Parker was able to spend time after hours with the musicians who were stretching the language of jazz uptown in Harlem, usually in Minton's Playhouse or Monroe's Uptown House. "When Charlie Parker came to New York, he had just what we needed," said Dizzy Gillespie. "He had the line and he had the rhythm. The way he got from one note to the other and the way he played the rhythm fit what we were trying to do perfectly. We heard him and knew the music had to go *his* way."

The importance of Parker's jamming with Gillespie, Monk, and the others has often been noted; but the importance of his big band experience cannot be overemphasized. In those bands Parker learned not only how to blend with other musicians and how to lead a section, he also became a master of setting riffs, those spontaneous motifs that were repeated as chants. Riffs were what gave Kansas City's jazz its reputation, they compressed the essence of the music into one vital unit of rhythm and tune. By playing for dancers, Parker discovered the world of rhythms that Afro-American audiences had invented. Backing singers as varied as McShann's blues crooner Walter Brown, the romantic balladeer Eckstine, and the unprecedented virtuoso Sarah Vaughan, Parker had three distinctly different approaches to the voice to draw from, all of which were incorporated into the epic intricacy of his melodic inventions. Jazz had always demanded that the player think and play his ideas with exceptional speed and logic, but Parker proved that everything could be done even faster. Unlike Tatum, Hawkins, and Byas, who were excellent technicians given to harmonically sophisticated arpeggios, Parker was primarily a melodist; his work brought lyricism to the chords and made rhythmic variations that matched the best of Armstrong and Young.

By casting aside vibrato, Parker introduced a sound many considered harsh at the time. But the ballad performances on Warner Bros.' *The Very Best of Bird* (the famous Dial sessions of 1946–47) establish that the hardness of his sound was modified by a charming skill for elucidating the riches of romantic fancy in a way that made his music both spiritual and erotic; this was the romantic talent that drew many women to this disordered but beguiling man from whom a high-minded sense of grandeur was delivered with imperial determination. That imperial aspect was also a part of his music's attraction awesome virtuosity of the sort heard in "Warmin' Up A Riff" or "Ko Ko" is always a protest against limitations. (Both performances are available on *Savoy Original Master Takes*.)

The small, curved brass instrument with cane reed and pearl buttons was throttled and twisted, until it allowed him to express a barely stifled cry that was ever near the edge of consuming rage, the pain of consciousness elevated to extraordinary musical articulation. Bird often sounds like a man torn from the womb of safety too soon. He resented the exposure that music demands, and yet he loved it, because there was no other way he could project himself. But this was no primal scream: the fearful force of Parker's music is always counterpointed by a sense of combative joy and a surprising maturity, by the authority of the deeply gifted. Parker brought the violent rage of the primitive blues (of Robert Johnson, for example) to the citadels of art inhabited by the music's greatest improvisors. For Parker, swing and lyricism were some sort of morale, the bars behind which the beast of hysteria was confined.

Will, in sum, was important to the art of Charlie Parker. He was, after all, a heroin addict. Those who know little about intoxication often fail to realize that the repetition of the condition is what the addicted love most. They seek a consistency that will hold off the arbitrary world. If a few glasses of whiskey, or a marijuana cigarette, or an injection of heroin will guarantee a particular state, the addict has something to rely on. As Parker told Doris, "When you have a bad day, there's nothing you can do about it. You have to endure it. When I have a bad day, I know where to go and what to do to make a good day out of it." Doris Parker also notes that the saxophonist often showed the strength to kick the habit, cold turkey, by himself at home. But the temptations ever present in the night world of jazz always overwhelmed him.

Charlie Parker's early fall resulted more from his way of making "a good day" than it did from race, the economic system, or the topsy-turvy world of his art. It was a tragedy played out along a dangerously complex front of culture and politics, something far more intricate than the crude hipster mythology of Eastwood's *Bird*. It was a fully American story of remarkable triumphs, stubborn misconceptions, and squandered resources that tells us as much about the identity of this country as it does about the powers of jazz.

Chronology

1920

Aug. 29   Born in Kansas City, Kansas to Adelaide and Charles Parker.

ca. 1931

Graduates from Charles Sumner Elementary School in Kansas
City, Kansas (based on the recollection of Rebecca Ruffin
Parker). The Parker family moves to Kansas City, Missouri (this
move may have taken place as early as 1927).
Enters Lincoln High School (this could have taken place in 1932).
Lincoln band director Alonzo Lewis assigns Parker an alto horn.
Parker eventually switches to the baritone horn. Later, he would
settle on the alto saxophone.

1934

April 10   Rebecca Ruffin and her family move into the Parker household at
1516 Olive Street, Kansas City, Missouri. Rebecca and Charlie
begin their courtship.

1935

Begins to play alto sax professionally. Tries to sit in at the Hi Hat
nightclub. Knows all of one song and eight bars of another; debut
is a failure.

June 7   Rebecca graduates from high school; Parker plays for the gradu-
ation ceremony, but does not graduate and instead drops out of
school.

1936

ca. 1936   Tries to sit in with Count Basie's group at the Reno Club. Basie's
drummer rejects Parker by tossing his cymbal at Charlie's feet.

July 25   Marries Rebecca Ruffin.

November   Injured in a car accident on his way to a Thanksgiving job. He suf-
fers a spinal fracture and breaks three ribs. One passenger dies
in the crash.

1937

ca. July	Rebecca first sees Charlie injecting himself with heroin.
Summer	Spends several months playing with George E. Lee's band at a summer resort in Eldon, Missouri. Studies harmony with guitarist Efferge Ware, learns several Lester Young solos note for note, and returns to Kansas City a strikingly better musician. Parker then meets pianist Jay McShann.
Fall	Parker and McShann work with saxophonist Henry "Buster" Smith. Smith becomes a mentor to Parker and also provides a model for Parker's saxophone style.

1938

Jan. 10	Rebecca and Charlie's son, Francis Leon Parker, is born.
mid-1938	Buster Smith leaves for New York City.

1939

Jan.–Feb.	Travels to New York City via Chicago. In Chicago, he is heard by vocalist Billy Eckstine, who is strongly impressed. In New York, Parker washes dishes in a club where Art Tatum often plays.
Dec.	Has a musical breakthrough while playing with guitarist Biddy Fleet at a restaurant in Harlem. He would later say of the moment, "I came alive."
late 1939	Parker and Fleet work in Annapolis, Maryland. Receives word that his father has died.

1940

	Returns to Kansas City in late 1939, or more likely early 1940. Joins the nine-piece group of Jay McShann, stays with the group until mid-1942. Trumpeter Clarence Davis informally records Parker playing solo alto saxophone, probably his first recording. McShann trumpeter Bernard "Buddy" Anderson introduces Parker to trumpeter John Birks "Dizzy" Gillespie, thus beginning a legendary affinity between the two modern jazz innovators. Asks Rebecca to "free him from their marriage." It's unclear if they ever legally divorced.
Aug. 9	An amateur recording is made of Parker with the McShann band at the Trocadero Ballroom in Wichita, Kansas.

1941

April 30	McShann's band makes its first commercial recordings for the Decca label in Dallas, Texas. For the first time, listeners around the country are able to hear Parker's new musical concepts.

1942

Jan.   The Jay McShann big band makes its debut at New York City's Savoy Ballroom.

Renews his acquaintance with Dizzy Gillespie and the two begin playing at New York jam sessions.

late 1942   Either forced to leave or quits the Jay McShann band.

Returns to New York, but retains informal ties to the band until the end of the year.

Dec.   Joins the Earl Hines big band, which already includes Dizzy Gillespie. The band needs a tenor saxophonist, so Parker switches to the larger horn.

1943

Feb.   Gillespie and Parker (playing tenor sax) are informally recorded for the first time while on tour in Chicago.

April 10   Marries Geraldine Scott while the Hines band is on tour in Washington, D. C. It's not clear if their marriage was legal, or later, if they ever divorced.

Around this time, Dizzy Gillespie leaves the band.

Parker leaves the Hines band and returns to Kansas City with his alto sax.

1944

Billy Eckstine, former vocalist with Earl Hines, decides to form a big band based on modern jazz concepts. Dizzy Gillespie signs on; Parker is reached in Chicago and agrees to play alto sax with the band. Joins them in New York.

ca. Aug.   Quits Billy Eckstine big band.

Sept. 15   Hired by guitarist Lloyd "Tiny" Grimes for first commercial recording date away from Jay McShann. Plays saxophone.

1945

Jan. 5   Parker and Gillespie are recorded commercially for the first time on a date led by pianist Clyde Hart. These records are the first chance for most listeners to hear their musical partnership.

Parker and Gillespie freelance around New York, working together whenever possible. When Dizzy leads a group at New York's Three Deuces night club, he chooses Parker to share the front line with him.

Begins to lead his own groups and in the fall hires trumpeter Miles Davis for an engagement at the Spotlite club.

Nov. 26   Makes his first recording under his own name for Savoy. Both Miles Davis and Dizzy Gillespie play trumpet.

Dec.	With Dizzy Gillespie and group, travels by train to Los Angeles to work at Billy Berg's club. This is the first opportunity for the West Coast to hear the modern music from New York.

1946

Jan. 28	Is recorded for the first time by jazz enthusiast Norman Granz, who will later become an important figure in Parker's career; at this Los Angeles concert Parker teams for the first time with his major early saxophone influence, Lester Young.
Feb. 5	Records with Dizzy Gillespie for Ross Russell's new Dial label. Russell will go on to record some of Parker's greatest studio performances.
July 29	Suffering from drug withdrawal symptoms, is barely able to play at a Dial recording session. At his hotel that night, he is arrested by Los Angeles police after a fire breaks out in his room. Ross Russell helps Parker to be committed to Camarillo State Hospital rather than being sent to prison. He is visited by Doris Sydnor, an acquaintance from New York who has moved to Los Angeles to care for him.

1947

late Jan.	Released from the hospital. Remains in Los Angeles for several months.
April 7	Leaves with Doris for New York via Chicago.
April	In New York, forms his most famous group, his "classic quintet." It most often includes trumpeter Miles Davis, pianist Duke Jordan, bassist Tommy Potter, and drummer Max Roach. The Parker quintet plays at Manhattan's Three Deuces night club and records for both Savoy and Dial.
Sept. 29	Appears at a Carnegie Hall concert with Dizzy Gillespie and an all-star group.
Dec.	Makes his first studio recordings for Norman Granz.

1948

	Charlie and Doris Sydnor marry.
Spring	The Parker quintet is included in a Norman Granz Jazz at the Philharmonic (JATP) touring group.
Sept. 3	Makes his first appearance at a new Manhattan night club called the Royal Roost. The club will be the home base for the quintet well into 1949.
Sept. 24	Makes his last recordings for the Savoy label.
Nov.	Joins another JATP tour, this time as a soloist in an all-star group.
Dec. 20	Norman Granz records Parker with the Afro-Cuban jazz band led by Frank "Machito" Grillo. This session marks the beginning of a

| | near-exclusive recording relationship that will last until Parker's death. |
| Dec. | Miles Davis quits Parker's quintet and is replaced by McKinley "Kenny" Dorham. |

1949

May	The Parker quintet flies to Paris for a series of appearances at the Festival International de Jazz. Parker reportedly meets "classical" saxophonist Marcel Mule and philosopher Jean-Paul Sartre. The encounters with receptive French listeners, musicians, and critics influences Parker strongly, and upon his return, he states to <u>Down Beat</u> magazine that he intends to return to Paris to study Western classical music.
Sept.	Joins another JATP tour as part of an all-star group.
Oct.	By this month, trumpeter Red Rodney (born Robert Chudnick) is clearly part of Parker's quintet.
Nov. 30	First records (for Granz) with a string section (violins, viola, cello, and harp), oboe (doubling on English horn), and a jazz rhythm section. This session is the realization of Parker's dream to record with instruments associated with Western classical music.
Dec. 15	Quintet is part of the opening weekend at a new New York night club. It is named Birdland in honor of the saxophonist.

1950

	Quintet breaks up. Parker begins touring more as a "single" (working with local rhythm sections) and with his string group.
May	Begins living with Chan Richardson. Although they do not legally marry, in every other sense this is Charlie's fourth and final marriage.
Sept.–Oct.	Tours the eastern United States as far as Chicago with his string ensemble.
Nov.	Travels to Sweden for a series of concerts accompanied by local musicians. Then flies to Paris for a planned concert but only participates in jam sessions before abruptly returning to New York. Arrested for possession of narcotics, probably near the end of the year.

1951

| | Given a suspended sentence for narcotics possession. As a result, his New York State "cabaret card" is revoked and he can no longer legally work as a leader in New York nightclubs. Makes several tours with his string group in the winter, spring, and fall, traveling as far west as St. Paul. |
| July 17 | Chan and Charlie's daughter, Pree, is born. |

267

1952

Feb. 24   Appears with Dizzy Gillespie on a television program in New York City. As of the publication of this book, the kinescope of this broadcast is the only truly "live" footage of Parker playing. (Parker was filmed at least one other time, but the music was recorded beforehand.)

May–July   Works with various local rhythm sections on the West Coast.

Aug. 10   Chan and Charlie's son, Baird, is born.

1953

                      Succeeds in getting his cabaret card restored.
                      Continues working as a single.

May 5   Appears in Toronto, Canada, with an all-star group including Dizzy Gillespie (trumpet), Bud Powell (piano), Charles Mingus (bass), and Max Roach (drums).

1954

Jan.–Feb.   Parker and Dizzy Gillespie join the Festival of Modern American Jazz and tour from coast to coast. When the tour ends in Los Angeles, Parker remains to work as a single.

March 6   Chan and Charlie's daughter, Pree, dies. Parker returns to New York City. Works in New York and tours the United States with a variety of accompanists.

Aug. 30   Swallows iodine and is admitted to New York's Bellevue Hospital. Readmits himself for emotional problems.

1955

                      Continues to tour and work in New York without a stable group.

March 4   Begins an engagement at Birdland with an all-star group including Kenny Dorham (trumpet), Bud Powell (piano), Charles Mingus (bass), and Art Blakey (drums). The weekend marks one year since the death of Pree, and Parker is in a fragile emotional state.

March 5   When an emotionally disturbed Bud Powell clashes with Parker on the bandstand, the engagement becomes a disaster and Parker leaves the club distraught.

March 12   According to his friend, patron, and ally, Baroness Pannonica "Nica" de Koenigswarter, Parker dies while watching television at her apartment in Manhattan's Stanhope hotel; his corpse showed the effects of a lifetime of narcotic and alcohol abuse. However, rumors soon surfaced that Parker had actually died as the result of a fight elsewhere in New York. More recently it has been suggested that he was shot at the Stanhope. Only de Koenigswarter's story is generally accepted as the truth.

Discography

All recordings are released under Parker's name unless stated otherwise.

Multilabel Compilation (1945–1953)

Yardbird Suite: The Ultimate Charlie Parker Collection, Rhino R2
72260. Although no Parker collection can truly be the "ultimate," this
two-CD set is by far the best Parker compilation. If you are just starting
to explore Parker's music, this is the place to begin. Its greatest strength
is that it includes music from all three of Parker's most important record
labels: Dial, Savoy, and the Verve group. It also has Dizzy Gillespie–led
Guild and Musicraft material and some live performances.
Unfortunately, the Dial recording of "Embraceable You" included is the
"B" take instead of the often-noted "A" take, which prominently uses
thematic improvisation. Highly recommended.

Apprenticeship Recordings (1940–1943)

Young Bird, Volumes 1 and 2, Média 7 MJCD 78/79 (French Import).
With the two Stash releases directly below now out of print, this excel-
lent imported two-CD set is especially worth looking for. It contains all
of the apprenticeship recordings discussed earlier in this anthology (see
pages 187–204) including the most complete version of "Honey &
Body" ("Honeysuckle Rose" and "Body and Soul") available. The
recordings vary in their audio fidelity. Recommended.
The Complete Birth of the Bebop, Stash ST-CD-535 (out of print).
Noncommercial recordings of varying fidelity, primarily pre-1945.
Includes what is thought to be Parker's first recording plus rare record-

ings of Parker playing tenor saxophone. A number of these early solos are lengthy and outstanding.

Early Bird, Stash ST-CD-542 (out of print). Noncommercial recordings of fairly good fidelity, most made by bands led by Jay McShann. Parker's solos tend to be short.

Blues from Kansas City, Decca GRD-614 (cataloged under Jay McShann's name). Studio recordings led by McShann that include short but famous solos by Parker.

Studio Recordings with Dizzy Gillespie (1945)

Shaw 'Nuff, Musicraft MVSCD-53 (cataloged under Dizzy Gillespie's name). Includes seven classic Guild and Musicraft recordings with Parker.

Dial Label Recordings (1946–1947)

The Legendary Dial Masters, Jazz Classics 5003. Here are Parker's excellent "master takes" for the Dial label, arranged chronologically. Reportedly, this set does not include the noted "A" takes of "Embraceable You" or "Klact-oveeseds-tene." Recommended.

The Complete Charlie Parker on Dial, Jazz Classics 5010. This four-CD set contains all of the excellent Dial masters found directly above, plus all of the related alternate takes. For serious Parker aficionados.

Savoy Label Recordings (1944–1948)

Note: As of this publication, Parker's excellent Savoy recordings are available in the United States only as poorly organized Savoy Jazz (Denon) reissues. A few of these are listed here. The best Savoy CD compilation is now out of print (see below, *The Complete Savoy Studio Sessions*).

The Charlie Parker Story, Savoy Jazz SV 0105. Includes the master and alternate takes of Parker's classic 1945 "Billie's Bounce," "Now's the Time," and "Ko Ko."

Charlie Parker Memorial, Volume Two, Savoy Jazz SV 0103. Includes the master takes of "Parker's Mood," "Constellation," "Milestones," and others.

Bird: Savoy Master Takes, Savoy ZDS-8801. This highly recommended two-CD set is unfortunately out of print at the time of this publication.

The Complete Savoy Studio Sessions, Savoy ZDS 5500 (out of print).

Similar in scope to the complete Parker on Dial set described above, this out-of-print three-CD complete Savoy set would be a must for serious Parker fans, if readily available; it is difficult to find as a used set.

Verve/Clef/Norgran Label Recordings (1946–1954)

Bird: The Original Recordings of Charlie Parker, Verve 837 176–2. A good one-CD introduction to Parker's work for Norman Granz's labels (Clef, Norgran, and Verve).
Confirmation: Best of the Verve Years, Verve 314 527 815-2. A more varied and more complete two-CD compilation of Parker's Granz recordings. Recommended.
Bird: The Complete Charlie Parker on Verve, Verve 837 141-2. This well-documented ten-CD set brings together all known Parker recordings for Norman Granz. Because of its many alternate takes, incomplete takes, and some studio chatter, this excellent set is primarily for devoted Parker fans.

Live Recordings

Jazz at Massey Hall, Fantasy OJCCD-044-2. Sometimes cataloged as by The Quintet. A classic 1953 concert in Toronto. Parker is in good form, as are Dizzy Gillespie, Bud Powell, Charles Mingus, and Max Roach. Recommended.

Interviews

The interview with Charlie Parker, Marshall Stearns, John Maher, and Chan Richardson Parker in this anthology has been issued on *Bird's Eyes, Volume Seven*, Philology W 80.2.
The interview with Charlie Parker and John Fitch (aka John McLellan) in this anthology has been issued on *Bird's Eyes, Volume Sixteen*, Philology W 846.2.
The interview with Charlie Parker, Paul Desmond, and John Fitch (aka John McLellan) in this anthology has been issued on *Bird's Eyes, Volume Eight*, Philology W 80.2.

Selected Bibliography

Nontechnical Books

Giddins, Gary. *Celebrating Bird: The Triumph of Charlie Parker*. New York: Beech Tree, 1987. A concise and accurate biography and nontechnical evaluation of Parker's music.

Miller, Mark. *Cool Blues: Charlie Parker in Canada 1953*. London, Ontario: Nightwood Editions, 1989. An account of Parker's two 1953 trips to Montreal and Toronto.

Reisner, Robert. *Bird: The Legend of Charlie Parker*. New York: Citadel Press, 1962. Interviews with friends and colleagues of Parker.

Russell, Ross. *Bird Lives!* New York: Charterhouse, 1973. Colorful but sometimes inaccurate and occasionally fictionalized biography of Parker.

Vail, Ken. *Bird's Diary*. Surrey: Castle Communications, 1996. The events of Parker's life, arranged as a timeline. Includes interviews with Parker, reproductions of Parker autograph materials, photos, and period reviews.

Woideck, Carl. *Charlie Parker: His Music and Life*. Ann Arbor: The University of Michigan Press, 1996. One chapter of biography followed by four chapters of musical discussion, arranged chronologically. Written musical examples are keyed to compact disc timings for easy location.

Chapters on Parker

Feather, Leonard. "Chapter 2," *Inside Be-Bop*. New York: J. J. Robbins and Sons, 1949.

Gitler, Ira. "Charlie Parker and the Alto Saxophonists," *Jazz Masters of the Forties*. New York: Collier Books, 1974 (reissued by Da Capo).

Harrison, Max. "Charlie Parker's Savoy Recordings," *A Jazz Retrospect*. Boston: Crescendo, 1976.

Hodeir, André. "Charlie Parker and the Bop Movement," *Jazz: Its Evolution and Essence*. New York: Grove Press, 1956.

Williams, Martin. "Charlie Parker: The Burden of Innovation," *The Jazz Tradition*. New York: Oxford University Press, 1970.

Technical Studies

Koch, Lawrence O. *Yardbird Suite: A Compendium of the Music and Life of Charlie Parker*. Bowling Green, Ohio: Bowling Green University Popular Press, 1988.
Martin, Henry. *Charlie Parker and Thematic Improvisation*. Lanham, Maryland: Scarecrow, 1996.

Owens, Thomas. "The Parker Style," *Bebop: The Music and Its Players*. New York: Oxford University Press, 1995.

Colleagues and Friends Remember Charlie Parker

Gillespie, Dizzy, with Gene Lees. "The Years with Yard," *Down Beat*, May 25, 1961.
Ramey, Gene. "My Memories of Bird Parker," *Melody Maker*, May 28, 1955.

Fiction and Humor

Grennard, Elliott. "Sparrow's Last Jump," *Harper's*, May 1947.
Perlongo, Robert A. "The Real Story Behind 'Charlie Parker with Strings,'" *Metronome*, August 1960.

Charlie Parker in the Jazz Press

"Bird Wrong; Bop Must Get a Beat: Diz," *Down Beat*, October 7, 1949.
Feather, Leonard. "A Bird's-Ear View of Music," *Metronome*, August 1948.

———. "A Fist at the World," *Down Beat*, March 11, 1965.

———. "Parker Finally Finds Peace," *Down Beat*, April 20, 1955.

———. "Yardbird Flies Home," *Metronome*, August 1947.

Hentoff, Nat. "Counterpoint," *Down Beat*, January 20, 1953.

"The Incredible Story of Parker in Paris," *Melody Maker*, December 9, 1950.

Levin, Michael, and John S. Wilson. "No Bop Roots in Jazz: Parker," *Down Beat*, September 9, 1949.

Permissions

"Parker at Birdland," by George T. Simon. Originally published in *Metronome*, July 1953. Copyright © George T. Simon. Used by permission of the author.

"Charlie Parker's Apprenticeship Recordings, 1940–43," by Carl Woideck. Excerpted from *Charlie Parker: His Music and Life*. Copyright © University of Michigan Press. Used by permission.

"A Rare Bird," by Max Harrison. Used by permission of the author.

"The Verve Sessions," by Phil Schaap. Used by permission of the author and Verve records.

"Dizzy Gillespie," by Barry Ulanov and Leonard Feather. Originally published in *Metronome*, October 1945. Copyright © R. Scott Asen, Metronome Archive. Used by permission.

"Tiny Grimes–Charlie Parker," by Barry Ulanov and Leonard Feather. Originally published in *Metronome*, October 1945. Copyright © R. Scott Asen, Metronome Archives. Used by permission.

"Charlie Parker's Ree Boppers," by Barry Ulanov, George T. Simon, and Leonard Feather. Originally published in *Metronome*, October 1946. Copyright © R. Scott Asen, Metronome Archives. Used by permission.

"Charlie Parker's Ri Bop Boys," by Barry Ulanov, George T. Simon, and Leonard Feather. Originally published in *Metronome*, October 1946. Copyright © R. Scott Asen, Metronome Archives. Used by permission.

"Charlie Parker," by George T. Simon and Leonard Feather. Originally published in *Metronome*, November 1946. Copyright © R. Scott Asen, Metronome Archives. Used by permission.

"Charlie Parker," by Barry Ulanov, Barbara Hodgkins, and Peter Dean. Originally published in *Metronome*, February 1949. Copyright © R. Scott Asen, Metronome Archives. Used by permission.

"Charlie Parker," by Barry Ulanov, Barbara Hodgkins, and George T. Simon. Originally published in *Metronome*, May 1950. Copyright © R. Scott Asen, Metronome Archives. Used by permission.

"Charlie Parker and Strings," by Barry Ulanov, Barbara Hodgkins, and George T. Simon. Originally published in *Metronome*, August 1950. Copyright © R. Scott Asen, Metronome Archives. Used by permission.

"Charlie Parker," by Barry Ulanov. Originally published in *Metronome*, September 1953. Copyright © R. Scott Asen, Metronome Archives. Used by permission.

Index

"Rhumbacito," 227–28
Rhumboogie, 32
rhythm, 20, 34, 214
  Afro-Cuban, 35, 48–49, 229
  Latin, 8, 20, 21, 35, 43, 48–49,
    223, 224, 229
  Parker's innovation in, 14–15, 16,
    17, 19, 21, 203, 207–9, 215,
    220
Rich, Buddy, 21, 229, 230, 231, 245
Rich, Sonny, 107
Richardson, Chan, see Parker, Chan
  Richardson
Richardson, Kim, 52, 82, 100, 107
Riddick, Dave, 75
Rite of Spring, The (Stravinsky), 152
Riverside Records, 45
Roach, Max, 19, 20, 42, 48, 56, 64,
  130, 176, 177, 184, 215, 222,
  232, 234, 236–37, 241, 242,
  244, 246, 247
Robinson, Willard, 235
Rochester, N.Y., 50
Rockets, 28
Rodney, Red, 6, 48, 107, 252
Roland, Gene, 106, 107, 108
Rollins, Sonny, 31, 47–48, 52, 53, 175
"Romance Without Finance," 33, 76
Roost Records, 47
"Rosetta," 218n
Ross, Annie, 234
Ross, Arnold, 226, 227
Ross, James, 95
Rostaing, Hubert, 43
"Round Midnight," 53, 182
Rouse, Charlie, 164
"Route 66," 54
Royal Roost, 31, 66, 210
"Royal Roost," 46
"Rue Chaptal," 46
Rugolo, Pete, 68
"running out of key," 138
Russell, Curley, 33, 65, 131, 165, 182,
  184, 231, 232
Russell, George, 44, 213
Russell, Ross, 37, 40, 41, 42, 58, 63,
  77, 151, 154–55, 160, 176,
  177, 243–44
  Parker's recordings for, see Dial
    recordings of Parker

Russo, Bill, 118
Rutgers University, Institute of Jazz
  Studies at, 142, 151

"St. Louis Mood," 201
salsa bands, 8
"Salt Peanuts," 34, 182, 239
Sandvik, Scott, 208n
Satie, Eric, 210
Saturday Review, 10
Savannah Club, 55
Savoy Ballroom, 6, 30, 62, 76, 125,
  138, 200–201
Savoy Broadcasts, 200–201
Savoy Hotel, 201
Savoy Records, 68
  Parker's recordings for, 20, 25, 33,
    35–36, 42–44, 58, 76, 77,
    105, 176, 177, 187, 198, 201,
    204–25, 239–42, 254,
    270–71
saxophone, see alto saxophone; C-
  melody saxophone; tenor sax-
  ophone
Schaap, Phil, 80, 109, 225–38, 246,
  254
Schildkraut, Davey, 45
"Schnourphology," 223
Schönberg, Arnold, 4, 64, 206
Schuller, Gunther, 8
Scott, Kermit, 163
"Scrapple from the Apple," 18, 19, 43,
  209, 214, 223
Selected Reports in Ethnomusicology,
  224n
"Señor Blues," 216n
"Sepian Bounce" ("Sepian Stomp"),
  30, 65–67, 68, 75–76
"sequencing," 12
"Serpent's Tooth, The," 53
"Seventh Avenue," 104
"Seven-Up," 68
Shavers, Charlie, 30, 233
Shaw, Billy, 35, 64, 182
"Shaw 'Nuff," 6, 34, 72, 182, 239
Shepp, Archie, 213n
"She Rote," 21, 48
"Shoe Shine Boy," 27, 199, 200
Silver, Horace, 216n
Simmons, John, 107

Thompson, Sir Charles, 37, 76
Thornhill, Claude, 234
Three Deuces, 24, 33–34, 63, 126, 130, 165, 231, 232, 239
"Thriving on a Riff," 35–36, 210, 213, 215, 216, 217
"Tickle Toe," 199
"Tico Tico," 49
Time, 9
Tinney, Allen, 30
"Tiny's Tempo," 33, 105, 216
TOBA (Theater Owners' Booking Association), 98
To Bird With Love (Bird), 252–53
tonality, 19, 77
"Topsy," 228
Torin, Symphony Sid, 182, 231
Toronto, 163, 184, 208, 271
Tovey, Donald, 209
Towers, Jack, 254
Town Hall, 55, 83, 87, 181–83
"Trane's Blues," 216n
Treadwell, George, 30, 76, 231
Treadwell, Oscar, 231
"Trio," 41
Tristano, Lennie, 8, 81, 116–17, 207, 213
Trumbauer, Frankie, 97
"Trumpet at Tempo," 155
Turk, Tommy, 48
"20th Century Blues," 37
25 Daily Exercises for Saxophone (Klosé), 123–24

Ulanov, Barry, 80, 109, 181–83, 238–46
"Up a Lazy River," 26, 74, 93, 94
up-tempo tunes, xi, 35–36, 43, 47, 190, 191, 197

Vail, Ken, 92
Vallee, Rudy, 37–38, 71, 73
Van Heusen, Jimmy, 193
Varäse, Edgard, 9, 121, 129, 225
Vaughan, Sarah, 31, 32, 34, 37, 76, 85, 126, 164, 202, 237, 239, 253, 261
Venora, Diane, 253
Ventura, Charlie, 31

Verve Records, 47, 48
Parker's recordings for, 20–21, 48–51, 56, 80, 109, 159, 176, 187, 225–38, 244–47, 254, 271
vibrato, 73–74, 191, 195, 202, 224, 261
Village Voice, 3, 174
"Vine Street Boogie," 75
"Visa," 24, 48

Waller, Fats, 17
Wallington, Billie, 53
Wallington, George, 131
Ware, Efferge, 27, 136, 198
"Warming Up a Riff," 36, 210, 217, 219, 261
"Way You Look Tonight, The," 43
Webb, Clifton, 46
Weber, Carl Maria von, 211
Webster, Ben, 6, 13, 14, 31, 51, 63, 73, 113, 140–41, 147, 148, 233
Webster, Freddie, 36, 165, 217
Weidemann, Erik, 53
Weinstock, Bob, 53
West, Harold "Doc," 33, 41, 182
"West End Blues," 16, 24
Wettling, George, 51, 68
"What Is This Thing Called Love," 18, 21, 49, 239
"What Price Love?," 191, 218n
WHDH radio, 109, 121
"When I Grow Too Old to Dream," 223
"When the Saints Go Marching In," 113
"Whispering," 33
Whitaker, Forest, 253–54
White, Charles, 198–99
White, Sonny, 162
Whittecombe, Art, 44
Who Walk in Darkness (Brossard), 178
"Wichita Blues," 195, 216n
Wichita Transcriptions, 23, 29–30, 194–96, 197, 199, 200, 201
Williams, Cootie, 32, 63
Williams, Edith, 74
Williams, J. K., 74
Williams, John A., 58

About the Editor

Carl Woideck is a saxophonist, musicologist, and writer. He teaches jazz, rock, and blues history at the University of Oregon in Eugene. Woideck's publications include the book *Charlie Parker: His Music and Life* (University of Michigan Press, 1996) and liner notes for Blue Note, Mosaic, Verve, and Prestige. He has also edited Schirmer's *The John Coltrane Companion* (1998).